W9-ANK-424

MILITARY
ETHICS

MILITARY ETHICS:
INTERNATIONAL PERSPECTIVES

Edited by
Lieutenant-Colonel Jeff Stouffer
and
Dr. Stefan Seiler

CANADIAN DEFENCE ACADEMY PRESS

Copyright © 2010 Her Majesty the Queen, in right of Canada as represented by the Minister of National Defence.

Canadian Defence Academy Press
PO Box 17000 Stn Forces
Kingston, Ontario   K7K 7B4

Produced for the Canadian Defence Academy Press
by 17 Wing Winnipeg Publishing Office.
WPO30607

Library and Archives Canada Cataloguing in Publication

Military ethics : international perspectives / edited by Jeff Stouffer and Stefan Seiler.

Produced for the Canadian Defence Academy Press by 17 Wing Winnipeg
Publishing Office.
Issued by: Canadian Defence Academy.
Includes bibliographical references and index.
ISBN 978-1-100-16318-5
Cat. no.: D2-264/2010E

1. Military ethics. 2. Soldiers--Professional ethics. 3. Military art and science. I. Stouffer,
Jeffrey M., 1962- II. Seiler, Stefan III. Canadian Defence Academy IV. Canada. Canadian
Armed Forces. Wing, 17

U22 M54 2010   174'.9355   C2010-980188-1

Printed in Canada.

1 3 5 7 9 10 8 6 4 2

ACKNOWLEDGEMENTS

Military Ethics: International Perspectives, the fifth of a continuing series of publications that focus on contemporary military issues, again speaks to the continued dedication and commitment of the members of the International Military Leadership Association (IMLA). As such, we would like to thank each of the contributing authors, not only for their continued interest in and support of the association, but also for their willingness to voluntarily participate toward the success of this publication. As with the previous volumes, the time and effort devoted to this project extend well beyond their normal responsibilities.

The success of any publication is also hinged to the production and technical support that is provided. To this end, we would like to again express our fullest appreciation and gratitude to Melanie Denis of the Canadian Forces Leadership Institute. The time constraints imposed on this volume, like the previous IMLA publications, requires considerable and skillful management. As always, Melanie's patience, tact, and technical skills to bring this project to fruition were greatly appreciated. As with previous volumes in this series, the staff of the 17 Wing Publishing Office are, without doubt, key to the transformation of the rough manuscript into this highly professional product.

TABLE OF CONTENTS

FOREWORD

I am pleased to introduce *Military Ethics: International Perspectives*, the fifth and latest volume in a continuing series of books produced by the International Military Leadership Association (IMLA) through the sponsored support and efforts of the Canadian Defence Academy and specifically, the Canadian Forces Leadership Institute. The IMLA, a mixture of civilian researchers and military personnel, has dedicated considerable effort over the last five years to collectively share and advance knowledge in areas of pressing interest to the respective militaries of its member nations. In this spirit, *Military Ethics: International Perspectives* focuses on the study of ethics and facilitates the continued development of military personnel to ensure that they possess the necessary capabilities to meet the ethical, character, and leadership challenges that often define contemporary operations. Through the presentation of theory, a variety of case studies, and applied research, this volume clearly demonstrates the importance of both the study and application of military ethics in today's world.

Military Ethics: International Perspectives greatly contributes to our understanding of ethics in general. Beyond this, it also illuminates how the various militaries represented in this book study, prepare for and approach ethical situations or, in other words, how military personnel are developed to effectively respond to the numerous and diverse situations encountered at home and in theatres of operation. This volume offers an opportunity to better understand how the militaries of IMLA member nations define and interpret ethically-demanding situations. Based on the individual contributions, there is clearly much to learn and more to research in this increasingly important and dynamic domain.

Military ethics is a subject that cannot be ignored if success is to be achieved through the highest standards of professionalism.

This series of publications which aims to contribute to the professional development literature and to support the professional development of military personnel, has garnered considerable attention and contributed to the growth and recognition of the IMLA over the last five years. Such a result is reflected in the tremendous support for this volume and stands in testimony to the interest that the international military research community is now extending to this specific forum. *Military Ethics: International Perspectives* represents another significant accomplishment of the international research community (IMLA) and the Canadian Defence Academy.

I hope that all will come away from this book with a more profound understanding of and appreciation for ethics in a military milieu. Readers are encouraged to contact the individual contributors and/or the Canadian Defence Academy to further discuss the contents of this volume.

J.P.Y.D. Gosselin
Major-General
Commander
Canadian Defence Academy

PREFACE

The core purpose of armed forces is the effective and adequate use of military force to achieve specific objectives. The use of military force influences the well-being of other people, directly or indirectly. Thus, military action is intimately linked to moral decision-making. In recent years, the spectrum of military missions has gradually shifted from classical warfare to counter-insurgency operations, peacekeeping and peace support operations as well as nation building activities. The widening range of modern armed forces' missions provides a formidable challenge to soldiers and officers on both a professional and a moral level. The moral dimension regarding military interventions is of vital importance on both the individual and the organizational and institutional levels. On the individual level, both the perpetrator and the victim of an immoral act are affected directly. The negative consequences for the victims of moral wrongdoings cover the gamut from humiliation and degradation to prolonged physical and mental harm, to torture and abuse and, finally, to death. Alternatively, the perpetrators also have to bear the consequences of their immoral behaviour: on the one hand, they can be brought to justice for their criminal misconduct and punished accordingly; on the other hand, they constantly have to come to terms with what they did and have to bear the lifelong responsibility for their misconduct. Moral misconduct also has far-reaching consequences at the organizational and institutional level. Individual soldiers' misconduct can jeopardize a whole mission and call into question the credibility of an entire institution. How, for example, can one credibly justify the bringing of freedom, peace, democracy and human rights to a country when these very values are trampled on by those entrusted to guarantee them? How can the hearts and minds of a civilian population be won if soldiers from foreign countries, who are on site to give them protection and freedom, cannot be trusted to behave in a morally correct way? How can soldiers be taught the purpose and the legitimacy, under international law, of a mission if the government or the army they command does not behave in a morally correct way? Or, how can an overarching cohesion between coalition partners develop if some of the partners do not comply with higher moral principles. It is therefore obvious that the moral dimension of military action has far-reaching consequences, not only on the ethical reflection of military actions, but also on the direct success of a mission.

Moral challenges can be found on the strategic, operational, and tactical levels. On a strategic level, these challenges appear when operation objectives are set or operation plans are developed. At the operational level, they can influence our actions when we define the means of achieving an objective or when we choose the operational means. At the tactical level, moral aspects especially influence a soldier's job when accomplishing specific missions.

Some cogent questions might illustrate these points: Is it correct to target and destroy an electrical power plant which is used for military as well as civilian purposes even though the plant is mainly operated by civilians? (strategic level). Should positively identified leaders of a terrorist group, who have been spotted in a densely populated area, be eliminated with accurate rocket fire even if innocent civilians could be harmed; or should the terrorists be captured by Special Forces, thus risking the lives of soldiers? (operational level). What does a soldier on patrol do when children are in the street playing with weapons and when he/she cannot accurately assess whether the children are just playing or posing a real threat? (tactical level). These questions illustrate that, in addition to such criteria as military efficiency and effectiveness, many military decisions raise serious moral issues. Therefore, a sound education in military leadership ethics is of the utmost importance on all the different hierarchical levels of the armed forces.

Most armed forces in democratic states are fully conscious of the need for ethical awareness training. Lessons learned from past mistakes as well as recurring problems have heightened the awareness of senior armed forces commanders and political leaders. In recent years, many armies have updated or developed new programs to increase the moral competence of both officers and soldiers. Major efforts have been made to optimize the effectiveness of training. The aim of this volume is to show the relevance of the topic seen from the scientists' and practitioners' perspective from different nations, who have different cultural and historical backgrounds and who are confronted with a mixed variety of problems related to military ethics. The book also demonstrates how different countries cope with the challenges of ethical awareness training at different levels within their hierarchy. I would therefore like to congratulate the International Military Leadership Association and the Canadian Defence Academy on their efforts and to encourage them to pursue this discussion further. Successful international military cooperation not only requires a common language, compatible communication and weapons systems; it also requires a certain level of commonality concerning moral values and norms, a basic moral trust in oneself, in the comrades of our own armed forces and those of coalition partners, as well as a deep conviction that they are fighting for a legal and morally legitimate cause. The present book, *Military Ethics: International Perspectives,* offers numerous interesting insights and should generate discussions that will foster our common cause.

Brigadier Daniel Lätsch, PhD
Director of the Swiss Military Academy at ETH Zurich

MILITARY ETHICS: INTERNATIONAL PERSPECTIVES

CHAPTER 1

Moral Professionalism within the Royal Netherlands Armed Forces

Miriam C. de Graaff, MSc
*Lieutenant-Colonel C.E. van den Berg, PhD**

> *"One of the soldiers in my platoon was not that good a soldier.*
> *He didn't exercise his skills or perform his drills correctly and,*
> *he was a danger to himself and the rest of the platoon. Yet be-*
> *cause of the bureaucratic system we could not get him out of our*
> *platoon. So one day I let my men do what they wanted to do:*
> *nag him so he would leave by his own choice. I did not give the*
> *orders to do so, but I knew that something was going to happen,*
> *and I did not prevent it from happening."*

(From an interview with a former infantry platoon commander about morality in his platoon.)

INTRODUCTION

In the Royal Netherlands Armed Forces, military ethics is part of the professional training and education of all military personnel. As the duty to act morally "responsible" is valid for all military personnel, the training focuses on the development of moral competence in accordance with the responsibilities of the different levels within the armed forces. The key reason for the increasing interest in ethics, and thus in moral professionalism, is its appeal

---

* The views expressed in this chapter are those of the authors and do not necessarily reflect the official policy of the Royal Netherlands Armed Forces. The authors would like to thank Miss Ninka Lenssen, MSc, for her critical perspective and remarks.

at the many "levels" of the Dutch military organization. From a political viewpoint, ethics proved to be a major issue in policy making and political discussions as ethical violations have received considerable media attention (e.g., policy and discussions regarding the Committee for the Investigation into Undesirable Behaviour, a committee concerned with the investigation of social misbehaviour within the Forces).[1] When Dutch general social norms are violated by an individual or a group of individuals, it is broadly discussed in the media; in order to keep a good organizational image, policy is formulated in an attempt to prevent ethical violations from happening. Also, in terms of education, training, and psychological support, ethics receives considerable attention. The troops are trained to become so-called "thinking soldiers", in order for them to be able to give full consideration to moral situations and to act accordingly in such situations. Another possible result of moral professionalism is its positive effect on the prevention of psychological problems caused for example, by moral dilemmas experienced during deployments.[2]

When discussing ethics with military personnel, it is not uncommon for them to question whether ethics is a field worth considering within the military context. Some feel that ethics is a field of interest for those who are not operational or practically active within the military field. They regard ethics as if it were some worthy disability, something for the armchair moralist, but not at all useful in the daily tasks of deployment. Besides, there is also the question as to whether or not there can actually be military ethics. After all, are violence, which the military organization applies as an instrument, and ethics not irreconcilable? Nevertheless, moral professionalism, and thus ethics, is part of the mindset of professional military personnel who make decisions in situations where the lines between good and bad are blurred.

MILITARY ETHICS: INTERNATIONAL PERSPECTIVES

Moreover, as broadly accepted today, in order to succeed in present day conflicts, soldiers should keep to the human high ground rather than the geographical high ground[3] and in order to do so, ethical considerations can make the difference.

This chapter discusses moral professionalism within the Netherlands Forces. Our goal is to demonstrate how moral professionalism ought to be an organizational virtue, and hence, that moral competence ought to be an essential military competence that is supported by the organizational system (i.e. the organizational structure, its objectives and the employees) in order to be functional and valuable.

The first section in this chapter defines the term moral professionalism as introduced by Verweij.[4] It also describes those things implemented by the Netherlands Forces to achieve moral professionalism. The second section provides a theoretical discussion on this theme and deals with the connection between the organization and the individual in relation to moral professionalism. Discussion and conclusions are offered.

ENHANCING MORAL PROFESSIONALISM IN INDIVIDUAL MILITARY ACTIVITY

The example given in the introduction of this chapter describes a situation in which it may be instinctively thought that moral professionalism is not at play. But what is moral professionalism? In this chapter, moral professionalism is defined based on Verweij[5] and the concepts of *moral competence* as introduced by Karssing:[6]

1. the capacity of an individual to be aware of the moral aspects of a situation;

2.   the ability to acknowledge his/her own moral standards and – in the given situation – the underlying values, rules and interests;

3.   a moral professional is able to evaluate the different alternatives and their consequences;

4.   a moral professional has the capability to make a judgement consistent with his/her moral considerations and act in accordance with this moral judgement; and

5.   the ability to communicate and explain the moral dimension to others and the ability and willingness to take responsibility for his/her own actions and decisions by communicating about the choices made.[7]

Thus, moral professionalism implies that an individual is able to recognize and deal with the moral dimensions of a situation. When an individual is not capable of recognizing the moral dimensions of a situation,[8] moral blindness emerges, which can result in the inability to make moral decisions.[9] Continuously reflecting on values, norms and interests in practice distinguishes an ordinary professional from a good professional.[10]

To become a professional in the Netherlands Armed Forces, an individual must participate in an educational program. This program is adapted to the level of functioning and fits the individual's personal development and the responsibility associated with his/her rank. This means, in relation to ethics, that all military personnel take part in ethics training programs, however, the emphasis of this training differs across ranks. Due to the responsibilities and complexities of commanders and staff officers at higher organizational levels, higher-ranking military personnel receive more training in military ethics. The focus of this training is to develop their moral competence so they can act in accordance with the complexity and accountability associated with their level of control and, hence, the impact of their decisions. However, as argued in this chapter, the actions of military personnel are also of (great) influence. This may range from effects on a personal to the strategic level, meaning that actions at an individual level can have effects at the strategic level.[11]

Educational ethical training programs for non-commissioned officers cover ethical decision-making (the so called Ethical Awareness-Model). Here, lessons focus on what is forbidden in the forces (e.g. alcohol abuse, drugs, smuggling, torture) and how to install appropriate norms for soldiers. Officers also receive military ethics programs as part of the curriculum at the various levels in their career (e.g., during the Advanced Command and Staff Course – military ethics is integrated into exercises and simulations and training that also covers moral dilemma's, different (theoretical) approaches in ethics, and the up and downside of power).

When Dutch forces are trained for a deployment, they participate in moral dilemma training programs that are integrated into several training sessions and exercises. This advanced training includes foreseeing moral aspects of military actions and creative thinking in solving moral issues. In these training sessions, military personnel are confronted with moral dilemmas similar to those they will probably encounter in the mission area (e.g., the strip searching of women by male soldiers – when contact between men and women is culturally thought unacceptable, although security demands intensive examination for weapons, explosives

etc.,). Moral dilemmas are prevalent in every layer of the organization irrespective of rank and represent part of the day-to-day-life
of any soldier. Even though the way moral dilemmas are handled
may have a significant impact on mission success, there is always
tension between the need to give attention to moral activity and
the need to train for the classical "real soldier activities" (i.e., basic
weapon skills and drills).

Karssing described two different management strategies that are
currently used in organizations in order to influence employees'
moral behaviour. The first strategy focuses on normative behaviour (i.e., rules). In this view, a strategy is chosen in which an
individual is encouraged to behave in a morally responsible way
because he/she wants to follow the (legal) norms stated by the organization. In order to encourage behaviour that is at first glance
morally right (at least legally just), the Netherlands Defence
organization formulated a code of conduct in order to regulate
individual activity in a way that is in agreement with the organizational view as to how one should behave (See Figure 1). A code
of conduct, however, does not enhance moral professionalism in
itself,[12] as stated: "a code is nothing, coding is everything".[13] An
improvement in moral professionalism may come to mind as a
justification for the code when a few "slips" are made. Nevertheless, it is more likely that good behaviour is carried out by individuals because they want to avoid the legal consequences of bad
behaviour as stated by the code of conduct. In other words, an
individual is not intrinsically motivated to do well but wants to
avoid being punished, and therefore, acts in accordance with the
code of conduct and other social and legal norms.[14]

1. **I am a member of a professional organisation.**

I will keep my knowledge and skills, including social skills, up to date. Therefore I can, even under difficult circumstances, perform well.

2. **I am a member of a team with a common task.**

I work together with colleagues and am both responsible for them as well as the team. I address others on their behaviour and accept when they address me on my behaviour.

3. **I am aware of my responsibilities.**

I do not harm the interests of the Armed Forces and in attitude, appearance and behaviour, I will give the right example. I will handle responsibility with the means given in my care and I will do so carefully and justly.

4. **I am integer and treat everybody with respect.**

I do not accept undesirable behaviour such as discrimination, (sexual) harassment and bullying, neither against me or others. I will respect to the rules and laws that apply to me and I will not misuse my power or position.

5. **I take care for a safe work environment.**

I feel responsible for the safety of others and myself. This accounts for all forms of safety like operational safety, information safety and a safe work environment. I won't use drugs. Alcohol may never influence the way I function.

FIGURE 1: Code of Conduct of the Netherlands Armed Forces, as stated by the Commander of the Armed Forces in 2007.

MILITARY ETHICS: INTERNATIONAL PERSPECTIVES

The second management strategy described by Karssing[15] focuses on stimulating individuals to put forth effort in making moral judgements regarding their own behaviour and their moral decision-making. It might be said that individuals are stimulated to become morally competent agents. In this view of moral activity, all individuals hold responsibility for their own behaviour. A code of conduct is not appropriate in this view because it does not make people think. A clear view of organizational values, education, mentoring and discussions, however, is of much use and value because individual considerations are needed to reach moral competence. Like the first strategy, this stimulating strategy is also applied within the Royal Netherlands Armed Forces. Developing moral professionalism within the military may be regarded as an attempt of the defence organization to develop this management strategy.

MORAL DEVELOPMENT IN MORAL PROFESSIONALISM

Moral professionalism is, on the one hand, a result of clear standards as set in a code of conduct as well as the ability to recognize them in actual situations. On the other hand, moral professionalism is the result of moral development. This means that military personnel are not only able to distinguish right from wrong, they are able to make decisions in ambiguous situations for reasons they can account for. Therefore, moral development is an important part of moral professionalism. In this section, the main theoretical views in use to enhance moral development are described.

As mentioned, the Netherlands Armed Forces uses an *Ethical Awareness-Model* (see Figure 2) to enhance moral professionalism. This Ethical Awareness-Model (as well as the entire view and policy of the Netherlands Armed Forces on ethics), implies that morality influences judgement and decision-making. It also implies that it is possible to integrate ethics within decision-making and that members can be trained to do so. After all, (cognitive) processes in reasoning are thought to precede decision-making and acting in accordance with decisions made.

The Ethical Awareness-Model raises the following questions:

1. What are the facts and which parties are involved?

2. What are the solutions and also their possible consequences?

3. Is my solution legal?

4. Have all interests been considered?

5. Is it acceptable?

FIGURE 2: Ethical Awareness-Model.

In several scientific fields (e.g., social psychology or philosophy), the morality of mankind is studied. Rest for example, describes morality from a social psychological point of view, tackling (moral) development, moral judgement, moral decision-making and behaviour.[16] His Four Component Model describes the psychological processes an individual completes in order to "behave morally." The four psychological processes from Rest's model include:

1. The individual is capable of interpreting a particular situation in terms of possible actions and consequences, for oneself and for others.

2. The individual is able to make a judgement about the fairness (or morally rightness) of a course of action.

3.   The individual must intend to do what is morally right by giving priority to moral values over other personal values.

4.   The individual must persevere in his [her] intention to act justly, in other words: to act morally responsible.

Like the Ethical Awareness-Model used within the Armed Forces, Rest's model, as well as Verweij's view on moral professionalism, rejects the concept that moral behaviour "is the result of a single, unitary process."[17] This means that, according to these views, an individual may be successfully demonstrating the elements of a particular process, but at the same time, not demonstrating the other processes adequately. In this situation, moral professionalism or complete moral development may have been ascertained.

In contrast to Rest, Kohlberg, a well-known psychologist, proposed a theory in which an individual goes through several levels that consist of six stages of moral development.[18] According to Kohlberg, decision-making depends on the (moral) development a person has been through (see Figure 3). This is a completely different view on moral decision-making than that of Verweij or Rest (i.e., in which the specific use of psychological processes by an individual in an ethical situation is important, and not his level of development). After all, a person may be well developed according to Kohlberg's stages and still not demonstrate moral professionalism because a specific process has not been carried out in its entirety or a specific component has been left out.

Kohlberg's Stages of Moral Development

In the first level of Kohlberg's 6 stage model (the preconditional level; stages 1 and 2) of moral development, one uses an egoistic perspective and is focused on doing right in order to prevent punishment or harm to oneself. In the second level (the conventional level; stages 3 and 4), social norms are becoming important: the perception of peers and other important individuals is the major reason to behave in a specific way. At this level, one can identify conformity to group norms and to systemic rules that are established for the interests of the group. The rules are lived by, without consideration or being checked, by the individual members of the group. In the transitional level – between level two and three – Kohlberg states that decisions are subjective because they are made using personal preferences and emotions. The third and highest level of moral development (the post-conventional and principle level; stages 5 and 6), represent the levels in which the individual internalizes rules and norms, and understands that decisions should be made in accordance with universally valid principles.[19]

FIGURE 3: Kohlberg's Stages of Moral Development.

As moral professionalism in the organization is supported by the existence of moral competence among all individuals within the organization, it is important to first clarify, from our point of view, what is moral competence. Karssing introduced the concept of moral competence.[20] His view on moral competence was translated for use within the Netherlands Armed Forces and is defined as the ability and willingness to adequately and carefully perform tasks by taking interests into account after consideration of the relevant facts (see Figure 4). Moral competence therefore, is not only achieved by possessing enough knowledge, but also through having the right attitude and capacity of skills. Moral competence does not stop at the point where people know what the right thing to do is, but continues insofar as people are willing and able to act in accordance with this knowledge.[21] Within the Netherlands Armed Forces, military instructors in ethics (mostly senior instructors, Sergeant-Majors and Captains with years of experience in the operational field), have the opportunity to participate in "Advanced-train-the-trainer military ethics" training (*verdiepingscursus militaire ethiek*). This training focuses on magnifying the moral competence of the participants and is based on the same elements that were mentioned by Verweij.

Moral Competence:

The Knowledge, Skills and Attitude related to:

a) Planned preparation on moral issues and dilemmas, (i.e., by anticipating such issues and dilemmas that are likely to occur during future missions);

b) The ability to recognise a moral issue when it occurs – awareness – which is dependent on perception and compassion related to fellow humans (empathy);

c) The ability to act professionally and adequately in problematic moral situations – judgement – skills that do not only concern coping with emotions (i.e., violated sense of justice), but also the skills and ability to oversee differing ethical aspects and arguments that can at times, be contradictory;

d) The ability to make resourceful and responsible choices for which one takes responsibility for (choice); and

e) The ability to explain choices that one has made in a way that all involved, including the ones who might have made another choice, see that the decision at hand has been made in a well-grounded and integer way (communication and accountability).

FIGURE 4: Moral Competence.

MILITARY ETHICS: INTERNATIONAL PERSPECTIVES

An employee in any organization can only act morally responsibly in those situations where the organization gives space to the employee to do so.[22] This means that an organization needs to consider the intent and range of tasks it wants the employee to perform and the means an employee has in order to carry out these tasks. Most employees want to perform well in their jobs.[23] The ends formulated in military operations are an important element to emphasize the need for moral competence in the Netherlands Armed Forces. After all, the end-state of a mission is formulated on a political level and therefore, all military actions need to contribute to this end. As such, the end-state needs to be in accordance with international and humanitarian law and the acts to reach these goals need to be accounted for in accordance with these laws. For soldiers who participate in missions, from commanders at the strategic level to those that plan at the tactical level, they must know, understand and apply the moral standards of their profession and the mission. They would, in the most desirable case, even be able to analyze, synthesize and eventually evaluate, create and outlive their moral standards for the mission at hand.

However, when considering the tasks an individual within the Armed Forces needs to perform, ambiguity seems to prevail. After all, between the code of conduct, the procedures, and the actual command or order, discrepancies are likely to arise. Procedures, codes, and even within the code of conduct, certain "values" may conflict with each other. For example, when short-term targets are to be reached under time-pressures, these targets may very well interfere with or conflict with the actual end-state to be achieved. So when a soldier needs to live by the rules of this code (or another specific set of principles such as the Rules of Engagement or the Geneva Convention), how can he/she do "right" when, even by applying the code, a simple solution may not be found? Or even worse, when he/she is in a situation in which a moral dilemma is experienced because two (or more) values, according to this code, conflict with each other?

During deployments, the individual (as well as the system formed by the organization and mission area), is confronted with their personal state of development of their moral competence. Morality and life are at stake when confronted with the dynamic complexity of deployment tasks. Moreover, because of the current organizational working method in operational activity, the responsibility for one's actions can no longer be displaced. After all, a key element of the so-called "*Auftragstaktik*" (i.e., the notion of decentralized command as it was first called within the German forces), is that decision-making is decentralized, meaning that even individuals in the lower levels of the chain of command can determine, to some extent, how activities will be carried out. Thus, "*Befehl*" is no longer "*Befehl*" (an order is no longer just an order). Individuals at every level of the chain of command need to deal with the fact that they must consider the situation, make decisions, and act accordingly.[24] As a consequence, the moral competence of any individual soldier can affect the decisions made and activities carried out. This can, however, be a very difficult and sometimes even tragic position to experience. On the one hand, we expect soldiers to be moral professionals who uphold high moral standards[25] and who reduce the use of force to the absolute minimum. On the other hand, situations encountered in today's missions are so complex that it might seem a mission impossible to be a moral professional. The characteristics of asymmetrical warfare and asymmetrical conflict, however, require a flexible and morally fit professional.[26]

Within the military organization, three norm-bases can be distinguished; 1) norms based on civil-military relations and cooperation (e.g. the Geneva Convention and humanitarian law); 2) norms based on the organizational criteria (e.g. Rules of Engagement); and, 3) norms based on the personal values of military personnel.[27] As mentioned, these different norms can lead to moral dilemmas that can be difficult to resolve. At times, military personnel are confronted with situations that have an extreme impact on their conscience (e.g., situations in which they are confronted with child soldiers). Three forms of relation between ones conscience and institutional norms can be distinguished.[28] In the first form, one finds absolutism. This means that the individual's conscience is a component of professional ethics and thus, the soldier may use his/her own personal values when executing tasks but still needs to comply to the organization even when his/her personal values conflict with organizational needs. The second form is situational. In this case, the individual is a component within the professional ethics and thus, may use his/her own personal values when executing tasks. In this situational form, however, the individual still needs to comply with certain organizational elements. The third form grants the individual the most freedom and is referred to as individualism. The basic element of professional ethics in this view is the interdependence of the personal values within the organization. According to this view, the institution is placed second; otherwise, it is argued, the tasks and the organization itself are distant from society.

The complex situation in which soldiers operate also involves the paradox created by the organization's goals and means. After all, the military tries to construct a safe environment of freedom, but reaches this end-state (mainly) by means of the use of legally permitted violence.[29]

MILITARY ETHICS: INTERNATIONAL PERSPECTIVES

DISCUSSION AND CONCLUSION

In this section, arguments are drawn from considerations mentioned above to specify the pros and cons of moral professionalism within the Royal Netherlands Armed Forces. Moreover, a final conclusion is extrapolated on how moral professionalism as an organizational virtue, evident in moral competence, is and ought to be embedded in current military operations and military management (i.e., policy).

In the discussion, different ideas on the question as to whether moral professionalism ought to become an organizational virtue in the military organization were reported. On the one hand, there are those that believe ethics and thus, moral professionalism, represent an undeniable element of the military profession. The first argument to support this view is that in current military operations (both during deployments abroad and during peace management operations in the Netherlands), one can only be a good military professional when one works in accordance with the military codes and with the end-state in mind. This means that (moral) considerations and judgements are always made in order to reach this end-state. While peace is the ultimate end state in current (UN/NATO) missions, one might argue that peace should not be reached with the use of (unnecessary) violence. One might even argue, like Scales,[30] that contemporary wars can be seen as psycho-cultural wars in which losing the human high ground due to moral intolerable acts, will detract from reaching the intended end-state. Therefore, by implementing moral professionalism, all military personnel should become better thinking soldiers which will hopefully help to reduce or prevent moral misbehaviour (i.e., such as the misbehaviour on the frigate Tjerk Hiddes of the Netherlands Navy or the treatment of prisoners at the Abu Ghraib prison). Equally important, the number of incidents (of misbehaviour) caused by the ambiguity and complexity of the situation could be reduced.

A second argument deals with moral reasoning and moral decision-making. After all, only when moral professionalism is demonstrated will personnel act morally responsible after reflecting on moral considerations and judgements that eventually led to moral decision-making. Since (the democratic) society wants its military personnel to behave morally responsibly, and the military organization is an instrument of this society; moral professionalism is necessary for the credibility and legitimacy of military activity and the military institution as a whole. Otherwise, civilian perceptions and support, which are absolutely necessary in operations, will be lost. Moreover, the military is at the service of society, meaning that the military should reflect the values, standards and rules of society. As a consequence, it is the organizations responsibility, carried out by its commanders, to bring home soldiers with stories they can talk about. Therefore, the organization should always communicate effectively on moral issues in a dialogue; a dialogue within the organization as well as those outside the organization.

A third argument deals with deployments. Thinking soldiers are needed in order to succeed on and end missions. In current missions, the military uses more and more decentralized decision-making, which means that *Befehl* is no longer *Befehl*. Even at the lower organizational levels, individuals deal with the fact that they are required to consider the situation, make decisions, and act accordingly. As a consequence, the actions of an individual soldier or corporal, or the decisions a group or platoon commander makes, can influence mission outcomes. This decentralizing of command – also referred to as *Auftragstaktik* – improves the speed and accuracy of decision-making.[31] "…[S]peed because commanders can act immediately without referring the decision to superiors; accuracy because commanders can act on local information unavailable to superiors."[32] So when decisions need to be made, individuals working in these lower level positions of the organization should, because of the consequences of their individual actions, be aware of the moral implications and the desired end-state of the mission. Thus, they should have well developed moral professionalism, otherwise, they may not be able to recognize all the moral aspects of the situation at hand and as a result, may not make a "just" decision and act morally responsible. Because it may not be assumed that all individuals have developed their moral competence to the required level, the organization needs to facilitate and nurture its soldiers to do so. Otherwise, wrong decisions can be made and moral misbehaviour might occur, making it impossible for the organization to reach the desired end-state.

However, moral professionalism as an organizational virtue is in need of some distinction. There are also those who criticize the use and practicality of moral professionalism within the military organization. For one, it seems that the organization does not want its personnel to truly behave in accordance with moral professionalism (meaning that they always take their own personal values into account when reasoning and acting). It seems as if the organization just wants its employees to hold specific ideals (values) and that they behave in accordance with specific attitudes. This might seem a good argument at first glance. After all, not everyone has high moral standards, so why not just give all military personnel a set of rules and principles to guide them? We believe morality must remain inherent to the profession of arms. Simply giving sets of rules and codes will likely lead to additional

problems and wrong decisions, as one may not be internally motivated to act responsibly. Thus, in order to make sure that all
activities are justified and morally responsible, the organization
should educate all military personnel on moral competence. This
might imply that the organizational culture has to change in order to demonstrate moral professionalism. For instance, military
personnel are trained to be loyal to the organization and their
colleagues (and therefore to the set of rules, codes and principles),
and not specifically to the military profession (and thus their own
moral considerations in relation with their task, moral standards,
and profession).[33]

When education and training are aimed at developing moral
competence (instead of convincing the servicemen to use a certain set of values and rules in decision-making), the individual
should become more capable in his/her decision-making. Using
the moral professional framework will become intuitive and automatic. This may possibly result in positive effects on intuitive
decision-making under time pressures. Arguably, this is what is
needed most in high demanding deployment environments –
where the luxury of time is often not available to truly consider
all aspects of the (moral) situation consciously. Morality should
be taken into account as part of intuitive decision-making instead
of just being considered the primary reaction of the individual in
a difficult situation. In addition, education and training in ethics
is important in order to enhance not only decision-making, but
the latter part of moral competence – the ability to communicate
about ones own actions and the ability to account for the results
of ones own military actions. Clearly, intolerable acts still occur.
Military professionals must have the ability to communicate about
their actions and take responsibility for the results of their actions.
Thus, education and training are of great importance to enhance
moral professionalism within the entire military organization.

The second argument that moral professionalism should not be considered an organizational virtue, has to do with the work ethic of the military organization. Since the organization always focuses on military effectiveness instead of personal effectiveness, moral professionalism demonstrated by servicemen is not facilitated by the organization in the current work ethic of the Netherlands Armed Forces. Examples that are heard in class-meetings of high-ranking military personnel often deal with making it easier for the organization to "do the right thing" in relation to military effectiveness. For example, morally responsible decisions made under time pressure, are overruled by higher-ranking commanders. Such as in the following example, described on one of the courses.

> *A company has prepared a cordon and search operation in cooperation with a national unit in order to find a possible weapon cache. The operation has been carefully prepared with moral guidelines to prevent indirect effects, like harm to the village population or collateral damage. Halfway through the operation, it becomes evident that the search will take longer than planned, so it won't be possible to search the whole village. As there are credible grounds for expecting weapons to be found, withdrawing before the search of the village is complete – the operation can't continue through the night – will most certainly lead to the removal of the weapons by the belligerents. The commander at the operational centre orders the bombing of the last houses in the village to prevent the smuggling of weapons, thereby rejecting the moral choices made earlier.*

The way the conduct of this operation was altered by arguing that military effectiveness is served, means that the moral grounds in choices and judgement were changed; hence, this requires accountability and communication by the decision-maker. In such cases, it might seem ineffective to use an individual or personal approach to achieve mission goals as there seems to be an overriding military rationale. However, this claim needs to be refined. It might also be argued that because of the enhancement of personal effectiveness through stimulating moral professionalism, military effectiveness will be augmented or increased. At first glance, it may seem impossible to reach the desired end-state when all military personnel use their own personal values in their activities. The question here is, how one can take a course of action to reach mission goals that are based on sound military judgement? Yet, as previously mentioned, when moral professionalism is demonstrated, personal values are considered in relation to the military profession. This means, that the moral considerations that are made will keep track of military effectiveness as well as the mission goals. Therefore, taking personal values into account will only bring more nuance and judgement into the situation. It might even be better at times to not achieve a mission goal, when it can only be reached in a morally irresponsible way. Will chaos, collateral damage, civilian losses and an angry local population stack up well against reaching a mission goal? Reaching an intermediate goal may also make reaching the end-state almost impossible. Therefore, nuance and thus, insight into personal values in relation to the military profession are needed in military decision-making. Moreover, to add to professional military moral judgement, accountability and communication about decisions across the hierarchical levels is necessary.

When moral professionalism fails, it might be argued, that there are no professional military personnel at all. The potential tension between the reality of the political and the operational level in the perception of military ethics strikes us as peculiar. Military

personnel at all hierarchical levels have to deal with the strain
between ethical considerations at the political level and its thorni-
ness in the fog of military operations. Profound lessons from military operations in the past few decades have taught us that ethics
cannot be taken away from the operational field. It would be
unrealistic to believe that military personnel would not encounter
morally challenging situations when they are conducting military
operations. Hence, as moral dilemmas are continuously present in
military operations, moral professionalism ought to be considered
an organizational virtue.

ENDNOTES

1   As a result of misbehaviour in the Netherlands Armed Forces, such
as the incident of sexual harassment on the Navy frigate Tjerk Hiddes, this
committee was set up in 2006 to investigate misbehaviour in the Netherlands Armed Forces.

2   Marten Meijer, "Morele vraagstukken en de geestelijke gezondheid van
uitgezonden militairen," *NGMT*, Vol. 62 (2009), 169-172.

3   Robert Scales, "Clausewitz and World War IV," *Military Psychology*,
21/S1, (2009), 23-35.

4   Desiree Verweij, *Geweten onder Schot* (Amsterdam: Uitgeverij Boom,
2010); and, Desiree Verweij, "Het belang van Militaire Ethiek voor de Kri-
jgsmacht," *Carré*, Vol. 28 (2005), 28-30.

5   Desiree Verweij, "Morele Professionaliteit in de Militaire Praktijk," in
Jos Kole and Doret de Ruyter, eds., *Werkzame Idealen – Ethische Reflecties
op Professionaliteit* (Assen: Koninklijke van Gorcum, 2007), 126-138; and,
Verweij (2005).

6   Edgar Karssing, *Morele Competenties in Organisaties* (Assen: Van Gorcum & Comp BV, 2000).

7   Peter Olstoorn, Marten Meijer and Desiree Verweij, "Managing Moral Professionalism in Military Operations," in Joseph Soeters, Paul C. van Fenema and Robert Beeres, eds., *Managing Military Organizations, Theory and Practice* (New York: Routledge, 2010), 138-149.

8   Verweij, "Morele Professionaliteit in de Militaire Praktijk."

9   Kim Hofhuis, Desiree Verweij and Joseph Soeters, "Moral Judgment Within the Armed Forces," *Journal of Military Ethics*, Vol. 6, No. 1 (2007), 19-40.

10   Jos M. H. Groen and Desiree Verweij, "De Onlosmakelijke Band Tussen Professionaliteit en Ethiek," *Militaire Spectator*, Vol. 177 (2008), 349-360.

11   Karssing, "Moral Competencies in Organizations."

12   Ibid.

13   Cees Homan, "Integrity in Uniform," in Fred A. H. M. van Iersel and Ted Th. A. van Baarda, eds., *Military Ethics: Moral Dilemmas of Military Personnel in Theory and Practice* (Budel, NL: Damon, 2002), 253-255.

14   Karssing, "Moral Competencies in Organizations."

15   Ibid.

16   James Rest, *Moral Development, Advances in Research and Theory* (New York: Praeger, 1986).

17   Ibid, 4.

18   Lawrence Kohlberg, *Essays on Moral Development Volume One; The Philosophy of Moral Development, Moral Stages and the Idea of Justice* (San Francisco: Harper & Row, 1981).

19   Ibid.

20   Karssing, "Moral Competencies in Organizations."

21   Jolanda Bosch and Eva Wortel, "Versterking van de Morele Competentie: De Verdiepingscursus Militaire Ethiek," *Militaire Spectator*, Vol. 178 (2009), 471-486.

22   Karssing, "Moral Competencies in Organizations."

23   Ibid.

24   *Befehl*, literally "order" in the sentence "*Befehl ist Befehl*" refers to strict obedience and following orders without the possibility to question or interpret them. This contrasts moral professionalism wherein military personnel need to account for their deeds and can not refer to given orders to deny their responsibility.

25   Olstoorn, Meijer and Verweij, "Managing Moral Professionalism in Military Operations."

26   Rudy Richardson, Desiree Veweij and Donna Winslow, "Moral fitness for Peace Operations," *Journal of Political and Military Sociology*, Vol. 32, No. 1 (2004), 99-113.

27   Sam Sarkesian and Thomas Gannon, "Professionalism: Problems and Challenges", in Malham M. Waking, ed., *War, Morality and the Military Profession* (Boulder: Westview Press, 1979), 127-141.

28   Ibid.

29   Verweij, "Morele Professionaliteit in de Militaire Praktijk."

30   Scales, "Clausewitz and World War IV."

31   Bruce Newsome, *Made Not Born, Why Some Soldiers Are Better Than Others* (Westport: Prager Security International, 2007).

32   Ibid, 67.

33   Verweij, "Geweten onder Schot."

CHAPTER 2

Ethics Research: Moral Psychology and its Promise of Benefits for Moral Reasoning in the Military

Principal Defence Chaplain Don Parker
*Dr. Peter Greener**

INTRODUCTION

Considerable effort has been applied by the New Zealand Military to the establishment and development of appropriate *Ethos and Values* over the last fifteen years. The Army, in particular, has sought to reinforce the role that all levels of command play in reinforcing its established values of "Courage, Comradeship, Commitment and Integrity".[1] This approach is matched by similar efforts in the Navy and Airforce.

However, it is our observation that the good intention implicit in the *Ethos and Values* approach has never been fully realized. Through a lack of overall coordination, the three individual Services initially identified and propagated different values and the teaching and reinforcement of these values was done through different channels.

Yet, in spite of the lack of an overarching strategy to propagate the New Zealand Defence Force (NZDF) *Ethos and Values*, learning

* The views expressed in this chapter are those of the authors and do not necessarily reflect the official policy of the New Zealand Defence Force.

and maturing can be seen though retrospective analysis. The Army gives a good case study in this regard. The initial *Ethos and Values* booklet produced in the mid 1990s contained eleven values. By 2002, these values had been honed down to "Courage, Comradeship, Commitment and Integrity". Through posters and lessons, these values were propagated by a very committed group of Senior Non-Commissioned Officers (NCOs) and, at times, the Chaplaincy Department. A significant development came when, in the redevelopment and implementation of a Leadership Framework in 2007, commanders at all levels were tasked with reinforcing these values.

Throughout this period of time, two linked questions have lingered in the minds of those who have been required to teach ethics and affirm the military ethos: how is the effectiveness of the *Ethos and Values* approach measured? Second, if the effectiveness of the *Ethos and Values* approach can be measured, do we have any assurances that we can make better soldiers, sailors, airmen and women?

This chapter attempts to address these questions by introducing insights provided by the field of Moral Psychology and by exploring whether there is an overarching theoretical frame which could be employed to help ensure the propagation of a coherent approach. The cornerstone work of Lawrence Kohlberg (1927-1987) will be considered, with specific attention paid to his "Six Stages of Moral Reasoning". Subsequent developments of this model by Neo-Kohlbergians will be discussed with reference to "The Four Component Model" and its relevance to the Profession of Arms.

To avoid the confusion that so often accompanies discussions on ethics and morals, a distinction is required. Throughout this chapter, the terms *Ethics* is primarily used to denote proper behaviour defined and required by a particular profession, whereas the term *Moral* is used more philosophically to denote what is considered "good" and "bad" in the general sense. It is acknowledged that further elaboration on this definition falls outside the immediate scope of this chapter.

To illustrate this distinction: it could be said that a soldier may be required, by virtue of adherence to the professional ethic of soldiering, to commit an act (e.g., apply lethal force) that many, including perhaps the soldier himself, would consider morally wrong.

Notwithstanding these definitions as stated, there will be variations dictated by the context below.

CONTRIBUTIONS FROM MORAL PSYCHOLOGY

Lawrence Kohlberg was born in Bronxville, New York in 1927. Coming from a comfortable background, Kohlberg was initially more interested in social action than academic study. As evidence of this, in the late 1940s he became second engineer on an old freighter that was smuggling Jewish refugees past the British blockade of Palestine.

Later, during his PhD studies at Chicago University, Kohlberg was exposed to and quickly engaged the theories of moral development in children as proposed by the Swiss Psychologist, Jean Piaget (1896-1980). Following the completion of his PhD in 1958, Kohlberg's academic career was to span Yale, Chicago and Harvard Universities from the mid 1950s to the late 1970s. He maintained his link with the nation of Israel by returning there in 1969 to study moral reasoning among the younger members of the collective settlements. Later, he contracted a serious illness while conducting research in Belize in 1971 and this brought debilitating bouts of pain and illness that were to accompany him for the rest of his life.

As a result of Kohlberg's work a whole new field of psychology was spawned, that of Moral Psychology. His Six Stages of Moral Reasoning[2] model was developed after researching individuals' responses to stories such as those typified by the well-known *Heinz Dilemma* (Figure 1). Given Kohlberg's commitment to matters of social justice, it is perhaps not surprising that for him, moral development was principally concerned with justice in the social field.

The Heinz Dilemma

A woman was near death from a special kind of cancer. There was one drug that the doctors thought might save her. It was a form of radium that a druggist in the same town had recently discovered. The drug was expensive to make, but the druggist was charging ten times what the drug cost him to produce. He paid $200 for the radium and charged $2000 for a small dose of the drug. The sick woman's husband, Heinz, went to everyone he knew to borrow the money, but he could only get together about $1000, which is half of what it cost. He told the druggist that his wife was dying and asked him to sell it cheaper or let him pay later. But the druggist said, "No, I discovered the drug and I'm going to make money from it." So Heinz got desperate and broke into the man's store to steal the drug for his wife.

Should Heinz have broken into the laboratory to steal the drug for his wife? Why or why not?

FIGURE 1: The Heinz Dilemma.

MILITARY ETHICS: INTERNATIONAL PERSPECTIVES

Kohlberg was clear that the stages of this model relate to the reasoning adopted by individuals and not the moral conclusions that are reached. Integral to this approach is the assumption that the *form and structure* of moral reasoning or arguments are distinct to the actual *content* of that reasoning. "How" one reasons is the important element in Kohlberg's Stage theory. As will be seen from the Heinz Dilemma in Figure 1, the justification that the individual makes for his or her particular response is the significant factor in Kohlberg's theory. The *form and structure* of individuals' responses to dilemmas such as those found in the Heinz Dilemma led Kohlberg to discern three levels of moral reasoning, each of these with two stages, as described below:

Level One is the *Pre-conventional Morality* level, so called so because at this stage, individuals do not really understand the conventions and rules of society.

- **Stage 1**: In this stage, "good behaviour" is associated with avoiding punishment. The sort of response made is: "Heinz should not steal the drug because he might be caught and sent to jail."

- **Stage 2**: This could be seen as the "you scratch my back and I'll scratch yours" stage. The sort of response that might be made is: "It is right for Heinz to steal the drug because it can cure his wife and then she can cook for him."

Level Two is the *Conventional Morality* level, so-called so because people in these two stages conform to the conventions and norms of society.

- **Stage 3**: At this stage there is a desire for group approval. Right action is one that would please and impress others.

30   CHAPTER 2

There may be an element of self-sacrifice in the reasoning but this provides the psychological pleasure that is constituted by the approval of others. Reasoning at this stage might suggest the following: "Yes, Heinz should steal the drug. He probably will go to jail for a short time for stealing but his in-laws will think he is a good husband."

- **Stage 4**: Right behavior at stage 4 consists in doing one's duty, showing respect for authority and maintaining the given social order for its own sake. A response to the Heinz Dilemma at this stage might be: "As her husband, Heinz has a duty to save his wife's life so he should steal the drug. But it's wrong to steal, so Heinz should be prepared to accept the penalty for breaking the law."

Level Three is *Post-conventional Morality* level, so-called so because the moral principles that underline the conventions of society are understood.

- **Stage 5**: At this stage, Right action is one that protects the rights of the individual according to rules agreed upon by the whole of society. Thus, while rules are needed to maintain social order, they should not be blindly obeyed. Rather they should be set up and reviewed by social contract for the greater good of society. A response at this stage might say: "Heinz should steal the drug because everyone has the right to life regardless of the law against stealing. Should Heinz be caught and prosecuted for stealing then the law (against stealing) needs to be reinterpreted because a person's life is at stake."

- **Stage 6:** Right action at this stage is determined by a decision of conscience in accord with self-chosen ethical principles appealing to logical comprehensiveness, universality and consistency. These rules are abstract and ethical and are not concrete moral rules such as the Ten Commandments. A suitable stage 6 response to the Heinz Dilemma might be: "Heinz should steal the drug to save his wife because preserving life is a higher moral obligation than preserving property."

As already noted, Kohlberg's framework for moral reasoning is seen to have a clear focus on Social Justice. His hypothetical dilemmas are considered by some to be representative of a very narrow slice of a very broad concept which is morality. To Kohlberg's credit, he acknowledged in his latter writings these very limitations in his work as well the assumptions that he was making.[3]

A CRITIQUE OF KOHLBERG'S WORK

As significant as Kohlberg's work has been, a critique of his work is required to address a number of recurring criticisms.[4]

Measurement. Can moral judgement be measured? Kohlberg developed a dilemma-based interview, using such dilemmas as the Heinz Dilemma (Figure 1). Known as "The Moral Judgement Interview" (MJI), this research tool was refined further by the Neo-Kohlbergians. Firstly as the "Defining Issues Test" (DIT) – a multiple-choice variation on Kohlberg's interview test. The DIT has been used in over 1000 studies, with participants numbering in the hundreds of thousands, across 40 countries.[5] The DIT has been further refined as the DIT-2.[6] Over a period of thirty-five years, a large number of studies have reinforced the validity and usefulness of these tests. In short, something is being measured. However, as indicated below, just what is being measured and what its relationship to good moral behaviour is still needs further refinement.

Developmentalism. Kohlberg's claim for the Six Stage Model is that it is developmental, clearly implying that the greater the age of the individual, the higher the stage of moral reasoning. Early studies using the DIT found through a longitudinal study that two significant issues arise in this regard: firstly, there is evidence that there are gains in moral judgement when age is considered. However, formal education is a more powerful predictor of moral judgement development[7] as evidenced in Appendix 1.

Is higher better? The issue that arises from Kohlberg's model is, "Who says higher is better?" In other words, why is it better to be on stage 6, say, than stage 1? It has been noted that not everything that comes later is necessarily better than that which came before (e.g., losing one's hair or teeth in old age!). Kohlberg's model has been criticized on this ground. Research has revealed that the subjects themselves elected to use higher levels of moral reasoning even when they had the choice to do otherwise. It would appear that "as people outgrow old ways of thinking – as they see them as too simplistic and inadequate – they still understand them but don't prefer them."[8]

Gender Bias. Kohlberg's theory has been criticized as being gender-biased (i.e., in favour of men). Carol Gilligan[9] criticized Kohlberg's theory on the grounds that women have a more caring/relational concept of what is "right" as distinct from the "justice" bias already noted in Kohlberg's thinking.

However, research as outlined in Figure 2 indicates that females consistently score higher in DIT testing than males. Recent studies, utilizing the DIT – 2 test[10] indicate that moral judgement scores do increase with level of education and are slightly higher for women.[11]

GRADE	MALES	FEMALES
Junior High	19.1	19.8
Senior High	28.7	30.4
College	44.1	45.9
Graduates	61.0	63.0

FIGURE 2: Average DIT P score Grouped by Education and Sex.[12]

Moral Universalism. Kohlberg's *moral universalism* has been criticized. He maintained that since reasoning *processes* are being measured – as opposed to particular forms of morality – then it is reasonable to expect that what is being measured can be found in all cultures, not just western cultures. Taking the DIT scores spread over countries as diverse as Iceland, Hong Kong, Australia and the USA (see Appendix 2), early evidence would suggest that moral reasoning development is universal (i.e., discernable in similar trends across different cultures). More recent research in this area by Neo-Kohlbergians has questioned this universalism and it is seen as an area that requires further verification.

Further challenges to Kohlberg's universalism come from the perspectives of Moral Philosophy. It is maintained that Kohlberg's original work was shaped by a very different philosophical environment than that which exists today.[13] In Kohlberg's day, it was more of a philosophical priority to find a *foundational philosophical principle*. This is simply no longer the case.

DOES ETHICAL EDUCATION ACTUALLY IMPACT MORAL JUDGEMENT AND REASONING?

Can moral judgement be stimulated by deliberate educational intervention? Meta-analyses of 56 moral intervention programs say yes, but only moderately (about the same effect as most college programmes).[14] What is of interest is that it has been found that it is never *too late* to educate morally and that University or Professional School students responded the best to such interventions.

Furthermore, subsequent studies have looked more closely at the impact of the environment (i.e., the *type* of institution) and other factors that might have an effect on moral reasoning. Significant differences were found between different types of institutions: post-conventional gains in moral reasoning were found to be significant in students progressing through a liberal arts university environment, whereas students progressing through a Bible University showed far fewer gains in this area.[15]

Does the measurement of moral judgement correlate with other measures of human development? Using the DIT measure, the following strengths of correlation were found:

- correlation with other measures of moral thinking is *significant*;
- correlation with most Personality Trait measures is *non-significant*;.
- correlation with IQ measures is *moderate*; and
- correlation with socio-economic status is *slight*.[16]

To return to the originally stated two-fold issue: does Kohlberg's work offer a suitable model for measuring the effectiveness of military ethics programmes and, if so, could better soldiers, sailors, airmen and women be made as a result of effort expended in such educational interventions?

Research undertaken by Kohlberg and Neo-Kohlbergians indicates that while the correlation between moral reasoning and moral behaviour is, in statistical terms, significant, it is a relationship that is *moderate* in strength only. This research goes on to indicate that other factors, both psychological and environmental are at interplay in ethical education.

On the grounds of this moderate correlation, it is tempting to question just what utility Kohlberg's work might have for those charged with moral or ethical education in the military context. If enhanced moral reasoning does not necessarily equate with superior moral behaviour – are we anywhere nearer finding a tool that can take the guess work out of our assessment of ethics education in the military? In short, is an evidence-based model of ethics education a viable option for use in the military context?

THE FOUR COMPONENT MODEL (FCM)

The response on the part of the Neo-Kohlbergians is hopeful. After a review of the ethical and moral educational material, Rest formulated a more comprehensive model of the areas which have an effect on moral behaviour.[17] Four major components were identified and it is from this structure that Rest's model takes its name. The four components determining ethical behaviour are deemed to be:

1. Moral Sensitivity,[18] more recently referred to as *Ethical Sensitivity*,[19] (i.e., the manner is which the moral situation is interpreted).

2.   Moral Judgement, more recently described as *Moral Reasoning and Judgement*, this component builds directly on the original work of Kohlberg and is measured by the DIT and DIT-2 and earlier variants. It is the component focused on by Kohlbergians until the development of the four component model.

3.   Moral Motivation, more recently described as *Moral Motivation and Commitment*, this component has to do with "putting moral values higher than other values – when other values such as self actualization or protecting one's organization replace the concern for doing what is right"

4.   Moral Character, latterly renamed as *Moral Character and Competence*. Rest saw this component as referring to ego strength and moral backbone.

In a paper summarizing the most recent findings (33 studies with approximately 6600 respondents) related to moral judgement development in five different professions (Medicine, Law, Veterinary Science, Dentistry and Nursing), the contribution of the DIT and Four Component Model (FCM) have been considered.[20] The author of this paper, Dr. Muriel Bebeau, has a strong background in Moral Psychology and as a Neo-Kohlbergian, she spent three decades developing ethics curricula for the American Dental Association, initially using the DIT but then progressing to researching the FCM itself. More recently, Bebeau spent time at West Point, where she had the opportunity to share her thinking with faculty there. In broad terms, Bebeau's research on the use of the FCM in professions, sheds light on the following:

Component 1 – Ethical Sensitivity. Defined as "the awareness of how our actions affect other people"[21] and "the ability to interpret the moral dimensions of an unstructured problem,"[22] this component addresses the issue of why people who should know better, have lapses and blind spots in their behaviour. The choice of ethical sensitivity as opposed to moral sensitivity is deliberate: what is to be measured is an individual's ability to conform to a preset professional code of ethics, not that individual's broader moral stance.

Studies have shown that across a wide-range of professions, those who are in training and even in practice, have anything but uniformly-developed sensitivity to profession-specific issues.[23]

How is ethical sensitivity assessed? One example of a measure of Ethical Sensitivity can be seen in the use of videos developed specifically to replicate professional issues directly related to the Dental Professional Code of Ethics.[24] Verbal responses were invited from participants; these were then transcribed and assessed by a number of experienced members of the dentistry profession. After this assessment process was refined, the following was found:

1.   Ethical sensitivity *can* be reliably assessed. As will be seen below, Bebeau is adamant that assessment of all of the components plays a prominent role in enabling improved moral and ethical behaviour in individuals.[25]

2.   Students, practitioners and the educating institutions all varied markedly in their scoring (some training institutions were more ethically attuned than others).

3.   Women have a slight edge over men in recognizing ethical issues.

4.   Ethical sensitivity *can* be enhanced through education.

5.   "Professionals may be skilled at interpreting the ethi-
      cal dimensions of a situation (ethically sensitive) but
      unskilled at working out a balanced view of a moral
      solution (moral judgment)."[26] In short, it is possible to
      break the pre-defined codes of practice of a given pro-
      fession by reasoning away the relevance of such rules
      and codes. If no one gets hurt, where's the problem?

Component 2 – Moral Reasoning and Judgement. Defined as
"the ability to reason through what ought to be done and settle
on a morally defensible action."[27] As noted, a considerable
amount of research has been undertaken by Kohlberg and the
neo-Kohlbergians in the area of moral reasoning and judgement.

Research in this area indicates:[28]

1.   Students need instruction in ethical reasoning. The abil-
      ity to reason ethically requires as much development as
      other professional/technical skills.

2.   Dilemma-based discussion is effective in enhancing
      moral reasoning, however, criteria and feedback are es-
      sential for overcoming student's relativistic perspective.[29]

3.   Essay results were not highly correlated with DIT
      scores.

4.   While a liberal arts education has a significant effect
      on a student's ability to reason morally, for this effect
      to be sustained throughout the period of professional

development and into the professional career, a deliberate and evidence-based ethics curriculum needs to be applied.

5. "There is extensive literature showing the relationship between moral judgement development and clinical performance."[30]

6. Self-assessment by students of ethical education intervention was very positive.

Component 3 – Moral Motivation and Commitment. In essence, this component refers to the professional identity that different professions attempt to establish and promote among its own professionals. Using a *Professional Role Orientation Inventory* (PROI) research revealed:

1. Students and professionals hold different conceptions of their role.

2. Students need explicit instruction in role concept.[31]

Research indicates that individuals' understandings of their professional expectations tend to change over time. Notably, the full integration of personal and professional values does not appear to take place until mid-life.[32] It is noted that individuals move through a range of attitudes; from a self-centered conceptualization of their identity through to a more self sacrificial one. Moreover, professional moral exemplars consider certain actions as ethically necessary, whilst others not in this category tend to see such actions as optional.

MILITARY ETHICS: INTERNATIONAL PERSPECTIVES

Further studies have indicated that students entering a profession do not just absorb values of the profession by *osmosis*. In the case of the dental profession students, even after ethics instruction, they were unable to clearly articulate the expectations of that profession.[33] Added to this, the informal processes of induction into the profession were found to encourage the perception of self-regulation and professional reporting as a sort of "telling tales out of school".

Bebeau reports on *whistle-blowing* as researched within a group of Scottish medical students. Of the students surveyed, only 40 percent indicated that one *should* report misconduct, while a mere 13 percent indicated that they *would*. Somewhat alarmingly, the number of students who indicated that misconduct *should* be reported diminished with the number of training years completed.[34]

Bebeau also outlines the research by Forsythe and colleagues on the development of the professional identity of officers in the US Army in the 21st century. Given her insistence that component effects be measured for the benefit of the professional involved, the PROI provides such a tool as evidenced in the following observation:

> …30% of West Point graduates (interviewed at various stages of the educational process) have not achieved key transitions in identity formation that would enable them to have the broad, internalized understanding of codes of ethics or the commitment to professional standards.[35]

The development of professional identity by *osmosis* or *enculturation* is deemed to be less effective than deliberate and explicit approaches to the development of moral motivation and commitment.

Component 4 – Moral Character and Competence: Interpersonal skills, problem solving skills, fatigue levels and ego strength (or weakness) all contribute to moral character and competence. Both students and professionals are found to vary widely in their levels of moral character and strength.

To enhance professionals' force of their own conviction (i.e., for professionals to have confidence in their own ability to make ethical decisions), opportunities to reflect on ethical practice should be provided on a frequent basis. Opportunities to self-assess their own development in this area have proven helpful in this regard.[36]

CONCLUSION

This chapter has sought to answer the two linked questions: how is the effectiveness of the *Ethos and Values* approach measured? If the effectiveness of the *Ethos and Values* approach can be measured, do we have any assurances that we can make better soldiers, sailors, airmen and women?

There is clear evidence to suggest that moral reasoning and judgement can be enhanced by ethics education. This has been well researched by moral psychologists. Furthermore, the effect can be measured.

Research has also shown, however, that improved moral judgement and reasoning does not necessarily lead to improved moral behaviour (i.e., the better soldiers, sailors, airmen and women that we require). In more precise terms: the relationship between moral reasoning and judgement and moral behaviour is *moderate* in strength only.

Neo-Kohlbergians, therefore, widened the scope of their research to include three other components that influence the moral behaviour of individuals. The Four Component Model (FCM) was developed to include the development of assessment of such components as: "Ethical Sensitivity", "Moral Motivation and Commitment", "Moral Character and Competence" as well as the already well-researched moral reasoning and judgement.

At the present time, the three new components have not been as well researched as moral reasoning and judgement. Bebeau cautions against neglecting these components, however, "…neglecting other abilities suggested by the FCM leaves professionals at risk. Individuals need to know whether they can reliably interpret ethical issues, articulate the norms, values, laws and codes that govern professional practice and implement defensible action plans effectively and efficiently. Instruction without measures to help students see their strengths and shortcomings, and to compare them to peers as well as to seasoned and exemplary colleagues, is unlikely to promote competence."[37]

In our search for better military personnel, the measurement of our ethical educational programs is critical to the effectiveness of those very programs. Reliable measurement tools such as the DIT, DIT-2 and the PROI will need to become part of the ethics educator's vocabulary and inventory.

Although ongoing research is required, for those charged with the delivery of ethics education, the FCM represents the most researched hope for an overarching strategy for an often under-coordinated field of expertise. We owe nothing less to our soldiers, sailors, airmen and women.

Appendix 1

DIFFERENT GROUPS ON THE DIT *P* SCORE

P-SCORE	GROUP
65.2	Moral Philosophy and Political Science grad students
59.8	Liberal Protestant Seminarians
52.2	Law students
50.2	Medical students
49.2	Practicing physicians
47.6	Dental students
46.3	Staff nurses
42.8	Graduate students in business
42.3	University students in general
41.6	Navy enlisted men
40.0	Adults in general
31.8	Senior High School students
23.5	Prison inmates
21.9	Junior High School students
18.9	Institutionalized delinquents

Appendix 2

A CROSS CULTURE STUDY OF AGE/
EDUCATION TRENDS IN MORAL JUDGEMENT[38]

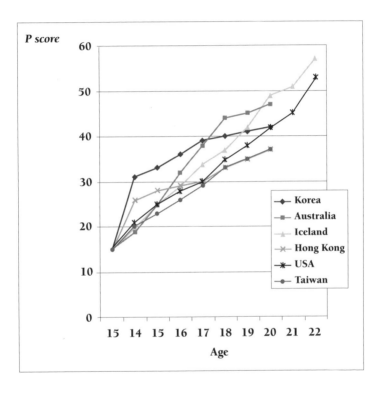

ENDNOTES

1   *The Army Leadership Framework* (Wellington: New Zealand Army, 2007).

2   Lawrence Kohlberg, *Essays on Moral Development, Vol. I: The Philosophy of Moral Development* (San Francisco, CA: Harper & Row, 1981).

3   Lawrence Kohlberg, "A Current Statement on Some Theoretical Issues", in Sohan Modgil and Celia Modgil, *eds.*, *Lawrence Kohlberg: Consensus and Controversy* (Philadelphia: Falmer Press, 1986), 499-500.

4   James Rest, "Background: Theory and Research," in James Rest and Darcia Narvaez, eds., *Moral Development in the Professions: Psychology and Applied Ethics* (Hillsdale New Jersey: Lawrence Earlbaum Associates, 1994), 1-26.

5   James Rest, Darcia Narvaez, Steve Thoma and Muriel Bebeau, "DIT-2: Devising and Testing a Revised Instrument for Moral Judgement," *Journal of Educational Psychology*, Vol. 91 (1999), 644-665.

6   Rest, "Background: Theory and Research," 15.

7   Rest and Narvaez, *Moral Development in the Professions*, 17.

8   Carol Gilligan, *In a Different Voice* (Harvard University Press, 1982).

9   Rest, Narvaez, Thoma and Bebeau, "DIT-2" Devising and Testing a Revised Instrument for Moral Judgement."

10   Yukiko Maeda, Muriel Bebeau and Steve Thoma, "Understanding the Relationship Between Moral Judgement Development and Individual Characteristics: The Role of Education Contexts," *Journal of Educational Psychology*, Vol. 101 (2009), 233-247.

11   Rest and Narvaez (1994), *Moral Development in the Professions*, 14.

12   James Rest, Darcia Narvaez, Steve Thoma and Muriel Bebeau, "A Neo-Kohlbergian Approach to Morality," *Journal of Moral Education*, Vol. 29 (2000), 381-396.

13   James Rest, *Moral Development: Advances in Research and Theory* (New York: Praeger Press, 1986).

14   Ibid., 234.

15   Rest and Narvaez, *Moral Development in the Professions*, 21-22.

16   Rest, "Background: Theory and Research," 1-26.

17   Ibid.

18   While adopting and researching the Four Components, Bebeau renamed the components. See Muriel Bebeau, "Evidence-based Ethics Education," *Summons*, (Summer 2005), 12-13.

19   Muriel Bebeau, "The Defining Issues Test and the Four Component Model: Contributions to Professional Education," *Journal of Moral Education*, Vol. 31, No. 3 (2002), 272-294.

20   Rest and Narvaez, *Moral Development in the Professions*, 23.

21   Bebeau, "Evidence-based Ethics Education," 12-13.

22   Muriel Bebeau, "Designing an Outcome-based Ethics Curriculum for Professional Education: Strategies and Evidence of Effectiveness," *Journal of Moral Education*, Vol. 31, No. 3 (2002), 271-295.

23   Muriel Bebeau, James Rest and Catherine Yamoor, "Measuring Dental Students' Ethical Sensitivity," *Journal of Dental Education*, Vol. 49, No. 4 (1985), 225-235.

24   Ibid., 13.

25   Rest and Narvaez, *Moral Development in the Professions*, 128.

26   Bebeau, "Evidence-based Ethics Education," 12.

27   Rest and Narvaez, *Moral Development in the Professions*, 129-132.

28   Bebeau, "Evidence-based Ethics Education," 12; and, Rest and Narvaez, *Moral Development in the Professions*, 132.

29   Bebeau, "Designing an Outcome-based Ethics Curriculum for Professional Education: Strategies and Evidence of Effectiveness," 279-280.

30   Ibid., 286.

31   James Rule and Muriel Bebeau, *Dentists Who Care: Inspiring Stories of Professional Commitment* (Chicago: Quintessence, 2005).

MILITARY ETHICS: INTERNATIONAL PERSPECTIVES

32   Muriel Bebeau, "Influencing the Moral Dimensions of Dental Practice," in James Rest, and Darcia Narvaez, eds., *Moral Development in the Professions: Psychology and Applied Ethics* (Hillsdale New Jersey: Lawrence Earlbaum Associates, 1994), 129-132.

33   Bebeau, "Evidence-based Ethics Education," 13.

34   George Forsythe, Scott Snook, Philip Lewis and Paul Bartone, "Making Sense of Officership: Developing a Professional Identity for 21st century Army Officers," in Don Snider and Gayle Watkins, eds., *The Future of the Army Profession* (New York: McGraw Hill, 2002). Quoted in: Muriel Bebeau, (2002), 285.

35   *Integrity in Scientific Research: Creating an Environment That Promotes Responsible Conduct* (Washington: National Academy Press, 2002).

36   Bebeau, "Designing an Outcome-based Ethics Curriculum for Professional Education: Strategies and Evidence of Effectiveness," 289-290.

37   Rest and Narvaez, *Moral Development in the Professions*, 19.

38   Rest, "Background: Theory and Research," 19.

CHAPTER 3

Beyond Good and Evil – or, A Genealogy of Ethics: Challenges for Professional, Unprofessional and Amateur Users of Force

Dr. Mie Augier
*Dr. Jamie MacIntosh**

> **"A man as he *ought* to be: that sounds to us as insipid as a tree as he ought to be."**
>
> **Nietzsche, *Will to Power***

INTRODUCTION

For some would-be realists the term *international law* might seem like an oxymoron. Conflicts prevail between States; the state of nature is untamed. Sovereign bodies either resolve disputes through secret diplomacy or combat decides their outcome. In the absence of law, arguing that morals and ethics are on stronger ground is difficult. Nonetheless, human practices of war and combat have rarely – if ever – been entirely devoid of customary practice and treaties. Whether regarded as primitive or advanced, the way people conduct themselves in combat and the principles societies articulate through war have evolved and will continue to do so. This is never a tidy process.

---

* The views expressed in this chapter are those of the authors and do not necessarily reflect the official policy of the British Armed Forces.

Between the mid-19th and mid-20th centuries, the Laws of Armed Conflict, as a register of morals and ethics, were upheld and debased to unprecedented levels. Shame and disgust at the Holocaust has not brought the evolution of ethics or morals to the end of history. Total War did give way to the Mutually Assured Destruction (MAD) terror of Total Peace for some. For others, so-called Low Intensity Conflict (LIC) kept the scourge war as virulent and intimate as ever. In the third decade since the end of the Cold War, there is little to suggest that ethics and morals can or will stop evolving.

Firms riding the flows of trade and capital have created global marketplaces. The interdependencies woven by globalization are now transnational, reaching far below inter-State relations. However, to presume, as was done in the early modern era, that the "doux commerce"[1] can tame human passions and the state of nature with pure rational interests may be rash. The geo-economic hegemony heralded as the *Washington Consensus* in the immediate post-Cold War era was a short-lived unipolar moment or perhaps even a mirage. In the wake of recent economic crises, outbursts of raw statecraft may again resurge as the multipolar world morphs to accommodate rising and declining powers.

Nonetheless, our capacity as a species to innovate is today without precedent. Debt, demographics, scarce resources and collapsing biodiversity will spur innovation further. This may even accord with human altruism – not least that of warriors – but innovation does not always lead to outcomes that are societally beneficial or healthy; and evolution and innovation is not always efficient.[2] How professional our societies are with these ethical challenges is an increasingly difficult question. Pleas for moral rectitude heralded by the word "*ought*" not only earned the disdain of

Nietzsche (for once in accord with the rationalist adherents of positive jurisprudence), but have also continued to demonstrate their practical weakness. Ultimately, these ethical challenges are not just questions for the military but the societies from which they hail and the other professionals with which they must work. Thus, the purpose of this chapter is to explore aspects of how strong professional ethics can promote societal resilience.

Bounds

The chapter takes an interdisciplinary approach for its minor genealogy of ethics. What enables the integration of multiple disciplines is a sharper focus on the insights evolutionary sciences have to offer. Dynamic networks are a recurring feature.

This approach does not fixate on the topical details of today's western military. The timeframe for evolutionary biology is more of an age than millennia. The cultures of civilizations can take centuries to grow and corrupt. Modern institutions that embody western jurisprudence and moral philosophy are very short-lived.

Meantime, our fitness for the challenges ahead – warriors or not – have little or no lead times to work with. Hierarchical organizations in which authorities can instil moral codes based on the myth of timeless virtues are severely tested by the reality of today. In other words, there has been a change in the organizational and evolutionary nature of the strategic competition – not just in wars and conflict but in other human areas, such as business. In business, the last decade has seen a variety of new organizational forms emerging (franchising, joint ventures, alliances, network firms, etc.). Consistent with this, business and organization theorists have argued for the evolutionary advantages of organizational structures that have no clear hierarchy and are relatively decomposed. This is particularly true in environments with high uncertainty.

Rather than re-invoking the myth of classical virtues, this chapter looks to the evolutionary and behavioural social sciences for a more realistic approach. The ideals of greater pure altruism or strict rational interests are shown to have less ethical or moral traction. Evolutionary evidence that concepts of parochial or reciprocal altruism owe most to our warrior ethos, point us towards a different conclusion on the professional use of force. The hard question is whether citizens – in or out of uniform – can be professional enough to learn with the grain of our evolutionary heritage given the scale and pace of the challenges ahead.

Assumptions

How ethics and morals relate is highlighted by the difference between training and learning. The questions arising from more indirect uses of force – military or otherwise – are not ducked. This is not just about learning the lessons of the current limitations to the comprehensive approach for countering terrorism and insurgency or the struggle to win a lasting peace through stabilization and reconstruction. Statecraft has always involved more forces than the military *per se*. The ethics of professionals and citizens using and enduring the application of increasingly indirect and complex forces have to be considered in more focused ways. Ethical abstraction has a purpose. These assumptions pave the way for understanding how professionalism can enhance societal resilience.

Structure & Flow

The chapter is structured to flow around four sections. The first section uses Boolean logic to explain how ethics and morals relate to one another. This is a devise for clarifying how professionalism, particularly where lethal and harmful forces amplify uncertainty, can be made coherent without succumbing to idealism or over-weening rationalism. The second section focuses on recent evolutionary insights and the heritage of altruism it ascribes to warriors. The third section considers aspects of professionalism in medicine and business administration. It then moves on to anticipate how the challenges ahead can evolve and how the use of force will involve citizens in ethical and moral questions, which are anything but unreal even if increasingly indirect. It will also touch on the perils of privatization, particularly where the use of forces is concerned. The final section considers how the embodiment of ethics and morals can scale through professionalism to organizations learning fitness in sufficient time through hierarchies and networks open to reality rather than that of closed institutions. This is a vital question if the prospects of citizens' professionalism enhancing societal resilience are more than a pious wish.

OF "AND" AND "XNOR": THE FUZZY LOGIC OF ETHICS & MORALS

Peter Singer provides a summary of three abiding themes in Ethics as:[3]

1. "disagreements over whether ethical judgements are truths about the world or only reflections of the wishes of those who make them";

2. "frequent attempts to show, in the face of considerable scepticism, either that it is in one's own self interest to do what is good or that, even though this is not necessarily in one's own interests, it is the rational thing to do"; and,

3. "repeated debates over just what goodness and the standard of right or wrong might be".

There are many twists and turns in the academic discourses on morality that, true to ethics as an abstraction, can only be given glancing reference at best. Within military ethics, the topic of this book, the question of ethics has of course occupied the minds (and the papers) of many contributors across countries, alliances and borders in recent times.

In the United Kingdom (UK), the *Values and Standards for the British Army* (2008) tries to place moral dimensions as central to military strategy and practice. This follows a pattern of academic and institutional interest in the topic of morality and ethics, which owed much to debate about the pattern of events in the Balkans, Sierra Leone, Iraq and Afghanistan. The three conferences and edited compendia produced over the turn of the millennium by Patrick Mileham, leading to his RUSI Whitehall Paper on *War and Morality*, evidence the level of concern.[4]

As with past centuries, the masses of moral material from which to distil ethics that will enable professional learning are daunting. This section will use Boolean logic to begin sharpening the focus on what an evolutionary perspective has to offer.

War is the lethal province of uncertainty. The pace, scale and intensity of events in combat, the uptake of innovation and the winning of the peace makes upholding laws a worthy but challenging endeavour. In such circumstances, moral behaviour is perhaps best not thought about. There is no time for educative debate. Training must assure us that as combatants, commanders and society's citizens, so far as is possible, that what is done, is right. Codified training for behaviour can be optimized to produce correct actions where time is short and pressures monstrous, but is up against a law of diminishing returns. Irrespective of how precise the codification for training is, the endless permutations of factors in events will reveal the limits of the most thorough training. Beyond moral training must come ethical learning, but it too, is no council of perfection.

The first, second and third order moral problems categorized by Patrick Milham's paper on military ethics creates a framework for ethical abstraction. Training for the first order moral problems has to be a sustained institutional effort. In combat between states, there are well codified principles for:

- discriminating combatants and their support from protected bodies and entities;

- what scale of force is proportionate to the circumstances; and,

- how needless cruelty is avoided in the way force is applied.

Keeping what is codified fit for our times is a capacity issue. Non-state combatants are a continuing problem yet to be resolved. Precision guided munitions have mismanaged expectations of proportionality among several constituencies – for and against their use. Whether ascribing to normative or consequentialist schools of morality, it is never easy to argue that lethal and injurious force can be more or less cruel. Overall, an exclusive focus on combat can be unhelpful.

Transitioning back and forth between war and peace, brings on more ethical challenges than applying tests of discrimination, proportionality and cruelty to combat. The harm done by indirect forces or their absence (e.g., the force of law as policing and criminal justice come to play their part in statecraft) is too often ignored. The overlap of civil and military forces in the twilight zone that is neither a well bounded interstate war nor peace, also presents major moral problems that cannot be ignored. They cannot be dismissed as second or third order consequences that require near "omniscience" that amounts to "guesswork". These challenges are of human making.

The politics of legislation during the last century or so have shaped the operational theatres of today. Operational commanders campaigning now, military or civilian, need not only to build on the assumption that moral training is assured (and will not breakdown in errors of strategic and irrecoverable consequence), but that they can also contribute to the drive for professional ethical education in real time. "Above my pay-grade" is a lame excuse for failure.

In these terms, Boolean logic helps differentiate moral training from ethical education for professionals. Moral training and ethical education are complementary and must work together, but are different. Tame moral problems that can be kept so, make wicked ethical challenges easier to focus on. It could also clarify what law-making (rather than just law-upholding) capacity is required; if the burden on moral training and ethical education is not to be overwhelming. However, if moral certainty is overextended, challenges become less tractable. Claims for universality can quickly tempt a backlash of moral relativism. This is why the West repudiated the Just War Doctrine after 1648. Escaping the trap of my just war being your unjust war and vice versa, took some realism that can still confound advocates of normative jurisprudence or classical virtues today. Boolean logic can provide ethical abstraction that clarifies the point.

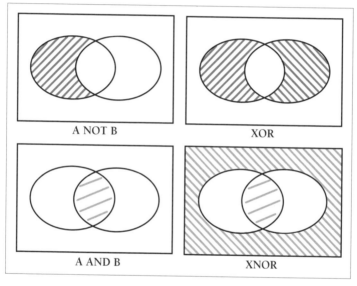

FIGURE 1: Four Venn Diagrams of Boolean Logic.

In terms of good and evil, most people will claim to be good rather than evil (A NOT B in Boolean logic, see figure above). In less loaded terms, moral training will strive to differentiate good from bad behaviour. Such work often wrestles with the overlap of good and bad but tends to exclude the middle (XOR). Where good and bad can be differentiated and moral training is required, it can be done. However, ethics requires more.

Whatever absolutes and universals we might wish to uphold, people's behaviour is the reality we need to contend with. This is not to invite moral relativism. An evolutionary approach is realistic. Bodies evidence good and bad (A AND B) behaviour through time, irrespective of intent or knowledge of what *ought* to be done. Individual bodies interact with others on various scales (groups, hierarchies, networks), all of whom are capable of being good and bad in the flux of events. Professional ethics therefore, needs to focus on XNOR, the interaction of bodies (capable of being good and bad) often coming from different cultures and brought together in contingent circumstances that throw up challenges beyond optimized moral training.[5] In Boolean logic, ethics is more about the fuzziness of AND and XNOR than A AND B and XOR.

Professionalism cannot take moral training for granted. However, ethical education has to wrestle with the uncertainties, fuzziness and ambiguity of evolving reality. This is where the challenge for professionals becomes hardest for anything but academic reasons. If institutions fail to maintain the fitness of moral and legal codes because of capacity and process bottlenecks or the politics of legislation, then ethical education is going to be more vital than ever.

EVOLUTIONARY INSIGHTS ON BEHAVIOUR

Scholars of ethics often contrast "*is*" with "*ought*" (the facts of what *is* done by people versus the norms of what they *ought* to do). Scholarly interest in the contrast of *is* and *ought* is not limited to moral philosophy. Labels for schools of ethics – Naturalistic, Emotivist, Utilitarianist, Intuitionist etc – may belong to moral philosophy but have more than a passing association with science. Darwin and Herbert Spencer drew strong connections between their evolutionary science and the moral philosophy of Jeremy

Bentham and J.S. Mill as Hedonistic Utilitarianism. Spencer may have been among the first to consider altruism but his crude Social Darwinism had shameful consequences. Eugenics and Nazism found value in Spencer's work and evidenced just how dangerous and vile *is* turning into *ought* can be.

The stains on Social Darwinism notwithstanding, bold claims for evolutionary ethics have been made since Nazism. For instance, during the 1970s, the socio-biologist Edward Wilson asserted that "scientists and humanists should consider together the possibility that the time has come for ethics to be removed temporarily from the hands of the philosophers and biologicized".[6] Conflating *is* with *ought* can lead to timeless naturalistic fallacies. Nothing so exaggerated, controversial or mistaken is intended here. Rather evidence, concepts, models and assumptions are all rendered open to falsification. Aside from good philosophy of science, falsification accords with Phillipa Foot's major contribution to ethics. Foot replaces the categorical imperative – so beloved by normative ethics built on Kant – with hypothetical imperatives.[7] This provides a more realistic approach for professional learning.

Evolutionary insights can avoid the naturalistic fallacy of collapsing *is* into a timeless *ought* by working towards hypothetical imperatives that are open to falsification. This process can begin by considering the evolutionary heritage of the words associated with ethics and morals; and even the concepts themselves reveal ambiguity. Whilst the Greek word "ethics" is more to do with conceptual and philosophical learning, the Roman origins of the word morals focus more on what is done. The two are not incommensurable but can easily be confused. Contemporary uses of these words often do little to help clarify how distinct and complementary they are or can be. Terms like "meta-ethics" perhaps add to the confusion.

MILITARY ETHICS: INTERNATIONAL PERSPECTIVES

Here, moral action will be presumed more fixed and customary; whereas ethics is more abstract enabling patterns to be discerned in behaviour and providing models that can support learning. Such learning is less about proving a truth as timeless or self-evident; it is more concerned with producing responsible understanding – through falsification – of how matters evolve. This is a realist not relativist or purist approach. Kantian categorical imperatives will either tempt conscious exceptions in the minds of elitists or be confounded by the good and bad brought out in anyone by events. Hypothetical imperatives can be explored responsibly together to produce community and social resilience.

Hypothetical imperatives may be paradoxical. These will certainly span different durations of time that co-evolve. For example, the evolution of neurological anatomy and physiology as well as the genetic selection of predispositions to altruism or selfishness work on quite different timescales from political institutions and the uptake of technology. All are evolutionary and interwoven as time moves on. There is no presumption of perfectibility in the end; teleology is more an issue of faith than reason. Until otherwise falsified, the process of evolution works through what are dissipative systems adhering to the second law of thermodynamics. Growth and decay are simultaneous. Three evolutionary strands of ethics are considered here:

1.   conflict as altruism's midwife;[8]

2.   the cost of learning to kill;[9] and,

3.   psychological experiments marking the ease with which badness can prevail.

Altruism has long been a keen topic of ethical enquiry. Recent interdisciplinary studies have added to the interest in the topic because they suggest that altruism has been selected over the ages by participation in combat. These studies combine archaeological studies of protracted periods with agent based computer modelling.[10] They do not suggest that pure altruism confers immediate or enduring advantage. Rather, it is in combination with what is termed parochialism that advantage accrues both in the heat of battle and across generations. Parochialism is selfish; it only favours people like us. Since diversity enriches learning and inheritance, parochialism alone has its downsides. Likewise, altruism may be a nicer quality but can disadvantage individuals and populations. The combination of parochial altruism may offer a healthy blend of *is* and *ought* or more moral selection and training to buy time for professional ethical learning.

In keeping with many studies of combat, evolutionary sciences are finding that qualified altruism is vital to survival in battle. Sharing warning cries, being prepared to lay down your life for brothers in arms and enduring hardship together equitably, all make sense to small units in the province of lethal uncertainty. These advantages are not limited to battle with other humans but also groups struggling through hostile environments. The combination of parochialism aggression towards outsiders with an altruisms impulse to share and cooperate are a war winning combination. Conversely, where selfishness and pure altruism can thrive separately in times of peace, they threaten a population at war. It is as well not to disadvantage parochial altruists in peacetime, because it is hard to tell how long peace will last.

Parochial aggression towards outsiders is not without its penalties. Whatever these heritable traits acquired over the ages by us humans and the evidence of our warlike tendencies that exceed any other species, there is also biological evidence that humans find it hard to kill – not least combatants. Investments in training during the 20th century did much to overcome the reluctance of soldiers to engage in combat. Increasing participation in combat has a price for survivors. Whilst some live long lives, even the healthy never recover from the knowledge of what it is to kill.

Taking care to avoid any moral equivalence, the cost of killing is even understood to have taken its toll on war criminals. Members of the *Einsatzgruppen* killing squads are documented as having nervous breakdowns, self-medicating with alcohol and drugs as well as indulging other ill-disciplined and depraved behaviour. Recent studies have described Perpetration-Induced Trauma Syndrome (PITS).[11] For the Nazi's, the threat of morale breaking down in units with links via very highly educated professionals to the highest command authority, may have spurred the uptake of more efficient and reliable bureaucratic and technological innovation with the formation of death camps. It may seem hard to comprehend how such technology and practices worked, particularly when its victims often describe the perpetrators as ordinary people.

Hannah Ardent's phrase "the banality of evil"[12] may have become overstated with time. However, a string of famous psychological experiments (some which would perhaps not pass an ethics committees scrutiny today), evidence how good and bad our behaviour is really capable of being when put to the test. For example:

- Asch's conformity experiment;

- Milgram's authority experiment;

- Zimbardo's Stanford Prison experiment;

- Moscovici's in-group / out-group experiment (not forgetting Jane Elliot's variation on the theme with Iowa school children); and,

- Darley and Latane's Bystander apathy experiments.

The impulse to moral outrage in easier times or at a distance fails to fully grasp the hypothetical imperative put so well by the line: "*All that is necessary for the triumph of evil is that good men do nothing*", attributed to Edmund Burke.[13] When the enforcement of law is weak or unfit for purpose, it takes moral and ethical courage to know how and when to refuse to conform, challenge authority, be inclusive and engage rather than be apathetic. Parochial altruists may have just the right blend of inherited traits to sacrifice themselves for the common good because such behaviour confers immediate and enduring advantage for individuals and the community. Whether this amounts to a customary norm or a learned ethic of responsibility is an important question. It is important not to forget the naturalistic fallacy that conflating *if* and *ought* into a timeless verity can produce.

Unsurprisingly, archaeological evidence suggests that periods of environmental stress are strong indicators of troubled times for humans. A population that has long enjoyed peace may have nurtured a preponderance of pure but untested altruists and selfish individualists. Such a population lacks fitness for environmental adversity as well as combat, which may be visited upon them whether wanted or not. What is less certain is how parochial altruism scales beyond small bands – perhaps depleted by protracted periods of peace – to larger organizations and how bodies learn.

MILITARY ETHICS: INTERNATIONAL PERSPECTIVES

Again, is parochial altruism more of a trained or innate customary norm or can professional ethics learn from more immediate events than genetic selection and cultural traditions?

Parochial altruism may be similar or related to what has elsewhere been described as reciprocal altruism.[14] This term has not been grounded in selection through combat and adversity, although it may account for behaviours in organizations that benefit from what parochial altruism provides a community. The sharing of information, resources and division of labour in organizations builds surpluses and choices that "cheaters" or "freeloaders" may exploit. Studies of reciprocal altruism evidence how powerful the reaction can be by members of a community to cheaters and freeloaders. Other studies are less confident that evolutionary traits (genetic or cultural) retain their fitness and adapt to changing organizational scale or scope activities.[15] Network organizations may enhance the value of reciprocators, particularly with enduring challenges[16] and more hierarchical organizations. It is not clear that parochial altruism born of small-bands can scale to small worlds and their prevailing power laws.[17] This assessment is vital to promoting and learning societal resilience.

ETHICS AND PROFESSIONAL CITIZENS

Ethical issues are also deeply psychological and can change over time. Experiences and events can push the boundaries of what people accept others to do. Thus, perceptions of what may seem right or ethical behaviour can change over time (and influenced for example by combat and other experiences).

One area that has seen increasing discussion is the area of business ethics. Ethics can have economic (and other aspects) and are often linked to our organizational and institutional/governance structure, something evident when unethical behaviour is found in rent-seeking/corrupt behaviour in monetary matters. And indeed, much of economic and business theories rest on notions of individuals as self-interest seeking and opportunistic; with little talk about social aspects and responsibilities of business organizations.

Ethics is also a concept that has been seen as foundational for professionalism. Indeed, the outrage at the events at Enron and in American financial institutions stimulated demands for rethinking the possible role of a code of professional ethics for a profession of management – and thus lead to attacks on modern business schools. For example: Robert Shiller wrote that the business curriculum could lead to an "ethical disconnect" and that the courses "often encourage a view of human nature that does not inspire high-mindedness".[18] Management professor Henry Mintzbergh has also criticized business schools for being part of the problem. He argued that MBA's tend to be arrogant and with a narrow focus on shareholder maximization, and he attributes the lack of social responsibility in business organizations to a focus on individual interests rather than social values and ethics (a focus attributable to elements in the MBA education). Thus, he finds, business schools are not the solution but part of the problem because they are corrupt systems, with corrupt and corrupting students, producing a "society of meanness."[19] Business schools have thus hastened to try and reform their curriculum and increase the emphasis on ethics and professionalism; another area with some conceptual ambiguity.

There is a large literature on professionalism; some of the most thoughtful contributions relates to Abraham Flexner, whose famous report by the Carnegie Foundation helped medical schools build on their professionalism. (Might it be time for a Flexner report for military education?). The Flexner report was a key to the transformation and professionalization of medical education in the early 20th century, improving medical education and medical practice, basing medical education in universities (and not vocational trainings) and their educational programs on solid scientific foundation. The background for the report was the poor state of medical education; mostly based on apprenticeships with little formal instruction and students having little academic preparation before becoming practicing physicians themselves. Although the practice of medicine before the Flexner report had improved somewhat from the days of barber-surgeons, even well-trained doctors had few diagnostic capabilities and their treatments often had little effects on the diseases they treated (some may argue that some recent wars were started because of poor diagnostic understanding of the situation). A Harvard biochemist was quoted as saying that "somewhere between 1910 and 1912, a random patient with a random disease, consulting a doctor chosen at random had, for the first time in the history of mankind, a better than fifty-fifty chance of profiting from the encounter."[20]

The realization of the poor state of medical education led to the articulation of the need for a detailed careful review. Supported by several professional associations (and financially by the Carnegie Foundation), a non-physician, Abraham Flexner, was chosen to do the study which would articulate fully the state of medical education and the need for reform. Working on the report from 1908 to 1910, he visited schools, reviewed medical education in Europe, the United States and Canada. The report both had specific suggestions for which schools to close (and which to improve), and the need to base medicine on science (and thus, medical education in universities) and a professionalization of medicine. One could only improve the practice of medicine through improving the academic and scientific standards of medical practitioners and medical education.[21] Flexner's emphasis on science and fundamental and academic knowledge was linked to the conception of the practice of medicine as a profession. He saw professionalism as an essential feature of good medical practice. Medical education was a professional field because it built on several sciences in a cross disciplinary and problem oriented way.

Flexner's (1915) criteria that he proposed for professionalism (also linked to the moral aspects were): (1) intellectual operations coupled with large individual responsibilities; (2) raw materials drawn from science and learning; (3) practical application, (4) an educationally communicable technique; (5) tendency toward self-organization; and, (6) increasingly altruistic motivation. For Flexner, professions should aspire to be "objective, intellectual and altruistic" and "devoted [more] to the promotion of larger nobler ends than the satisfaction of individual ambitions."[22]

Flexner's concept of professionalism spans across different levels, thus, must have implications for military organizations too (as well as their operations). Alfred North Whitehead in his discussion of *Adventures of Ideas*, recognizes the problems of defining a concept which is linked to both science, ideas, and nature and practice:

> The term Profession means an avocation whose activities are subjected to theoretical analysis, and are modified by theoretical conclusions derived from that analysis. … the practice of a profession cannot be disjoined from its theoretical understanding and vice versa.[23]

Professionals (in this sense) are linked to specialized knowledge that is not readily accessible to, or interpretable by, non-
professionals. Thus, a famous report on business education noted:

> ...the crucial criterion of a profession is ... the existence
> of a systematic body of knowledge of substantial intel-
> lectual content and the development of personal skill in
> the conscious application of this knowledge to specific
> cases.[24]

The link between professionalism and fundamental research-
based knowledge underlies the tendency of for instance, medical schools (and business schools) to associate themselves with
the keepers of fundamental knowledge – the universities, as well
as the tendencies for the guardians of knowledge – the universities – to seek to control professional education. In our context,
this underscores the importance of research for establishing and
maintaining professionalism in military organizations (as well
as in operations), and to rely on fundamental knowledge in our
building of strategic capabilities.

Another aspect of professionalism is trust; not just individual but
mutual or social trust. Richard Dannatt wrote in his foreword to
Values and Standards in the British Army[25] that the good reputation
of the organization "derives from, and depends upon, unequivo-
cal commitment, self-sacrifice, and mutual trust." Professionals
(whether in military or medicine or business or elsewhere) exhibit
a commitment to social responsibility in conduct that takes pre-
cedence over personal or group gain; a concern beyond oneself.
Social trustworthiness should be differentiated from the trustworthiness that is usually discussed in the modern economic and
psychological literature, which deals primarily with interpersonal

trust – the reliability with which a person does what they say they will do. Social trustworthiness is the reliability with which a person acts with the community's interests at heart. Members of a profession or professional organization such as the Army, are bound by autonomous rules of behaviour that reflect the altruistic demands of a professional identity, rather than the demands of an employer, client, or authority, or the temptations of individual self-interest. Thus, lawyers recognize obligations to justice that may conflict with the demands of clients; physicians recognize obligations to proper medical care that may conflict with the demands of health insurance companies; our soldiers, officers and commanders in military organizations recognize obligations of service to a higher cause, often a nation, even at high personal sacrifices. Mary Parker Follett wrote: "The word 'profession' connotes … a foundation of science and a motive of service."[26] In a military context, seeing beyond oneself also includes admitting one's own shortcomings; as one officer in the *Study of Military Professionalism* observed: "It takes a great deal of personal courage to say 'the screw-up occurred here' rather than passing the blame to the lower level."[27]

UNDERSTANDING ORGANIZATIONS

In 1831, General Carl von Clausewitz wrote that business is war. Leo Tolstoy, a few decades later, searched for a theory of war, in much the same way that management scholars have been searching for a theory of business. Tolstoy explored the role of leadership, history and organizational capabilities. Clausewitz and Tolstoy are frequently quoted in the modern management literature for their pioneering insights on business strategy. Like war, business involves competition. But the rules of engagement aren't the same in business as in war. For instance, you cannot burn down your competitors' plant, appropriate their intellectual property, or poison their workers. In business, one tries to outflank competitors by starving them of the best customers or the most talented personnel so that their profits fall and they cannot generate the means to compete with you. In essence, in business you win by engaging in actions and making investments that one way or the other will result in depriving your competitor's of resources whilst making the best use of one's own resources. The legal system and regulations govern how you compete. Another difference is that in warfare, citizens can suffer intense fallout from the invading enemy. In short, externalities or "collateral damage" can be more ubiquitous and damaging in warfare than in business.

Regardless of the differences, recent events (in both military and business) require understanding different organizational structures and systems that are highly complex, and have significant elements of decomposability. Most complex systems are hierarchical and the components at each level are not independent of each other, but there is much denser and more rapid interaction within the components at any level than between components at that level. Such systems are said to be nearly decomposable.[28] When Simon first introduced this idea, it was intended to contribute to our understanding of a central and fundamental property of multi-celled organisms – but it is potentially central to our understanding of some of the mechanisms of some organizational structures, too. This fundamental property is the fact that such organisms consist of a hierarchy of components, such that at any level of the hierarchy, the rates of interaction within components at the level are much higher than the rates of interaction between different components. Such systems are nearly decomposable.[29]

Organizations are prime examples of nearly-decomposable systems and probably the most powerful tool that humans have found to cope with and organize their limited rationality by combining their thinking powers. The near decomposability of organizational structures is a means of securing the benefits of coordination while holding down its costs by an appropriate division of labour among sub-units. Moreover, complex systems, such as organizations, must be created such as to meet the needs of coordination and the prospects for the emergence of an effective complex system, are much greater if it has a nearly decomposable structure than if the interconnections are less departmentalized. Thus, nearly decomposable systems have built in flexibility and competitive advantages that help them survive the evolutionary competition. They have learning advantages too which are central for gaining and maintaining strategic capabilities.

Developments in the studies of organizational behaviour and strategy theory may thus help provide a foundation for the development of an evolutionary and realistic conception of the strategic competition that our military organizations face. It is important, however, that they build on behaviourally realistic assumptions.[30] That is, that we see the world as it is, not as we wish it to be. For while rational strategy models would categorize as acts and decisions, the evolutionary and behavioural perspective see it as outputs of the complex interaction of decision-makers and organizations, and portions of organizations, functioning according to (sometimes standard) patterns of behaviour. Faced with the problems of explaining for instance the behaviour of terrorist networks, one could then better identify the relevant organizational structures, individuals, values and networks (involved in conflicts or attacks) likely to be involved in the sequence of decisions and in the process of carrying out the actions, and the (behavioural, ethical and psychological) characteristics of the individuals engaged in these activities. We would then also understand better the

patterns of organizational behaviour from which the action probably emerged and try and make anticipations of which organizations would likely to be involved in future actions and patterns of
these organizations. Also important would be to try to determine
the organizational culture of the relevant enemy organization and
the way that culture influenced the behaviour of the individuals.
Such information would likely improve our understanding of the
current future security environment and of where ethical issues
may themselves be the source of conflict (and thus try and avoid
them). It might even help us also create a better culture of ethic
and professionalism in our own organizations.

CONCLUSION

"Virtute enim ipsa non tam multi praediti esse quam videri volunt"
(Few are those who wish to be endowed with virtue rather than to seem so).

Cicero, *De Amicitia* (XXVI)

This chapter argues for a shaper focus on realism in ethics. Vacil-
lating between the bounded rationality of what *is* and the idealism of why things *ought* to be better, has and will continue to be
fruitless. Such vacillation merely tempts outbursts of relativism
and murderous expediency. Rational facts and ideal norms have a
tendency to timelessness, whether seeking an end-time or perfect-
ing a universal law. It is no more realist to indulge cynicism or
relativism. Instead, this chapter has explored what evolutionary
science might contribute. Some of the key points and implications
that deserve further elaboration for the implications for ethics in
a military context are:

1.   Boolean logic expressed in Venn Diagrams gives a very
     simple and sharp focus on where attention is needed for

morals and ethics to work with reality. Moral training may instill unthinking behaviour that is fit for certain circumstances. Continuous professional education is vital to ethics. The Venn diagrams signpost the kinds of scholarship in ethics and morals that is realist because uncertainty and time are acknowledged as always already present.

2. Evolutionary ethics may offer ways to develop professional education for ethical responsibility that builds on the appropriate selection, training and retention of moral norms, but does not overextend reliance on these. Such developments cannot assume that the genetic and cultural traits accrued over ages – in particular parochial or reciprocal altruism – are either present in sufficient strength, learnable in sufficient time or indeed fit for the scale and scope of prevailing organizational forms.

3. Examining and building on professionalism at all levels in our education and organizations may help produce a culture of ethics (although wars and conflict will always be around).

4. The strategic competition between organizations (in both military and business) can be understood as a complex dynamic process involving issues of organizational adaptation, learning, and the development and deployment of strategic competencies under the conditions of rapid technological change, high uncertainty and the behavioural assumptions of bounded rationality, etc. This implies greater attention to the organizational structures used by potential and actual enemies. It also

implies greater attention to organizational innovation and the importance of developing flexible capabilities as well as greater attention to developing a code of ethics and professionalism embedded in the culture of our military organizations.

The strategic interaction is about the co-evolution and co-adaptation of organizational and individual and technological capabilities and the competitive landscape, which include current and potential enemies/competitors. It is also about developing flexible competencies that can quickly be reconfigured to different potential enemies.[31]

One of the potential difficulties in achieving a greater sense of ethics is that with more decomposed structures, not only do organizations change; there is a lot more room for ambiguities about what the appropriate codes of ethics are, the right legal frameworks, and so on.

If we keep hanging on to cold war old style organizations and not adapt to change, we are unlikely not just to not professionalize and "ethicalize" our military organizations – we are unlikely to be able to keep ahead in military, economics, and other ways.

ENDNOTES

1   Albert Hirschman, *The Passions and the Interests: Political Arguments for Capitalism Before its Triumph, The 20th Anniversary Edition* (Princeton NJ: Princeton University Press, 1997).

2   James March, *The Ambiguity of Experience* (Cornell: Cornell University Press, 2010).

3   Peter Singer, *Ethics, in the Encyclopaedia Britannica* (Chicago, 1985), 627-648.

4   See Patrick Mileham (ed.): *War and Morality* (proceedings of a RUSI conference "Morality in Asymmetric War and Intervention Operations," held on 19-20 September 2002 (RUSI Whitehall Paper 61. London: Royal United Services Institute, 2004).

5   Alain Badiou, *Ethics: An Essay on the Understanding of Evil*, trans. Peter Hallward (London: Verso, 2001).

6   Edward Wilson, *Sociobiology: The New Synthesis* (Cambridge, Massachusetts: Harvard University Press, 1975), 27.

7   Paul Thompson, "Evolutionary Ethics, Darwinian Ethics and Ethical Naturalism," *Human Evolution*, Vol. 5 No. 2, (1990), 133-138.

8   Samuel Bowles, "Conflict: Altruism's Midwife," *Nature*, Vol. 456, No. 20 (2008), 326-327.

9   Dave Grossman, *On Killing: The Psychological Cost of Learning to Kill in War and Society* (Boston: Little, Brown & Co., 1996).

10   Jung-Kyoo Choi and Samuel Bowles, "The Co-evolution or Parochial Altruism and War," *Science*, Vol. 318 (2007), 636-640; Samuel Bowles, "Did Warfare among Ancestral Hunter-gatherers affect the Evolution of Human Social Behaviours," *Science*, Vol. 324 (2009), 1293-1298; and, Monique Bogerhoff-Mulder, Samuel Bowles, Tom Hertz, Adrian Bell, Jan Beise, Greg Clark, Ila Fazzio, Michael Gurwen, Kim Hill, Paul Hooper, William Irons, Hillard Kaplan, Donna Leonetti, Bobbi Low, Frank Marlowe, Richard McElreath, Suresh Naidu, David Nolin, Patrizio Piraino, Rob Quinlan, Eric Schniter, Rebecca Sear, Mary Shenk, Eric Smith, Christopher von Rueden and Polly Weissner, "Intergenerational wealth transmission and the Dynamics of Inequality in Small-scale Societies," *Science*, Vol. 326 (2009), 682-688.

11   Rachel MacNair, *Perpetration-Induced Traumatic Stress. The Psychological Consequences of Killing* (New York: Authors Choice Press, 2002).

12   Hannah Ardent, *Eichmann in Jerusalem: A Report on the Banality of Evil* (London: Penguin Classics, (1994).

13   The original source for this quote was not found and it is likely attributed or based on a paraphrase of Burke's ideas.

14   Robert Trivers, "The Evolution of Reciprocal Altruism," *The Quarterly Review of Biology*, Vol. 46 (1971), 45-57.

15   John Tooby, Leda Cosmides and Michael Price,"Cognitive Adaptation for n-person Exchange: The Evolutionary Roots of Organizational Behaviour," *Managerial and Decision Economics*, (2006), 103-129.

16   Rui Vilela Mendes, "Network Dependence and Strong Reciprocity," *Advances in Complex Systems*, Vol. 7 (2004), 357–368.

17   Duncan Watts, *Six Degrees: The Science of a Connected Age* (London: Vintage Books, 2004).

18   Robert Shiller, "Who Wall Street Learns to Look the Other Way," *Wall Street Journal*, Op-Ed, February 8, 2005.

19   Henry Mintzberg, *Managers Not MBA's* (London: Pearson Education, 2004), 153.

20   Stephen Ayers, *Health Care in the United States: The Facts and the Choices* (Chicago: American Library Association, 1996), 12.

21   Abraham Flexner, "Medical Education in the United States and Canada: A Report to the Carnegie Foundation for the Advancement of Teaching," *The Carnegie Foundation for the Advancement of Teaching Bulletin*, No. 4, New York City: OCLC 9795002, <http://www.carnegiefoundation.org/publications/medical-education-united-states-and-canada-bulletin-number-four-flexner-report-0>.

22   Abraham Flexner, "Is Social work a Profession?," In *Proceedings of the National Conference of Charities and Correction at the Forty-second Annual Session Held in Baltimore, Maryland*, (1915), 56.

23   Alfred Whitehead, *Adventures of Ideas* (Cambridge: Cambridge University Press, 1933), 72.

24   Robert Gordon and James Howell, *Higher Education for Business* (New York, NY: Columbia University Press, 1959), 71-72.

25   Richard Dannatt, "Values and Standards in the British Army," retrieved from <www.army.mod.uk/documents/general/v_s_of_the_british_army.pdf>.

26   Mary Follet, *Dynamic Administration. The Collected Papers of Mary Parker Follet* (New York: Harper and Brothers, 1940).

MILITARY ETHICS: INTERNATIONAL PERSPECTIVES

27   The Army War College's Study on Military Professionalism (United States Army War College, Carlisle Barracks, Pennsylvania, 1970).

28   Herbert Simon, "The Architecture of Complexity" in Herbert Simon, ed., *The Sciences of the Artificial* (Cambridge: MIT Press, 1962).

29   To characterize, consider the following metaphor: Imagine a large building, with very many rooms with thick walls, each room divided into smaller cubicles with thinner walls. Then, some external disruption occurs, causing the temperature in each cubic centimetre of air to be different from each adjoining cubic centimetre; each cubicle exhibiting a sizable temperature difference from each adjoining cubicle; each room from each adjoining room, and the whole set of rooms from the outdoors. We hold the outdoor temperature constant and shut off the heating and air conditioning, close all doors and see what happens. Rapidly, the temperatures of all the air particles in any single cubicle will become essentially equal. But in the end of an hour, the temperature of all the cubicles in a given room will be the same. By the end of eight hours, the temperatures of all the rooms will be about the same. And by the end of the day, all the rooms will be at the same temperature as the outside air. Never mind that the exact times of equilibration of the place would depend of the Newton coefficient of heat transmission through the walls and ceilings; the sequence is clear. Such a system is the archetype of a nearly decomposable system. It can be thought of as a boxes-within-boxes hierarchy with an arbitrary number of levels. Its special characteristic is that equilibrating interactions within boxes at any level take place much more rapidly than do interactions between boxes at that same level, and similarly all the way to the top of the hierarchy – all this without explicit direction or leadership from any positions of "power" or authority.

30   James March and Herbert Simon, *Organizations 2nd Ed* (Oxford: Blackwell Publishers, 1958).

31   James March, "Rationality, Foolishness, and Adaptive Intelligence," *Strategic Management Journal*, Vol. 27 (2005), 201-214.

CHAPTER 4

Ethics in the 21ˢᵗ Century Profession of Arms: A Context for Developing Leaders of Character

Colonel Joseph Sanders, PhD
Lieutenant-Colonel Douglas Lindsay, PhD
Dr. Craig A. Foster
Colonel James Cook, PhD*

INTRODUCTION

The Profession of Arms is in the midst of an extraordinary transformation. Historically, military might was proven by massing armies against each another and fighting until the dominance of one side was established. Modern warfare and military operations reveal a much different type of battlefield. The terminology that once defined our workspace in the military such as "battlefield", "standing armies", and "economies of scale" has been supplanted by terms like "coalition forces", "peacekeeping operations", and "information operations". This changing context has imperative implications regarding the training of future military forces. One of these specific implications (and the focus of this chapter) involves the decision-making process at the individual and tactical level. Decisions that were once made at senior levels are now

---

* The views expressed in this chapter are those of the authors and do not necessarily reflect those of the United States Air Force Academy or the Department of Defense.

dispersed throughout the military hierarchy. Accordingly, all
military members on the "battlefield" of today must be prepared
to make decisions that do not only influence the success of the
immediate mission, but the completion of the overall theatre
mission. For example, a young sergeant that is leading a squad
through a village in Afghanistan can no longer assume that the
impacts of his/her actions are limited to that geographical location. Poor decisions, such as those that lead to civilian casualties,
could destabilize military-civilian relations locally and diplomatic
relations internationally. Thus, even when operating at a tactical
level, improperly executed decision-making can destabilize the
broad military mission.

The unprecedented importance of tactical-level decision-making
necessitates that our forces behave consistently within the rules
of engagement associated with the area of operations, but also
by certain ethical and moral principles – principles that take into
account the culture of the country in which they are operating.
Therefore, old models of simply training a set of leader skills and
competencies are useful, but no longer sufficient. Rather, service
members must recognize that the situational flux has accelerated
to a point that leader strategies that work one day might not work
the following day. Taken further, leaders cannot be guided solely
by cognitive knowledge, they also require a broader set of fundamental principles related to their sense of self and being. Service
members with the right state of *being* create a capacity for growth
and application versus a set of competencies that might fail as
the situation changes around them. Specifically, this involves being, feeling, thinking, and behaving ethically and effectively even
when encountering novel and often critical situations (as is common to the military profession). To the point, force development
must focus on its service member's fundamental character. In the

present chapter, we address this issue by discussing the United States Air Force Academy's program of developing future officers with the necessary set of fundamental leadership and ethical principles. We begin with a model for developing leaders of character to operate in the current military context. We conclude by reviewing implications of this approach for the profession of arms in the 21st century.

ETHICS IN A CHANGING MILITARY CONTEXT

In his seminal work *The Soldier and the State*, Huntington delineates the profession of arms with respect to three dimensions: expertise, responsibility, and corporateness.[1] He described expertise as a set of specialized knowledge and skills that are required for a unique field of human endeavour. While acknowledging the vast differences in functions and duties, Huntington concludes that the central *expertise* that defines the military profession is the "skilled management of violence." The military profession also has a *responsibility* to the greater society. Members of this profession are not primarily motivated by money or profit, instead they are inspired by a sense of obligation to master and apply their craft for the benefit of society. Finally, military professionals must maintain a sense of *corporateness* – that is, a feeling of unity and collectiveness with other military professionals. The distinct traditions, uniforms, and bureaucratic structure of the military serve to preserve the "select" membership of the profession.

Huntington's classic depiction of the military professional underscores the dramatic changes taking place in the military profession.[2] The 21st century military professional context is marked by increasing complexity, uncertainty, and asymmetrical threats.[3] Such trends have expanded the knowledge and skill requirements for officers. According to Snider, the expertise of the military officer has expanded beyond military-technical to include ethical-moral, political-cultural, and human development.[4] Snider also notes that the demise of the Soviet Union, the end of the Cold War, and the events of September 11 have caused the military to rethink its social responsibilities. Instead of merely protecting their status in the world order, the United States and its allies are now responsible for leading, and in some cases accommodating, world order. Further, joint and coalition operations have redefined "corporateness." Amidst these changes, knowledge and expertise in military ethics has seemingly become omnipresent.

It is not surprising then that military members are expected to observe and preserve a particular set of ethical precepts; the precepts presumably guide military professionals by requiring that they understand explicitly their core organizational values and behaviour in ways that may be distinct from larger society and other professions. According to Gabriel, as the military operates in the larger context of the society it serves, its members must create space where their actions are influenced primarily by the values of the profession of arms.[5] In particular, military ethics form the core values for a profession that is engaged in a very specialized duty that may require the sacrifice or taking of life. Gabriel notes that military ethics is a social enterprise that is more concerned about conforming to professional standards than following personal guides for behaviour (i.e., character).[6] Gabriel also asserts that in order to make pragmatic ethical decisions, military professionals must develop a philosophical ethical foundation that guides ethical behaviour.

Consistent with this theme, service academies, war colleges, and other military educational institutions in the United States

recognize this imperative to help each officer develop and re-
fine a "moral compass." All teach the Western just-war tradition
that began to develop no later than Thucydides and arguably
emerged much earlier.[7] The seven or eight traditional principles
governing the resort to war, gathered under the heading of *jus ad
bellum* – just cause, right authority, right intention, proportionality of ends, last resort, reasonable hope of success, the aim of
peace, and (some would add) public declaration of intent to go to
war – remain the focus of often intense analysis and debate carried
on at every level of U.S. military education. The same is true of
the ethics of actually fighting wars. The just-war tradition places
principles such as non-combatant immunity and proportionality
of means under the heading of *jus in bello*.

Yet, a variety of historical events call into the question the
overarching utility of these just-war principles. During the Cold
War, for instance, many scholars and public officials doubted
whether *ad bellum* principles such as proportionality and reasonable hope of success could possibly be observed when strategic
nuclear weapons loomed behind NATO and Warsaw Pact military
strategies. Retrospective analysis of attacks during the Second
World War, especially the bombings of Hiroshima and Nagasaki
led similarly to penetrating reconsiderations of just-war principles. Conflicts on the Korean Peninsula and especially in Vietnam
tore at the nation's conscience. Once the Soviet Union collapsed,
Western nations struggled to understand how the just-war
tradition might apply to peacekeeping operations, especially
ones that violated post-Westphalian concepts of sovereignty for
the sake of safeguarding human rights, as in Kosovo. After the
attacks of 11 September 2001, new concepts emerged to accommodate the threat of asymmetric warfare conducted with unprecedented tempo and destructive potential. Going far beyond the

long-recognized right to neutralize pre-emptively an imminent threat, for example, the U.S. National Security Strategy of 2002 asserted an unprecedented prerogative to wage "preventive war" in order to forestall the eventual development of a serious threat. Ongoing operations in Afghanistan and (after March 2003) Iraq continue to stoke the debate.

It is not surprising then that the U.S. military educational establishment has developed a strong interest in the obligations that occupying powers should bear. A new category of principles – the *jus post bellum* – has entered the literature and military classrooms. What obligations does an invading power bear toward the country it has occupied? The "decapitation" of the Iraqi government, for instance, and the accompanying devastation of infrastructure during more than seven years of war and insurgency, has left many Iraqis with no or little electricity in their residences, diminished access to health care and education, and a constant vulnerability to sectarian violence. Who, if anyone, bears responsibility to remedy these and other problems? As the task of rebuilding becomes increasingly daunting, the development of a rational *jus post bellum* has become of urgent interest to U.S. military officers. Scholarship in this area remains critical as ineffective and dated analogies abound, especially to the occupation post-Second World War Germany and Japan, societies that were used to centralized control and that enjoyed a high degree of homogeneity. In contrast, the next several years will see the United States and its allies attempt to stabilize and modernize an Iraq that is essentially a colonialist's faction fractured along tribal and religious lines. Afghanistan shares Iraq's tribal parochialism and faces the added challenge of forbidding topography as well as primitive transportation and communications infrastructures.

MILITARY ETHICS: INTERNATIONAL PERSPECTIVES

Awareness of these and other ethical principles remains a critical component of developing a military professional who can make effective decisions in a rapidly changing military environment. These ethical precepts provide a good foundational understanding of rules and consequences, and serve as an ethical guide regarding how members of the profession should think and behave. At the same time, even this brief review of just-war principles demonstrates the potential folly of relying solely on a cognitive awareness of ethical precepts as a guide for military professional behaviour. The ever-changing discussion of ethics and just-war theory demonstrates that ethical dilemmas shift as the nature of warfare changes; thus, ethical principles that apply to warfare today, might not necessarily apply to warfare tomorrow. Likewise, military professionals might encounter specific situations that are not clearly explicable based on broader ethical precepts.

Moreover, military professionals encounter a plethora of psychological pressures that can undermine, or eliminate, the benefits of good ethical training. First, the nature of warfare and military operations can cause military members to neglect the influence of their ethical belief systems. This can occur as military professionals experience painful events that cause ethical reason to be supplanted by desire for revenge. Second, military operations, particularly those in theatre, can corrupt the appropriate application of military ethics. The overwhelming desire for survival, for example, could lead military members to justify actions that would be seemingly unethical in a non-military environment (see, for example, attitude change models like cognitive dissonance).[8] Some incidents of fragging, for example, presumably seemed "ethical" to those doing the fragging, but would appear unethical to many outsiders. Third, the corporateness of military members and the tight emotional bonds that characterize operational military

units probably make military professionals particularly suscep-
tible to conforming to group norms.[9] Unethical group behaviour
can thereby create unethical individual behaviour. Fourth, the
concept of de-individuation could exacerbate the conformity to
unethical group behaviour; de-individuation is a process where
personal values and beliefs are minimized psychologically causing
individuals to conform more to existing situational or group pressure.[10] Military operations provide several factors that can create
heightened states of de-individuation, namely anonymity, physiological arousal, and reduced cues related to the self (e.g., remind-
ers of one's personal life and value system). Fifth, the immediate
and long-term stress of military operations can cause military
professionals to lose their resilience and experience failures to
effectively regulate their behaviour in accordance with personal
values.

Military professionals must therefore be equipped not only with
ethical training, but with the personal fortitude to resist situational factors that disrupt ethical principles. We believe that the
foundation for consistent ethical behaviour resides in developing
a simpler form of ethical consistency at a deeper character level. As
militaries advance into the 21st century, its educational institutions
must become increasingly concerned about who the members of
the profession must "be." Pfaff maintains that officers of character
must be "more concerned with being the right kind of person who
does the right thing, at the right time, in the right way and is not
as concerned with the act itself."[11] With character, the focus is not
on ensuring that one resolves two conflicting rules but instead on
"being" a certain kind of person. Military officers must place their
commitment to be socially responsible, and supportive of the corporate organization at the centre of their professional identities.
Snider provides even greater clarity in his discussion of multiple

military professional identities by asserting that one of a military officer's primary identities is being a "leader of character."[12]   We agree, but we also believe that the concept of "character" is frequently used too ambiguously for training purposes. To remedy this, we now turn to the notion of character specifically.

CHARACTERIZING CHARACTER

The term character is derived from the Greek word *kharassein*, which meant to engrave or inscribe.[13] When applied to people, character refers to the human qualities that have been engraved within an individual.[14] The Greek notion of character has evolved to mean moral goodness as a function of an individual's essence. However, Aristotle cautioned that good is not automatic, but must be habitually and socially constructed. Aristotle believed that character can be objectively good or bad, depending on whether one's values, choices, and practice have long been good or bad. He believed his judgements in this regard are demonstrably true rather than matters of mere opinion. Aristotle was interested in these issues because he thought they influenced the sometimes arduous process of moral practice that leads to a stable and objectively good character. Fond as he was of metaphor, Aristotle reminds us that one learns to play musical instruments through practice, but that practice alone does not guarantee desirable outcomes. Practice in the incorrect way, and one becomes a truly poor musician. Aristotle believed that individuals become good by practicing good actions, and that a person may have knowledge of good behaviour, but lack the disposition to act good based on that knowledge.[15] For Aristotle, to be virtuous was the ultimate pursuit of human fulfillment and reflected the excellence of a person's character.[16]

A number of modern scholars have provided additional details about character and virtue. Peterson and Seligman argued that character contains three levels of abstraction.[17] At the top level are core virtues, which consist of core universal qualities valued by moral and religious philosophers throughout history: wisdom, courage, humanity, justice, temperance, and transcendence. Character strengths reside at the next level. Peterson and Seligman referred to these as the "psychological ingredients" or processes that define the virtues.[18] Character strengths provide individuals with distinct paths for manifesting core virtues. The final level entails situational themes, which are the contextual elements that contribute to the likelihood that an individual will display certain character strengths (consistent with our notion that individual ethical principles can be disrupted by the situation). Similarly, Wright and Huang described character as those impenetrable habitual qualities within individuals that constrain and lead them to desire and pursue personal and societal good.[19] Peterson and Park contended that character is best defined as a multi-dimensional construct that is determined by personal and social factors.[20] Lickona asserted that good character consists of "knowing the good, desiring the good, and doing the good-habits of the mind, habits of the heart, and habits of action."[21] Berkowitz proposed that character involves an individual's capacity to consider right versus wrong, experience moral emotions, engage in moral behaviours, and believe in the moral good.[22] In essence, character relates to how individuals think, feel, believe, and act.

These definitions and descriptions shape the conceptual focus of how character has been studied and developed over the years. While attempts to define and describe character have been somewhat holistic and all-encompassing, the practice of character development has emerged from research that has been steeped in isolated approaches. According to Berkowitz, each group from these diverse approaches views character as "flourishing in narrow realm, embraces models that directly address that realm, implements programs designed to affect that realm, and uses different criteria for choosing labels for their respective realm."[23] Likewise, Rest asserts that our theoretical tendency to divide the character field into multiple approaches has been more of a liability than an asset.[24] To address this duality of perspectives, Berkowitz has advanced a more integrative perspective that synergistically incorporates components from several approaches.[25]

Central to Berkowitz's conceptualization of character development is the moral self system, which includes moral identity and some aspects of conscience.[26] Persons with mature moral identities view themselves as moral agents and being virtuous is primary in the construction of their self-concepts. Berkowitz describes conscience as both structure and content – with the structure of conscience being the degree to which an individual has internalized moral values and rules and content refers to an individual's specific beliefs about what is right or wrong.[27] The moral system consists of the virtues, values, and beliefs and the extent to which individuals maintain these constructs as part of their self-concept. Berkowitz also notes that this dynamic self system overlaps with other components of the moral person. He divides these parts into three frequently recognized components of psychology: affect, behaviour, and cognition.[28] He suggests that each of these components has moral and non-moral domains, where the non-moral domains consist of foundational and supporting elements for the moral domain.[29] Consistent with Berkowitz's emphasis on both cognitive and behavioural components, Likona and Davidson's conceptualization of character suggests that character consists of two capacities, moral character and performance character.[30,31]

They define moral character as "those qualities needed to be ethical – to develop just and caring relationships, contribute to community, and assume the responsibility of democratic citizenship" while performance character is described as "those qualities needed to realize one's potential for excellence – to develop one's talents, work hard, and achieve goals."

LEADERS OF CHARACTER

Consistent with the aforementioned responsibilities to society and each other, military professionals must not only have character, but must engage volitionally in creating proper and good behaviour, both personally and interpersonally. Consequently, character is intertwined with being a good and effective leader, because military professionals must create good behaviours in themselves and others.[32] According to Wakin, most leadership definitions merely produce a list of traits and attributes that ostensibly clarify the parameters of being an effective leader, but seldom highlight the more essential element of being a good or moral leader.[33] He suggests that good leaders have moral purpose in addition to all the other qualities that inspire trust and confidence in themselves and others. Brown, Trevino, and Harrison likewise posit that effective leaders must be concerned fundamentally with the moral well-being of themselves and others, and must also possess the ability to communicate and manage others' ethical behaviours.[34] Rost argues similarly that such leaders are morally purposeful and intentionally enhance their relationships with others, their influence on others, and their intended impact on organizations and societies.[35] Together, these tenets suggest that a leader of character should be defined in terms of both moral (i.e., good) and functional (i.e., effective) dimensions. Not only must the leader of characters be good and do good, they must also be effective at developing others to be good and do good, thereby creating positive and just outcomes.

In this vein, we define leader of character as *a moral person, who is purposefully committed to knowing, caring, and doing in such a way that he or she expands the moral and performance capacities of self and others toward a positive change.* The leader of character is first and foremost a moral person who has internalized the commitment to be good, do good, and cause good results. The development of self and others is a distinguishing function of a leader of character. Leaders of character intentionally strive to benefit others in their relationships. Rost describes this notion effectively through his depiction of the mutually purposeful relationship.[36] Mutually purposeful relationships are created through non-coercive means where both leaders and followers share a commitment to a common vision. These relationships are purposeful in the sense that they add moral and functional meaning to the lives of the leader and others in the relationship. Ultimately, leaders of character are people of consequence. Not only do they influence others through caring, thinking and behaving, but they lead others toward the fulfillment of a favourable future that was not otherwise going to happen.[37] They assume and internalize the responsibility of creating a more ethical and moral environments while enhancing the effectiveness of organizations and society.

Leader of Character Development Model

In Figure 1, we advance a model for being and developing leaders of character. The model rests heavily on the work of Berkowitz who suggested that this type of model can also be used as a template for understanding and supporting the development of character in specific human functions.[38] In our case, we focus on the function of being and developing leaders. The leader of character model uses Berkowitz's conceptualization as a template to understand the developmental components of character, and incorporates an expanded and revised version of the "Be-Know-Care-Do" leader development model advanced by Snook.[39] Consistent with our definition, our model suggests that a leader of character is first and foremost a moral person who: internalizes moral and functional identities and responsibilities (Be); understands moral and functional cognition (Know); experiences the moral and functional affect (Care); and who ultimately displays moral and functional behaviour (Do).

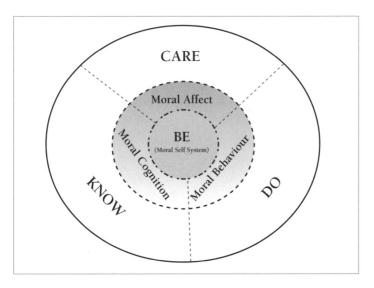

FIGURE 1: The Be, Know, Care, Do (BKCD) Model to Develop Leaders of Character.

We believe that the Be, Know, Care, and Do (BKCD) are best con-ceptualized as capacities because leaders have the potential to in-crease (or decrease) their abilities even in these fundamental areas.

Daft, for example, notes that developing leader capacity is broader than learning a skill for planning or managing others, and deeper than a reflection on leader styles and traits.[40] Instead, it is a holistic approach that involves expanding the potential of the whole person. Just as the biological capacity of our lungs is increased through exercise, a leader's capacity to morally and functionally be, know, care, and do can be developed deliberately. Our model is grounded in the historical and theoretical traditions of character and leader development.

Philosophical Grounding

Aristotle believed that the knowledge of moral facts and the ability to reflect productively on moral issues were prerequisites to moral development and maturity. In turn, moral maturity is necessary to enjoying happiness of the most robust kind. In this teleological (or goal-based) approach, Aristotle spends much of his *Nicomachean Ethics* helping the reader understand the meaning of living a life of virtue. (It is interesting to note that the Greek *areté*, usually translated as virtue, can also be translated as *excellence*, one of the key words in the Air Force's Core Values). That said, Aristotle also emphasized that moral knowledge and reflection, no matter how accurate and potent, do not suffice to live the best possible life. "Our present discussion does not aim, as our others do, at study; for the purpose of our examination is not to know what virtue is, but to become good, since otherwise the inquiry would be of no benefit to us."[41] As a scientist and careful observer of the human condition, Aristotle was always interested in function. The human being's proper function is not merely to know, but to act and act with a certain state of mind, just as the "Do" and "Care" portions of the BKCD model would have it: "...[T]he human function is activity of the soul in accord with reason..."[42]

The concepts of doing and caring in the BKCD model might be taken most generally as acting in accordance with one's moral insight while caring about how one's actions (or inactions) affect others. Interpersonal influence, after all, is inevitable when humans live collectively, which is consistent with the Aristotelian conception of human nature where each person is a *zoon politikon*, a *social* animal. To care about one's action – the co-requisite to caring about others – is to be in the right frame of mind. Even an action that has good results does not signal that the doer is necessarily a good person who does the right thing for the right reason. The morally immature person, though not someone whom Aristotle would call good, can nonetheless perform a good act. Hence, Aristotle is quick to point out metaphorically that "one swallow does not make a summer." Furthermore, the caring that signals good character cannot be concerned only for one's family and close friends; the moral citizen strives to fulfill the role of caring leader. "For while it is satisfactory to acquire and preserve the good even for an individual, it is finer and more divine to acquire and preserve it for a people and for cities."[43]

In sum, Aristotle urges students and teachers of ethics to understand the role that each element of a sort of proto-BKCD model necessarily plays in the quest to create moral leaders. First, we must *know*. However, because the aim is to live fulfilled lives of service to society, military professionals cannot stop at merely knowing; they must also *do* the right thing for the right reason (*care*), and practice right action to the extent that habits develop, habits so strong and comprehensive that they define what each of us has come to be internally committed to (*be*). Aristotle consolidates the model's elements in this way: "...[W]hat is true of crafts is not true of virtues. For the products of a craft determine by their own qualities whether they have been produced well;

and so it suffices that they have the right qualities when they have been produced. But for actions in accord with the virtues to be done temperately or justly it does not suffice that they themselves have the right qualities. Rather, the agent must also be in the right state when he does them. First, he must know [that he is doing virtuous actions]; second, he must decide on them, and decide on them for themselves; and, third, he must also do them from a firm and unchanging state."[44]

Theoretical Grounding

Leader of Character – Being. The capacity of "being" refers to the core identity and fundamental disposition of a leader of character. Several scholars have explored the link between self systems and leader development.[45] These authors point to the importance of helping leaders develop fulfilled, meaningful, and authentic identities. In other words, effective leaders are self-aware and behave consistently with their values, beliefs, thoughts and emotions in accordance with their true selves. Such leaders take responsibility for their actions, and incorporate heightened levels of transparency into their decision-making and behaviour; their verbal and non-verbal behaviour matches their true feelings and they avoid false or misleading statements. In so doing, these leaders not only have the capacity to be true to themselves, but they are also true to their roles and responsibilities as leaders.[46]

In the BKCD model, the leader of character must develop a moral identity to be objectively good. Nucci defines moral identity as "the ways, and the extent to which, individuals integrate their morality into their subjective sense of personal identity."[47] According to Lapley, moral identity is the extent to which notions of "being" (i.e., being compassionate, being good, being just) are deemed central, essential and important to one's self understanding.[48] Lapley suggests further that moral identity is an internalization of one's moral commitments. Moral commitments reside more fundamentally than cognitive schemas and representations, because they shape the essence of who people are at the centre of the self-concept.[49] Moral persons become moral leaders when they assume responsibility for the impact of their actions and the actions of their followers.[50] This commitment or responsibility is a natural extension of the self system. In fact, this process can render a person's affective, behavioural, and cognitive components as relatively superficial, because rather than merely thinking and behaving "good", a leader of character is good foundationally. For effective leaders of character, being moral is a fundamental commitment; what follows is an attempt to wholly align how they think, care, and act with this central notion of being good.

Leader of Character – Knowing. A critical part of aligning these peripheral components with the notion of "being" begins with an expanded functional capacity to understand and reason effectively. Cognitive ability has been associated frequently with effective leadership.[51] According to Tichy and Bennis, making judgement calls is the primary job of the leader.[52] They assert that leaders who do not make effective decisions cannot be effective. In addition, Daft outlines five cognitive capacities that are essential for effective leaders: independent thinking, open mindedness, systems thinking, mental models, and personal mastery.[53] Leaders who think independently continuously re-evaluate previous learned ways of doing things. They also engage in critical questioning and interpretation of data and events. These leaders can set aside preconceptions and suspend opinions for the sake of taking another perspective. These leaders can also engage in systems thinking – the ability to see the pattern of the whole versus only the independent parts.[54] They can use a variety of mental models (systems of assumptions, perceptions, and biases) to make sense of their world. Finally, Senge also highlights the notion of personal mastery to describe a leader's capacity to create a personal vision, face reality, and manage the tension between the two in a disciplined manner.[55]

Naturally, leaders benefit from an expanded and effective cognitive capacity, but this alone is not sufficient to make leaders effective over the long term. Book-smart leaders who behave inconsistently with an authentic commitment to be good will potentially inhibit their ability to achieve truly great outcomes, expose their fundamental principles to others, or suffer from the self-regulation requirements of being one way but thinking in another. Instead, leaders of character must be able to engage the moral aspect of cognition. This perspective focuses on an individual's ability to discern right from wrong, evaluate personal and social values, and make appropriate decisions. Although several theoretical frameworks support this approach, Kohlberg's theory of cognitive moral development has had the greatest influence on research in this area.[56] Kohlberg describes six stages of innate development through which a leader can progress.[57] He suggests that during the early stages of development, leaders tend to make decisions based on personal interests, but as they advance in their moral development they acquire more sophisticated ways of thinking and begin to wrestle with the social and universal implications of their decision. According to Berkowitz, moral cognition also includes the knowledge of moral facts.[58] Thus, moral cognition consists of both process and content elements. He suggests that cognitive process entails the leader's capacity to make moral judgements whereas moral knowledge relates to the leaders capacity to understand and apply moral content to the moral decision-making process.

Leader of Character – Caring. Leaders of character have the functional capacity to care about others, their feelings, and motives in such a way that they have a positive influence on followers. Although caring about followers is often linked to effective leadership, the concept of servant leadership perhaps most strongly emphasizes this point by noting that effective leaders must care and even place follower's needs over their own needs.[59] Spears argues similarly that a leader's primary means of influence is through caring for and ensuring that the needs of their followers are being met.[60] Leaders of character build rapport by demonstrating genuine concern for follower's physical, emotional, and spiritual well-being.

The ability to care about and connect emotionally with followers is enhanced when leaders possess greater levels of emotional intelligence. Emotional intelligence refers to working effectively with personal emotions and the emotions of others. Common emotional intelligence themes include the ability to recognize and work with others' emotions and be aware of personal emotions. Indeed, some researchers assert that emotional intelligence is the primary determinant of leader effectiveness.[61] An easily overlooked component of emotional intelligence involves the individual ability to regulate personal emotions and remain energized towards personal goals. In this respect, emotional intelligence can have an additional connection to caring about others and following ethical principles. By being self-aware and having a capacity to preserve through challenging times, the emotionally intelligent leader maintains a greater ability to demonstrate courage in the traditional sense of behaving admirably in dangerous circumstances or in the workplace sense of having managerial courage.[62] For example, emotionally intelligent leaders are more likely to question unethical behaviour in the workplace, despite being afraid of doing so.

Scholars also suggest that moral effect is a critical capacity for leaders of character to develop.[63] Hoffman's concept serves as the seminal work on centralizing affect as the prime component of moral development.[64] According to Hoffman, expanding a person's empathetic capacities will enhance a person's character by allowing them to experience feelings that are more aligned with another person's situation than their own.[65] Based on Berkowitz, the leader of character's moral affect capacity includes "both other-focused emotions such as empathy, sympathy, and compassion and emotions of self-reproach such as guilt and shame."[66]

Leader of Character – Doing. To this point, we have argued that leader behaviour must be consistent with a leaders cognitive and affective capacities and an extension of a leader's commitment to be a good and moral person. We have made these arguments because inconsistency between any of these concepts creates non-transparency and a fractured sense of purpose. Nonetheless, it is important to note that leader verbal and non-verbal behaviour is the only aspect of leadership directly witnessed by others.

Leaders can be depicted as having to choose between doing the "right thing" and the best thing for the broader organization. Motion pictures like *Wall Street* portray the effective businessperson (at least by profit-making standards) as an unethical leader. Yet, displaying ethical behaviour might enhance, rather than detract, from leader effectiveness. Bass and Avolio provide a framework of effective leader behaviour in their conceptualization of transformational leadership.[67] The transformational leadership framework is particularly relevant to the BKCD model as it describes leader behaviour both in terms of behaving in good and purposeful ways generally as well as creating purposeful relationships with followers. Bass and Avolio suggest that effective leaders function as strong role models and cause followers to want to emulate them through idealized influence. These leaders also effectively set high expectations to inspire motivation and commitment to a shared vision. In addition, effective leaders have the functional capacity to stimulate followers' creativity and innovation. Finally, effective leaders enhance their relationships with followers by demonstrating individualized consideration. They listen actively to followers and provide coaching and mentoring, based each follower's individual needs.

Berkowitz describes in more detail the link between moral leader behaviour and leader effectiveness.[68] He notes that leader behaviour is evaluated by followers in a social context. For instance, if leaders behave in a manner that is "kind," they may be deemed by others to have good character, but if they act "cruelly" others may conclude that the individual has bad character. An understanding of the mediating and moderating environmental variables, along with an emphasis on the impact of "modelling" on shaping moral behaviour, are central to expanding the leader's moral behaviour capacity.[69] Specifically, this capacity is concerned with how leaders acquire and manifest moral behaviour. According to Berkowitz, a leader's moral behavioural capacity would consist of behaviour that promote justice, enhance the welfare of others, and protect human rights.[70] To illustrate, a moral leader might make charitable contributions, spend time volunteering, and support policies that protect the underprivileged.

DEVELOPING LEADERS OF CHARACTER: THE UNITED STATES AIR FORCE ACADEMY

The United States Air Force Academy (USAFA) is a four-year undergraduate institution whose primary mission is "To educate, train, and inspire men and women to become officers of character, motivated to lead the United States Air Force in service to our nation." Upon graduation, cadets receive a Bachelor's of Science Degree and, with rare exception, an obligation to serve between five to nine years as a United States Air Force (USAF) officer depending upon occupational specialty (i.e., pilot, intelligence, and engineer). In so doing, USAFA provides a substantial portion of the commissioned officers in the USAF. Therefore, USAFA is centred on two complementary goals: provide a high quality undergraduate education and prepare cadets for being officers in the Air Force. Accordingly, USAFA cadets have numerous academic, athletic, and military responsibilities, many of which offer formal or information leadership opportunities. At the core of the cadet experience is the idea of development. The institution operates under the assumption that leadership and character are capacities that can be increased. The challenge is to ensure that all institutional programs and experiences contribute successfully to professional development.

While USAFA has been developing leaders of character for over 50 years, it has recently reestablished an emphasis in this domain. In particular, USAFA has recently created a Center of Character and Leader Development (CCLD) with the purpose to "Advance the understanding, practice, and integration of character and leadership development in preparation for service to the nation in the profession of arms."

Application of the Model

The BKCD model reflects a new approach to this idea of development at USAFA. While many of these pieces have been accomplished for years, USAFA has struggled to integrate its formal programs and informal experiences into a cohesive developmental plan. Previous USAFA leaders have relied heavily on educational classes (academic leadership courses) and experiences (leadership positions in the cadet wing) to develop leadership, while using specific workshops and an institutional honour oath to develop character. These endeavoors have been effective, but lacked the synergy needed to maximize their influence. This is due in large part to different mission elements owning separate pieces of this developmental process. For example, the Dean of the Faculty is responsible for the education of the cadets whereas the Commandant of Cadets is responsible for most formal leadership positions. While this is understandable due to staffing requirements and structural necessity, it has been a barrier to building a cohesive plan for creating ethical and character development. To remedy this situation, the CCLD has been given responsibility for integrating these different programs across mission elements to leverage the strengths of each program, while eliminating the redundancies.

The BKCD model has been diagnostic and prescriptive in regards to the existing program at USAFA; it has highlighted areas that have been seemingly ineffective and provided a course of action to enhance the development process. The first of these is the cognitive piece (knowing). Because USAFA is a four-year undergraduate degree-granting institution, it is positioned to have a strong influence in developing cadet knowledge. Cadets are required to take a core set of courses that span several academic disciplines (e.g., philosophy, behavioural sciences, engineering, mathematics, english, and so forth). This significant core curriculum approach is used to help develop cadets' intellectual capacity in a variety of domains that are related to their Air Force careers. Because the primary mission of USAFA is to produce leaders of character, all cadets complete a required academic course in leadership. This course takes a developmental approach to the learning of leadership and uses their cadet experiences in leadership positions as the frame of reference for learning how to lead effectively.[71] The course focuses primarily on using cadet's immediate situation to help cadets develop themselves and those around them to be more effective. While this approach to leadership education is in the initial stages of implementation, early assessments reflect positive feedback toward the concept.[72]

FRESHMAN	SOPHOMORE	JUNIOR	SENIOR
Behavioural Science	Chemistry	Aeronautical Engineering	Astrological Engineering
Chemistry	Economics	Leadership	English
Computer Science	Engineering Mechanics	Biology	Management
Engineering	English	Electronic Systems	Military Strategic Studies
English	Law	History	Social Science
Foreign Language	Military Strategic Studies	Math	
History	Physics	Philosophy	
Math	Political Science	Engineering Option	
Math (2)			
Physics			

FIGURE 2: Core Curriculum at USAFA by Academic Year.

This required leadership course is supplemented by additional courses similarly designed to facilitate individual development (Figure 2). For example, cadets complete an introductory course in the behavioural sciences. In this course, they begin developing critical thinking and additional skills allowing them to process their social worlds in enriched ways. They also complete courses in political science, philosophy, and engineering which provide a disparate set of intellectual experiences ranging from the abstract to the practical and from the humanities to the hard sciences. This educational process (knowing) is intended to expose cadets to various concepts that increase their capacity with respect to their moral cognition and enhance the knowledge that is required for effective leadership.

The second area, the moral self system (being), is also foundational to the developmental process at USAFA. At the centre of this area is the Honour Code: "We will not lie, steal, or cheat, nor tolerate among us anyone who does." This is given to cadets when they enter USAFA and is the standard by which their actions are measured. As with many militaries, the cadets come from the population at large and therefore have varied backgrounds and belief systems. For some, the Honour Code is synonymous with their current state of being. For others, the Honour Code is a guide that they should reach before they graduate and become USAF Officers. Thus, USAFA has developed a process that handles infractions of the Honor Code. In most cases, Honour Code infractions result in a corresponding developmental process. In some cases, Honour Code infractions result in dismissal.

The USAF's core values also contribute to cadets being. These values are Integrity, Excellence, and Service Before Self. These are the core principles that USAFA cadets should embrace. They provide clear expectations of how USAF airmen conduct themselves. Because USAFA offers a developmental process of increasing capacity, cadets are expected to face challenges as they endeavour to uphold these values. Yet, even when they are challenged, USAFA leaders must ensure that they have the necessary support in place to help cadets pursue their developmental goals and understand this development is critical to the overall team.

Knowing and being are critical, but ultimately useless without the third area, behaving. Cadets must be able to take moral action in the execution of their leadership positions. To address this point, there are several formal positions that allow cadets to practice and develop leadership during their tenure at USAFA. These leadership positions occur in academic, athletic, and military contexts. Cadets can test their leadership in positions such as instructor pilots, intercollegiate team captains, intramural coaches, military supervisory positions, and community programs administration. Failure to behave effectively in these positions should result in feedback from cadets, staff, or both. Through these opportunities, cadets not only practice the skills critical to effective leadership, they are also exposed to the idea of moral motivation (care).

The fourth and final area, caring, is a challenging capacity to develop for several reasons. First, cadets are deeply invested in their own development in regards to becoming an effective leader. To some degree, this necessitates a self-focused perspective as cadets must evaluate whether they are working effectively with others. Yet, at the same time cadets are attempting to develop this capacity in themselves, they are being asked to develop it in others as well. Second, USAFA leadership positions often require cadets to lead their peers. This is a significant issue as cadets frequently lack the position power associated with formal leadership positions in the operational military.[73] Cadets must therefore rely on influence and persuasion in not only the execution of their leadership responsibilities but also in the personal development of moral and ethical capacity in their followers. Finally, cadets are often motivated toward personal achievement because it has the greatest influence on important outcomes, namely job selection. This can undermine cadet motivation to help others achieve because providing too much assistance to others takes time away from earning good grades, preparing for physical tests, and effectively completing military responsibilities.

One way that USAFA has approached this idea of caring is through multiple character development programs run by the CCLD. These programs take place throughout the cadet's term at USAFA and each program has a particular focus to help develop cadets along the lines of being, caring, and doing. The courses are Vital Effective Character Through Observation and Reflection, Respect & Responsibility, Responsible Officership Performance Enhancement, Leaders in Flight Today, and the Academy Character Enrichment Seminar. Through this phased approach, USAFA can expose cadets to a process that helps them to understand not only their role in the leadership dynamic, but how they can care for their subordinates. Cadets are encouraged to realize that effective leadership goes well beyond the traditional skills they bring as leaders.

To summarize, while USAFA has taken great strides to ensure cadet development in all aspects of the BKCD model, it is important to recognize potential areas for improvement. It is also important to note that USAFA is not only trying to increase the capacity of the individual cadets, but also increase their abilities to have a positive influence on those that they lead. A chief goal at USAFA is to develop a comprehensive assessment strategy that will measure current and future success in regards to the various aspects of the BKCD model. Ultimately, USAFA must ensure that its cadets graduate with all the necessary capacities they will need to serve competently in the Air Force.

FUTURE IMPLICATIONS

Leadership and character are critical capacities in educating and training future military leaders. Unfortunately, military forces face a more dynamic environment than existed previously. It is a difficult endeavour to train these forces for an uncertain future. Ironically, it is the dynamic environment that makes the moral self system vital. Because military leaders cannot predict the future military environment, they must focus on the remaining asset that they can control: the individual leader. The individual has become the stable force in an unsure future.

With this in mind, we can examine a few of the trends that have arisen over the past few years that can at least give us some indication as to the environment our forces will face. First, there seems to be a greater emphasis on enduring officer virtues and less on military doctrine. This is not to say that we should not have rules of engagement codified for our forces. In fact, due to the legal and ethical implications existing in the current wartime environment, these remain imperative. However, many military contexts have shifted from definable to nebulous. To illustrate, if an individual is in a tank fighting another force across the battlefield, the "enemy" is easily identifiable as the person across the battlefield shooting back. This is a rather straightforward form of warfare. However, this is much less likely in current forms of warfare. Often, troops progress from street to street trying to clear the area from the enemy, and the enemy has not outfitted themselves in a traditional uniform (or by sitting in a tank). Troops must often quickly evaluate the situation and determine how to respond in that particular situation (which could be vastly different than the previous situation they were in). To make matters worse, civilian casualties occur easily in this urban environment. This creates recurring dilemmas involving the delicate balance between force protection and minimizing civilian casualties. Naturally, it is exceptionally difficult to train soldiers to operate in such an environment. However, we contend that developing the proper moral self system in soldiers increases the likelihood that they will act in an appropriate manner. Although it might be natural for a soldier to immediately return fire, the responsible act is to assess the broader situation to determine the appropriate reaction. The actions of a single soldier could have strategic consequences, especially when relations are strained in that arena.

A second trend follows this concept of the individual soldier having a strategic impact. It is becoming increasingly evident that the U.S. Military requires strategic and global thinkers instead of just parochial thinkers. Individual leaders certainly need to have competency in their individual level of expertise, but this too is not a sufficient level of knowledge to wage warfare today. The individual must understand how his or her job fits into the overall operation. In addition, because most U.S. military operations occur internationally, United States service members must also understand the culture in which it is operating. The values, beliefs, and ideals that many military professionals have, will not always translate into the culture in which they are conducting military operations. Failure to understand and appreciate these differences can drastically undermine effectiveness. In these situations, soldiers must understand that those around them may be operating with a different moral self system than their own. Service members need to be sufficiently adept in their cultural understanding so they can recognize these differences and operate with them in mind.

Consistent with this notion of cultural awareness is the issue of cultural intuition. In the United States Air Force, we have spent decades ensuring the technical competence of our military personnel. We educate, train, and equip our troops to be highly proficient at their jobs. This is a critical component of daily business when troops are in garrison or deployed. The U.S. Military must place the same level of focus and dedication on being culturally adept. We are not suggesting that soldiers working in Afghanistan must understand everything about that culture (as that would not be feasible), but failing to gain a basic understanding of the culture will result in misunderstandings when dealing with the local population. To borrow a commonly used phrase, it is hard to "win the hearts and minds of the people," when one does not know how those people feel and think. By increasing the quality of the military professional's moral self-system, one also builds their capacity to understand (and appreciate) the same self-systems in others.

Finally, the U.S. Military must recognize that it has become difficult to act unilaterally as a nation in world-wide efforts. Indeed, there has been a clear increase in the number of coalition actions that have taken place over the past two decades. This necessitates our military forces to build effective partnerships with its military allies. Again, achieving this goal requires that U.S. military professionals understand other nations' perspectives. This understanding is vital to ensuring that both parties' goals are met through the cooperation. If this does not happen, the very nature of the coalition is at risk.

CONCLUSION

Warfare is becoming increasingly complex. Ironically, this change has placed more, rather than less, importance on the tactical level service members required to carry out military operations in this enhanced context. While it is impossible to directly control all the events that occur on the battlefield, the one area where the military profession has the most direct impact is at the level of the individual soldier, sailor, and airman. Military ethics assists in this endeavour by providing a guiding foundation of rules and precepts to which military members can adhere. This is critical as these ethical principles help to define and shape behaviour. However, this knowledge (*know*) is no longer enough as militaries should also understand how its members behave (*do*), consider their troops and people more generally (*care*), and conduct themselves foundationally (*be*). The BKCD model is a starting point which we can address these areas and increase the moral capacity (and ultimately effectiveness) in all our forces.

ENDNOTES

1   Samuel Huntington, *The Soldier and the State* (Cambridge, MA: Harvard Press, 1957).

2   Ibid.

3   Brian Burton and John Nagl, "The Future of the Military Officer: Strategic Context," in John Nagl and Brian Burton eds., *Keeping the Edge: Revitalizing America's Military Officer Corps* (Center for a New American Security, 2010) 9-18.

4   Don Snider, "Multiple Identities of the Professional Army Officer," in L. Matthews ed., *The Future of the Army Profession* (Boston: McGraw-Hill, 2005) 139-146.

5   Richard Gabriel, *The Warrior's Way: A Treatise on Military Ethics* (Kingston, Ontario: Canadian Defence Academy Press, 2007).

6   Ibid.

7   Gregory Reichberg, Henrik Syse, and Endre Begby, *The Ethics of War: Classic and Contemporary Readings* (Oxford: Blackwell, 2006).

8   Leon Festinger, *A Theory of Cognitive Dissonance* (Evanston, IL: Row & Peterson, 1957).

9   Solomon Asch, "Opinions and Social Pressure," *Scientific American*, Vol. 193 (1955), 31-35.

10   Leon Festinger, Albert Pepitone, and Theodore Newcomb, "Some Consequences of De-individuation in a Group," *Journal of Abnormal and Social Psychology*, Vol. 47 (1952), 382-389.

11   Tony Pfaff, "Multiple Identities of the Professional Army Officer," in L. Matthews, ed., *The Future of the Army Profession* (Boston: McGraw-Hill, 2005) 153-161.

12   Snider, "Multiple Identities of the Professional Army Officer," 139-146.

13   Gene. Klann, *Building Character: Strengthening the Heart of Good Leadership* (San Francisco: Jossey-Bass, 2007).

14   Gail Sheehey, *Character: American's Search for Leadership* (New York: Morrow, 1988).

15   Malham Wakin, "Professional Integrity," *Air Power Journal*, Vol. 10 (1996), 23-29.

16   Alejo Sison, "Leadership, Character, and Virtue From an Aristotelian Viewpoint," in T. Maak and N. Pless eds., *Responsible Leadership* (New York: Taylor & Francis, 2006) 108-121.

17   Chris Peterson and Martin Seligman, *Character Strengths and Virtues: A Handbook and Classification* (New York: Oxford University Press/Washington, D.C.: American Psychological Association, 2004).

18   Ibid.

19   Thomas Wright and Ching-Chu Huang, "Character in Organizational Research: Past Directions and Future Prospective," *Journal of Organizational Behavior*, Vol. 29 (2008), 981-987.

20   Christopher Peterson and Nansook Park, "Character Strengths in Organizations," *Journal of Organizational Behavior*, Vol. 27 (2006), 1149-1154.

21   Thomas Lickona, *Educating for Character: How Our Schools Can Teach Respect and Responsibility* (New York: Bantam Books, 1991), 51.

22 Marvin Berkowitz, "The Science of Character Education," in W. Damon, ed., *Bringing in a New Era in Character Education* (Stanford, CA: Hoover Institution Press, 2002), 43-63.

23 Marvin Berkowitz, "The Complete Moral Person: Anatomy and Formation," in M. Dubois, ed., *Moral Issues in Psychology: Personalist Contributes to Selected Problems* (Lanham, MD: University Press of America, 1997), 13.

24 James Rest, "The Major Components of Morality," in W. Kurtines and J. Gewirtz eds., *Morality, Moral Behavior, and Moral Development* (New York: Wiley, 1984), 34-38.

25 Marvin Berkowitz, "Moral and Character Education," in T. Urdan, ed., *APA Educational Psychology Handbook: Vol 2, Individual Differences, Cultural Variations, and Contextual Factors in Educational Psychology* (Washington, DC: American Psychological Association, in press).

26 Ibid.

27 Ibid.

28 Ibid.

29 Ibid.

30 Ibid.

31 Thomas Lickona and Matt Davidson, *Smart and Good High Schools: Integrating Excellence and Ethics for Success in School, Work, and Beyond* (Washington, D.C.: Character Education Partnership, 2005).

32 Sean Hannah, Paul Lester and Gretchen Vogelgesang "Moral Leadership: Explicating the Moral Component of Authentic Leadership," *Authentic Leadership Theory and Practice: Origins, Effects, and Development Monographs in Leadership and Management*, Vol. 3 (2005), 43-81; Scott Snook, *Leader(ship) Development* (Boston: Harvard Business School Publishing, 2008); and, Linda Trevino and Michael Brown, "Managing to be Ethical: Debunking Five Business Ethics Myths," *Academy of Management Executive*, Vol. 18 (2004), 69-81.

33 Malham Wakin, "Does Good Leadership Require Good Character?," *Journal of Character and Leader Scholarship*, Vol. 1 (2009), 43-46.

34   Michael Brown, Linda Treviño and David Harrison, "Ethical Leadership: A Social Learning Perspective for Construct Development and Testing," *Organizational Behavior and Human Decision Processes,* Vol. 97 (2005), 117-134.

35   Joseph Rost, *Leadership for the Twenty-First Century* (Westport, CT: Praeger Publisher, 1991).

36   Ibid.

37   Thomas Cronin, *The State of the Presidency* (Boston: Little, Brown, 1980).

38   Marvin Berkowitz, "Moral and Character Education" (in press).

39   Snook, *Leader(ship) Development.*

40   Richard Daft, *Leadership: Theory and Practice* (Fort Worth, TX: Dryden Press, 1999).

41   Aristotle Cite (1103b25ff.; tr. Terence Irwin here and below).

42   Aristotle Cite (1098a7; emphasis added).

43   Aristotle Cite (1094a7 ff.).

44   Aristotle Cite (1105a30 ff.; translator's parenthetical).

45   Christopher Branson, "Effects of Structured Self-Reflection on the Development of Authentic Leadership Practices Among Queensland Primary School Principles," *Educational Management Administration & Leadership*, Vol. 35 (2007), 225-246; Hannah et al., "Moral Leadership: Explicating the Moral Component of Authentic Leadership," 43-81; Snook, *Leader(ship) Development*; Fred Walumbwa, Bruce Avolio, William Gardner, Tara Wernsing & Suzanne Peterson, "Authentic Leadership: Development and Validation of a Theory-Based Measure," *Journal of Management*, Vol. 34 (2008), 89-126; and, Phillip Woods, "Authenticity in the Bureau-Enterprise Culture: The Struggle for Authentic Meaning," *Educational Management Administration and Leadership*, Vol. 35 (2007), 295-307.

46   Adrian Chan, Sean Hannah, and William Gardner, "Veritable Authentic Leadership: Emergence, Functioning, and Impact," *Authentic Leadership Theory and Practice: Origins, Effects, and Development Monographs in Leadership and Management*, Vol. 3 (2005), 3-41.

47   Larry Nucci, *Education in the Moral Domain* (New York: Cambridge University, 2001) 128.

48   Dan Lapsley, "Moral Self-Identity as the Aim of Education," in L. Nucci and D. Narvaez eds., *Handbook of Moral Character Education* (New York: Routledge, 2008) 134-154.

49   Agusto Blasi, "The Development of Identity: Some Implications for Moral Functioning," in G. Noam and T. Wren eds., *The Moral Self* (New Baskerville, MA: The MIT Press, 1993) 99-122.

50   Hannah et al., "Moral Leadership: Explicating the Moral Component of Authentic Leadership," 43-81.

51   Robert Sternberg, "A Systems Model of Leadership: WICS," *American Psychologist*, Vol. 62, (2007), 34-42.

52   Noel Tichy and Warren Bennis, *Judgment: How Winning Leaders Make Great Calls* (New York: Penguin Group, 2007).

53   Daft, *Leadership: Theory and Practice*.

54   Peter Senge, *The Fifth Discipline: The Art and Practice of the Learning Organization* (New York: Doubleday Currency, 1990).

55   Ibid.

56   Arthur Chickering and Linda Reisser, *Education and Identity*, 2nd ed. (San Francisco: Jossey-Bass, 1993); Carol Gilligan, *In a Different Voice: Psychological Theory and Women's Development* (Cambridge, MA: Harvard University Press, 1982); Lawrence Kohlberg, *The Philosophy of Moral Development: Essay on Moral Development* (San Francisco: Harper & Row, 1981); and, Trevino and Brown, "Managing to be Ethical: Debunking Five Business Ethics Myths," 69-81.

57   Kohlberg, *The Philosophy of Moral Development: Essay on Moral Development*.

58   Marvin Berkowitz, "Moral and Character Education" (in press).

59   Joseph Boyett and Jimmie Boyett, *Beyond Workplace 2000: Essential Strategies for the New American Corporation* (New York: Dutton, 1995); Robert Greenleaf, *The Servant as Leader: A Journey Into the Nature of Legitimate Power and Greatness* (Mahwah, NJ: Paulist Press, 1991); and, Diane Larkin,

Beyond Self to Compassionate Healer: Transcendent Leadership (Ann Arbor, MI: Bell and Howell-UMI, 1994).

60   Larry Spears, *Reflections on Leadership: How Robert K. Greenleaf's Theory of Servant-Leadership Influenced Today's Top Management Thinkers* (New York: John Wiley & Sons, Inc., 1995).

61   Daniel Goleman, Richard Boyatzis and Annie McGee, *Primal Leadership: Realizing the Power of Emotional Intelligence* (Boston: Harvard Business School Publishing, 2002).

62   Chris Rate, Jennifer Clarke, Douglas Lindsay and Robert Sternberg, "Implicit Theories of Courage," *Journal of Positive Psychology*, Vol. 2 (2007), 80-98; Sandra Walston, "Courage Leadership: How to Claim Your Courage and Help Others Do The Same," *Training and Development*, Vol. 8 (2003), 58-60.

63   Martin Hoffman, Empathy and Moral Development: Implications for Caring and Justice (New York: Cambridge University Press, 2000); Larry Nucci, *Education in the Moral Domain,128; and, Lynn Swaner, Educating for personal and social responsibility: A planning project of the association of American colleges and university* (Review of the Literature, 2004).

64   Hoffman, *Empathy and Moral Development: Implications for Caring and Justice.*

65   Ibid.

66   Marvin Berkowitz, "Moral and Character Education" (in press).

67   Bernard Bass and Bruce Avolio, *Improving Organizational Effectiveness Through Transformational Leadership* (Thousand Oaks, CA: Sage, 1994).

68   Marvin Berkowitz, "The Complete Moral Person: Anatomy and Formation," in M. Dubois, ed., *Moral Issues in Psychology: Personalist Contributes to Selected Problems* (Lanham, MD: University Press of America, 1997), 13.

69   Albert Bandura, *Social Foundations of Thought and Action: A Social Cognitive Perspective* (Englewood Cliffs, NJ: Prentice Hall, 1986); Marvin Berkowitz and Michael Fekula, "Educating for Character," *About Campus*, Vol. 4 (1999), 17-22; and, Donald McCabe, Linda Trevino and Kenneth Butterfield. "Honor Codes and Other Contextual Influences on Academic Integrity: A Replication and Extension to Modified Honor Code Settings," *Research in Higher Education*, Vol. 43 (2002), 357-378.

MILITARY ETHICS: INTERNATIONAL PERSPECTIVES

70   Marvin Berkowitz, "Moral and Character Education" (in press).

71   Douglas Lindsay, Craig Foster, Robert Jackson and Anthony Hassan. "Leadership Education and Assessment: A Developmental Approach," *Journal of Leadership Education*, Vol. 8 (2009), 163-176.

72   Douglas Lindsay, Anthony Hassan and David Day, "Leadership Education and Experience in the Classroom: A Case Study," *Journal of Leadership Education*, Vol. 8 (2009), 32-40.

73   John French and Bertam Raven, "The Bases of Social Power," in D. Cartwright and A. Zander, eds., *Group Dynamics* (New York: Harper & Row, 1959).

CHAPTER 5

Preparing Values-Based Commanders for the 3rd Generation Singapore Armed Forces

*Lieutenant-Colonel Psalm B.C. Lew**

> *"Nothing creates loyalty and national consciousness more speedily and more thoroughly than participation in defence and membership of the armed forces… the nation building aspect of defence will be more significant if its participation is spread out over all strata of society. This is possible only with some kind of national service."*

> **Dr. Goh Keng Swee, 1967, Singapore's First Minister for Defence**

INTRODUCTION

As a nation, Singapore is unique in many ways. Its geo-strategic position at the crossroads of the world's busiest trade lanes has created a multi-ethnic and multi-racial society which is still attracting many foreign talents. Singapore's small size and population and lack of natural resources necessitate a unique approach to its defence via the implementation of National Service (NS) to meet its security requirements. Here, the Singapore Armed Forces (SAF) is both the guardian of the country's national interests and sovereignty as well as a national institution that brings together

---

* The views expressed in this chapter are those of the author and do not necessarily reflect the official policy of the Singapore Armed Forces.

people from all walks of life.[1] The practice of conscription in the past four decades has created the "NS citizen soldier" – a unique form of military professionalism where the 250,000 National Servicemen (NSmen)[2] are part of the main fighting force alongside the 50,000 active personnel. While most other Armed Forces that practice conscription normally have units that are all active personnel or reservists, the SAF has deliberately integrated active and NSmen with each other. For example, Singapore Infantry Brigades command a mix of active and NSmen units. The Brigade Headquarters is also staffed by active personnel and NSmen.[3] Therefore, sustaining the NS today and into the future requires that the SAF actively engage its NSmen. This requires that the SAF maintains the highest order of values in both managing its NSmen and in the way it fulfills its mission. Values and ethics in the SAF are not just desirable outcomes – they are vital to sustaining the commitment to the defence of Singapore.

CHALLENGES CONFRONTING THE SAF

Since the September 11 attacks on New York, global acts of terrorism and political instability in South East Asia have created an uncertain security landscape. From the plans uncovered in the Al Qaeda headquarters (HQ) in Kabul to bomb the Yishun Mass Rapid Transit System (MRT) station to the recently discovered Jemaah Islamiah terrorist plot to attack the Orchard MRT Station right in the heart of the city, Singapore remains a terrorist target.[4] As the SAF transforms from its 2nd to its 3rd Generation,[5] it needs to raise, train and sustain units capable of conventional war-fighting as well as having the capacity to wage full spectrum operations in support of Singapore's national interest and regional security. Examples include the anti-piracy missions in the Gulf of Aden and the Straits of Malacca as well as the Protection of Installations

(POI) at Singapore's Jurong Island – the world's second largest oil refining centre that supplies the entire Asia-Pacific region. Beyond an upgrade in hardware such as networked combat systems and platforms, the SAF's 3rd Gen transformation into a force capable of full-spectrum operations meant that its commanders and personnel need to deal with complex dilemmas that are inherent in uncertain security landscapes and asymmetric warfare.

At the same time, education literacy in Singapore has improved tremendously. As of 2009, approximately 70.3% of the adult population had received tertiary education as opposed to 41.5% a decade earlier.[6] A better-educated population of NSmen means that the SAF has an opportunity to build an entire Armed Force of *Thinking Soldiers*. For the NSmen, it is not unusual for a rifleman with a doctorate degree to serve under a platoon commander with only a diploma. This situation suggests that NSmen and indeed the rank and file within the SAF are more likely to seek clarification for the orders they receive. It is expected that orders that are poorly thought through, illogical or even unethical would most certainly be met with requests for clarification and even resistance in some cases. As such, SAF Leaders will need to lead by example and demonstrate a higher standard of ethics and values-based behaviour to complete missions and inspire commitment to the defence of Singapore.

THE CONCEPT OF MILITARY PROFESSION IN THE 3RD GEN SAF

Before describing ethics for commanders, it is important to first consider the purpose and task of the military profession in Singapore. For the SAF, Samuel Huntington's[7] concept of only considering Regular Officers as members of the profession of experts in the management of violence is inadequate. Huntington's concept no longer explains the requirement of the full spectrum of expertise and responsibility of the SAF today; a force capable to "Destroy" the opponent, "Deter" aggression, "Contain" a threat and "Ameliorate" humanitarian crisis.[8] In this effort, both SAF Officers and other ranks have similar social responsibilities.

In the task to "Destroy", NSmen are part of the main fighting force and not just a temporary supplement (i.e., active units have a significant number of NSmen and NS commanders). In the task to "Deter", NSmen serve annual rotations to fulfill POI duties at key installations in Singapore alongside active units on completion of their unit evaluation. In fact, NSmen in the seventh-ninth years of their unit's NS Training Cycle[9] will at times have a deeper expertise in performing multi-faceted tasks than active personnel. With the revision to the SAF Act in 2007,[10] even Sergeants (both active and NSmen) deployed in any operation to aid a civilian authority are permitted to take any measure including the use of lethal force to protect life and infrastructure. Here, they gain full access to police powers under the Singapore Criminal Procedure Code.

In the task to "Contain'", NSmen participated in several national events/crises. For example, in the Severe Acute Respiratory Syndrome (SARS) crisis in 2003, NSmen took part in the SAF's quarantine management and contact tracing efforts. In the task to "Ameliorate", since the independence of Singapore, NSmen have participated in relief operations to render aid to civilian authorities in every major disaster in Singapore's history.

Although not made explicit in any SAF manifesto, any person (whether regular or NSmen; Officer or otherwise) that has taken the SAF Oath of Allegiance and who subscribes to the SAF

Pledge, is considered a full member of the military profession. It is through these NSmen, who are both citizens and soldiers, that the military profession in Singapore is woven into the country's social fabric. For all Singaporean males, National Service is considered a rite of passage to adulthood and it is an issue close to the hearts of the people. So much so that when a famous Singapore-born concert pianist in London tried to return to Singapore after defaulting on National Service, he was met with such public uproar that he had to cancel his concert and remain in the UK.[11] For many permanent residents, NS is also part of the rite of passage to citizenship.[12] As such, the number of immigrants in the NS is increasing. It is no longer a surprise to see an NSman of European descent or first generation immigrants from Asian countries training alongside Singaporeans. Very few countries in the world share the same sense of the profession where the Military epitomises the values and belief systems held by its citizens since the profession is formed by its people. A physical manifestation of the integration of the military profession into the Singaporean social fabric[13] is evidenced from the local saying that in every neighbourhood and apartment block in Singapore, a few sets of military uniforms would always be hanging out to dry, especially on weekends when the soldiers returned home. Therefore selecting, developing and building every new generation of values based commanders for the SAF, is in itself part of the nation building effort to strengthen social cohesion and national identity.

The SAF subscribes to seven Core Values; Loyalty to Country, Leadership, Discipline, Professionalism, Fighting Spirit, Ethics and Care for Soldiers. The demonstration of these values through role modelling in operations, training, and garrison life is the central core of the profession in the SAF. These values describe the SAF ethic – the commonly accepted belief system that guides

behaviour among SAF NSmen of different ethnicity, religion and
backgrounds. The standard is to help SAF commanders and their
men understand the ethics of the military profession – about what
is morally right and what is not.

MORAL AUTHORITY OF COMMAND

For the military to command is to provide the planning, coordination, and control of soldiers in the application of lethal force. As
described by the SAF Core Values of Leadership, every NSman
is expected to demonstrate leadership, but only the commander
is entrusted with the formal powers to direct the forces under
command to shoot and kill the enemy. The SAF definition of command and leadership makes this distinction clear.

> **Command** *refers to the authority vested in an individual of
> the armed forces, by virtue of rank or assignment, for the
> planning organization, direction, coordinating and control of
> military forces subordinated to him. Command also includes
> responsibility for health, welfare, morale and discipline of as-
> signed personnel, and responsibility for the effective employ-
> ment of organic resources.*[14]

> **Leadership** *is defined as the process of influencing people to
> accomplish the mission/task, inspire their commitment, and
> improve the organization.*[15]

The popular comic book hero *Spiderman* popularized the quote
"With great power comes great responsibility". Although a *cliché*
term glamorized by Hollywood, it is this sense of wielding greater
power that makes the privilege of command sacrosanct. From the
platoon HQ where only the commander gives the order to start

firing on the enemy to the Division Command Post where only the commander gives the approval to commence an operation against an aggressor, this sense of a moral authority that comes with a greater responsibility is transient across ranks and time.

For an NS armed force like the SAF, legal authority in command is never sufficient because it can lead to compliance due to the fear of punishment. Further, command may break down when the instruments of punishment are absent. In a nation of five million people where 250,000 are currently members of the SAF, commanders (both regular and NSmen) will find that their subordinates may be their friends, clients, or even superiors outside the military. Hence, in the SAF, command by legal authority alone can lead to a personal conflict of interest – a personal ethical dilemma, especially when one has to choose between acting in the interests of the profession or in the interests of personal relationships.

Therefore, beyond legal authority, a commander must possess moral authority or a moral quotient based on a set of values to lead and unify soldier's commitment to the mission by inspiring soldiers with the values associated with command decisions. This allows the execution of command to be effective regardless of the type of relationships or social dynamics a commander may have with the soldiers. The account of Major (ret) Ang Taw Hai, the commander of the stand-by force activated for disaster relief when a hotel in Singapore collapsed in 1986 due to structural problems, serves as a fine example. Despite having to deal with discipline problems earlier, Major (ret) Ang had no difficulty during the operation and his men worked 2 days and nights to clear debris with little sleep or mechanical tools.[16] At that time, Major (ret) Ang possessed a moral authority drawn from the SAF Core Values of Loyalty to Country and Professionalism; a citizen's duty to first serve the country and its people and where previous problems are put aside and the attention to duty comes to the fore. All he had to do was to remind his soldiers of Rule 2 in the SAF Code of Conduct, "At all times, we must bear in mind that we are the protector of our citizens."[17] The result was an unprecedented demonstration of motivation and performance by his men. His experience showed that Values Based Command is effective in an NS armed force.

EVOLVING CONCEPTS OF VALUES AND ETHICS IN THE SAF

One of the first SAF manifestos to be published was the 1967 SAF Code of Conduct.[18] The release of this Code coincided with the development of the 1st Generation SAF. The six codes prescribed a set of rules, standards and obligations of all SAF NSmen. When the SAF Code of Conduct was launched, the following declaration was made to clarify its intent, "Members of the SAF have a unique role; they are not only the ever-vigilant guardian of our nation but are also required to be an example of good citizenship… therefore, I Goh Keng Swee, on the authority of the Army Board of Singapore hereby prescribes the Code of Conduct for members of the SAF. I prescribe that every member of the SAF shall abide by the Code of Conduct and measure up to the standards embodied therein."[19] It is clear from the declaration that the Code of Conduct adopted a deontological ethics approach,[20] through six maxims to guide each soldier's behaviours, to describe what is morally right and what is not. However, as with all theories of deontological ethics, its does not deal directly with a person's moral character and it certainly does not help one consider the moral consequences of one's own moral actions.

SAF CODE OF CONDUCT

1)   *We always honour our Nation. We will do everything to uphold it & nothing to disgrace it.*

2)   *At all times, we must bear in mind that we are the protector of our citizens.*

3)   *We are loyal to the Armed Forces and we take pride in our unit, our uniform, our discipline, our work, our training and ourselves.*

4)   *We must be exemplary in our conduct. We respect others, and by our conduct win the respect of others. We are courageous but not reckless.*

5)   *We are devoted to duty but not to ourselves.*

6)   *We guard our weapons as we guard secrets.*

The SAF Code of Conduct was driven by necessity; Singapore was a young nation and did not have a professional officer caste described by Samuel Huntington in *The Soldier and the State*. There was an urgent need to use the Code of Conduct to ensure that a sense of dignity and purpose prevails throughout the SAF until such a time that the tradition of the military profession matured (possibly over generations). So for the next few decades, the SAF went about its business guided by the SAF Code of Conduct.

In the late 1980s, as the military began its transformation from a 1st to a 2nd Generation SAF, the idea to create an "Institute of Excellence"[21] that would eventually serve as the home of the SAF

Officers Corps emerged. In creating this Institute, the idea was also to identify a set of SAF Core values in order to create a common set of attributes for SAF Officers. After a series of rigorous discussions, the SAF Core Values of Loyalty to Country, Leadership, Discipline, Professionalism, Fighting Spirit, Ethics and Care for Soldiers were formalized and subsequently promulgated in 1996.[22] These Values were also incorporated into the SAF's Knowledge-Abilities-Qualities (KAQ) model of Leadership under Qualities along with 12 other qualities of leadership.[23]

The seven SAF Core Values took a Virtue Ethics[24] approach to describe what is morally right and what is not. This was accomplished by emphasizing the attributes of the SAF commander and leader. The SAF Core Values complemented the Code of Conduct by describing the aspirations of the military profession and how its members ought to be as opposed to the Code of Conduct which are behavioural maxims. Thus the virtue ethics and the deontological ethics described by the Core Values and Code of Conduct complement each other. However, in dealing with the ethical dilemmas of a complex security environment, the moral consequences of actions must be considered.

ETHICS AND VALUES INCULCATION FOR THE 3RD GENERATION SAF

As the military profession in Singapore transforms into a 3rd Generation SAF, there are several key frameworks to help NSmen rationalise their understanding of ethics and values. Since 2003, the SAF Leadership Framework[25] (see Figure 1 below) has guided commander's discussions about leadership in the SAF. Of the four components of leadership described by the "triangle", the Core Values is placed at the bottom because it is meant to be the foundation of all leadership practices in the SAF. The "circle" describes the context (i.e., the SAF's Mission and Purpose, Operating Environment and Desired Outcome), that shape how SAF Commanders lead and operate. Here, the three factors in the "Circle of Leadership" framework suggest that moral consequences are just as important. This however could not be adequately supported by the deontological ethics approach of the Code of Conduct and the virtue ethics approach of the SAF Core Values.

FIGURE 1: The SAF Leadership Development Framework.[26]

Hence today, other than the manifesto of the seven Core Values, ethics in the SAF comprises a three level model of SAF Core Values inculcation[27] (see Figure 2 below), and the skill of ethical reasoning – one of 14 skills in the SAF Leadership Competency Model (LCM) in the competencies component of the SAF Leadership Development Framework (see Figure 1 above). Everyone in the SAF begins with the SAF Core Values inculcation model at Level 1 where values inculcation begins through clarification and alignment of the organizational values with that of the individual's personal values. At Level 2, they come to understand the threats to values-based functioning.[28] At Level 3, they make choices through the application of values. Ethical reasoning, as defined in the SAF, involves engaging in ethical thinking and reasoned argument about what is right and wrong; it also upholds and applies ethical reasoning principles and processes to all contexts, even in the face of adversity.

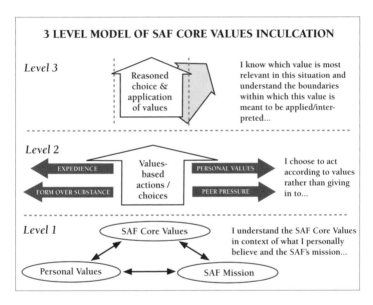

FIGURE 2: SAF Core Values Inculcation.[29]

Level 1 of the SAF Core Values inculcation takes virtue ethics and personal philosophy one step further; as a misalignment of the mission intent, personal and core values in a commander creates ambiguity that can potentially result in bad moral choices. More importantly, the clarification of a personal command/leadership philosophy as a result of aligning personal to core values for the commanders helps them establish their moral authority in order to command their men effectively. For the NSmen, this is an extremely important step of helping them fully engage and become a full member of the profession.

Level 2 of the SAF Core Values inculcation brings an understanding of social psychology into the development of ethical values based behaviors. The theories of Conformity as described by Asch[30] and the theories of Social Learning by Bandura,[31] help SAF NSmen understand the social influences that prevent them from translating a personal moral intent into positive action. Through an understanding of how these factors shape moral reasoning, it would mitigate their effects on later moral actions.

Level 3 of the SAF Core Values inculcation brings Level 1 and Level 2 together in daily practice so that the NSmen are able to see the relevance of the SAF Core Values in every aspect of operations, training and garrison life. More than just an outcome, the daily application of values by SAF commanders ensures that the central concepts of the military profession is reinforced daily and in doing so, it creates a reinforcing effect on the sense of profession in the SAF. The outcome of such an effort is an authentic understanding and demonstration of professionalism. Such preparation is necessary for a young nation to quickly create and strengthen a military tradition that would help the SAF complete its mission and when necessary, secure a swift and decisive victory.

ETHICS AND ETHICAL REASONING FOR THE 3RD GENERATION SAF

Ethical reasoning – one of the 14 skills in the SAF Leadership Competency Model (LCM) exists beyond Level 3 of the SAF Core Values inculcation as it involves determining what is morally right and what is not. This moral judgement (see Figure 3 below) is made through clarifying moral intent and exercising moral motivation to achieve moral action based on Rest's[32] Four Component Model of Moral Judgement. It is through the SAF Core Values inculcation that the SAF NSmen gains moral awareness and understands moral intent. The responsibility that comes with command is the moral authority that provides the moral motivation for thoughts and concepts to be translated into action. The SAF Leadership Competency Model of ethical reasoning is where consequentialist ethics approaches to the study of moral judgement can be supplemented by outcome driven principles to help the SAF derive positive moral consequences.

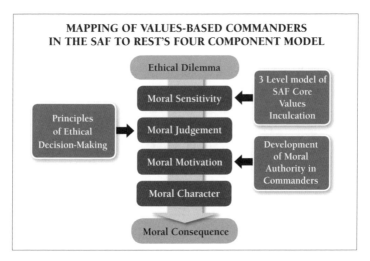

FIGURE 3: Ethics for SAF Commanders.[33]

PRINCIPLES OF ETHICAL DECISION-MAKING FOR COMMANDERS

The principles of ethical decision-making described here are drawn from well-known military philosophers such as Sun Zi and Clausewitz. A deliberate choice was made to avoid religious principles given that it would be difficult to identify universal principles that would meet the full spectrum of the eight official religions and four major ethnic groups in Singapore. Being principles, it is not a model for ethical reasoning.[34]

Principles of Ethical Decision-Making for Commanders

1.   A Commander must show the necessary care and empower his soldiers.

2.   A Commander must possess the moral courage to make the right choices and serve without thoughts of seeking personal glory and retreats without fear of punishment.

3.   A Commander's decisions are well thought through and he is bold and tenacious but yet has shown compassion for non-combatants and protected persons.

4.   A Commander must adapt to changing situations and always weigh favourable and unfavourable ethical factors in his deliberations.

5.   A Commander must remind his troops that they are a force for good and his concerns must always be the protection of the people's welfare and the upholding of our national interests.

Principle 1: Sun Zi said that when a Commander "treat[s] his troops like beloved sons they will be willing to support and die with him."[35] This analogy is especially true for an NS Armed Force and the litmus test for every command decision is whether the soldiers were equipped and empowered to deal with complex problems. This is the crux of the SAF Core Value of "Care for Soldiers"[36] and it is meant to support the moral consequence of looking after one's own men well, even under adversity.[37]

Principle 2: In his work *On War*, Clausewitz describes courage as "a feeling, like fear; the latter looks to the physical preservation, courage to the moral preservation."[38] Indeed, moral courage in the face of ambiguity is a key part of exercising the SAF Core Value of leadership. Lieutenant-General (ret) Ng Jui Ping, in his reflections on managing the hijack of Singapore Airlines Flight SQ117, said that "between the time that I gave the order to start the process of assaulting and the actual lifting up of the ladders... and the beginning of the assault, I had a few minutes. In that few minutes, I was composing a letter I would write if the assault in any way would end in disaster."[39] In spite of his feelings concerning the possible loss of lives, Lieutenant-General Ng's moral courage to stand up to the hijackers allowed him to achieve a moral consequence where the hijackers were taken down with no collateral damage. His example showed how moral courage helped to preserve the honour of the country against overwhelming odds.

Principle 3: Sun Zi said that some of the negative attributes of a commander are recklessness and being overly compassionate.[40] As such, SAF commanders must balance the SAF Core Values of Professionalism, Discipline and Fighting Spirit; they have to be measured yet bold and tenacious while possessing compassion for protected persons.[41] Major (ret) Surajan was the Commanding

Officer of the Republic of Singapore Ship (RSS) ENTERPRISE in the late 1970s when his ship encountered Vietnamese boat refugees trying to land illegally in Singapore. Despite the condition of the refugees, he could not give in to recklessness or compassion and let them pass because he had to be professional and protect Singapore's borders. Hence, he came up with a bold plan to give the refugees all his supplies, except for some bare necessities to sustain his personnel, before taking firm action to turn them away.[42] His example demonstrates how tenacity and boldness in a well thought through plan can help to create a positive moral consequence for his own conscience while maintaining mission imperatives.

Principle 4: Given the asymmetric threats of today, a commander has to adapt his methods to meet the changing environment and yet manage the many ethical considerations. During a peacekeeping mission to Timor in 2000, Colonel (ret) Surya's medical team was in a remote area when a nearby UN patrol was surrounded by a rioting mob.[43] He weighted the ethical and unethical outcomes of assisting or not assisting. Eventually, he made the decision to organize his team as a combat patrol to assist as he felt it was unethical to refuse assistance when the lives of the other patrol were at risk. Should the other UN patrol suffer fatalities due to his refusal to help, the moral consequence for Singapore, the SAF, and for himself, would have been disastrous. His account reflects the balance for adaptability and the SAF Core Values of Ethics where the outcomes of each moral action need to be compared and weighed to achieve a larger utilitarian good.

Principle 5: Today, the effect of the *Strategic Corporal*[44] cannot be overstated and the alignment of command decisions even at the lowest levels to the strategic intent is important. Further, it must reflect the values of "Loyalty to country" (i.e., "upholding of the interests of the nation.")[45] For example, during the 2004 Post Tsunami Humanitarian Assistance and Disaster relief (HADR) mission to Aceh, Major (NS) Supramaniam was one of the few NS present; he said he was very proud of Singapore's actions and "that we [the SAF] were doing the right thing [that] the SAF was an agent for good."[46] Later on during Hari Raya (a Muslim Holy day), Major Supramaniam was initially concerned that his NS Malay driver would be homesick, yet to his surprise the driver replied that he was privileged to be there and would happily stay longer if asked.[47] Commanders reminding themselves and the men that the military is a force for good not only reinforces the commander's moral authority, it also helps to guide decisions and actions on the ground toward a positive moral consequence for the entire military profession.

VALUES INCULCATION AND ETHICS IN TRAINING AND EDUCATION

Since 2008, a concerted effort has been made to embed SAF Core Values inculcation into the training curriculum of all leadership schools. In the SAF's initial efforts, the practices of *Storytelling*[48] and *Reflection-Journaling*[49] were found to be very important in helping leaders clarify and align their own values with the SAF Core Values. This led to the development of the SAF Centre for Leadership Development (SCLD) training concept of designing weekly learning cycles of values based leadership. With each learning cycle of goal setting – reflection – summarization, the faculty uses daily training opportunities and garrison activities to increase moral awareness (see Figure 4 below for an example used with Officer Cadets). In addition, leaders holding command appointments in field training exercises receive coaching and facilitation as individuals and as teams to better enable them to appreciate the moral consequences of their actions and improve their moral judgement skills. Here, the principles of ethical decision-making serves as talking points to facilitate self-reflection and team conversations between the teaching faculty and the leaders they are developing.

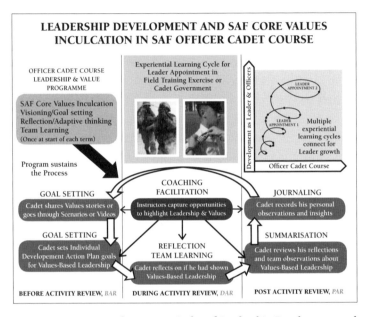

FIGURE 4: Experiential Learning Cycles of Leadership Development and SAF Core Values Inculcation for Officer Cadets.[50]

Describing principles to military leaders are by themselves insufficient. In order to be able to reason ethically, military commanders need to be given a broader education on the complexity of the issues which are inherent in an uncertain security environment. In military ethics education, commanders are supported by the SAF's Continuing Education (CE) effort to provide a broader learning experience within formal SAF courses as well as courses provided by local universities to help drive life-long learning in the military profession. Educational topics being studied for integration into the SAF CE effort include the study of philosophy from Aristotelian virtue ethics to Kantian deontological ethics. This helps commanders become clearer about their own life purpose and therefore, be better equipped to frame their own command philosophy and help them sustain their own moral motivation. Engaging in philosophical discourses also helps military commanders make better sense of the principles of ethical decision-making when confronted with an ethical dilemma. Here, military history complements philosophy by helping commanders understand past experiences and the current realities of conflict. Topics such as law, politics, regional studies and religion helps commanders understand the concepts of morality as seen from different perspectives and thus, increases their moral awareness and in-directly, enables them to make better moral judgement decisions.

Finally, experiences in social and moral psychology such as the infamous Stanford Prison Study lends a clinical yet realistic perspective on why soldiers in the battlefield could behave unethically.[51] Here, theories from Developmental Psychology such as Kohlberg's theory of Moral Development[52] and Bandura's theory of Social Learning[53] will help commanders understand how behaviours are shaped, thus, allowing them to be effective in shaping their soldiers' beliefs and concepts of what is morally right and what is not. This understanding of the cognition and behaviour of individuals will enable SAF commanders and their followers to make informed choices, both in operations and in training.

COMMAND ROLE MODELS

To facilitate the transition from schoolhouse to combat unit, the Battalion, Company, Platoon and Section level "Assuming Command" program consists of a series of dialogues and workshops that emphasize moral authority over legal authority. In fact, the SAF *Army Command Effectiveness Manual* describes the "Assuming Command" program to have 3 priorities: the clarification of personal values; the management of command transition; and the development of command philosophy to build both moral authority and moral awareness. Here, role modelling plays an important role in the development of junior commanders. Confucius advocated that "the person in the highest position should act with integrity. If he sets a good example, would others dare not to follow?"[54]   Hence, every level in the chain of command, whether Regular or NSmen, has to "talk the talk" and "walk the walk". In the context of the SAF, the men may potentially be connected to the commander outside of the military. Thus, the overall moral character of a commander within and beyond his uniform, has an impact on whether he commands with moral authority.[55]

CONCLUSION

A commander cannot rely on legal authority alone to inspire commitment and it is through a values-based approach to command that the SAF Core Values are translated into decisions and actions when it is guided by the principles of ethical decision-making. These principles empower commanders with the moral authority to inspire citizen soldiers to be committed to the defence of Singapore. As an SAF Commander gets better at achieving positive moral consequences through moral authority, he achieves a unity of command and alignment of intent and as described by Sun

Zi, "He who is able to unite himself with his officers and men as one mind, spirit and purpose will win."[56] This will allow the SAF as an NS armed force to effectively complete its mission and uphold Singapore's national interests amidst the challenges of the 21st Century.

ENDNOTES

1   See Singapore Government Press Statement Speech by the Minister of Defence, Dr. Goh Keng Swee, in moving the second reading of the National Service (Amendment) Bill in the Singapore Parliament on Monday, 13th March, 1967, Document Number: PressR19670313b retrieved on 20 May 2010 from <http://www.a2o.com.sg/a2o/public/search/index.html>.

2   All Singaporean males who reach the age of 18 are conscripted to render National Service (NS) to the country. NS comprises two years of full time service and 10 years of NS liability during which they render service up to a maximum of 40 days per year. Upon completing 10 years of NS liability, they will enter MINDEF Reserve (MR). In essence, everyone is a National Serviceman. Those serving full-time are known as National Servicemen or NSFs as opposed to NSmen who are serving their annual liability.

3   Tim Huxley, *Defending the Lion City: The Armed Forces of Singapore* (Talisman Publishing, 2004), 123-125.

4   Wahyudi Soeriaatmadja and Lynn Lee, "Orchard MRT station targeted by terrorists," *The Straits Times*, May 19, (2010), (Singapore: Singapore Press Holdings).

5   The aspiration for the 3rd Generation SAF is to build an Armed Force that is capable of full-spectrum Operations, focused on the people and the values that make up the SAF. It would be integrated and networked across the services supported by advances in administration, planning and in the development and deployment of technology. See *C4I Asia Conference 2008 Keynote Address by Lieutenant General Desmond Kuek, Chief of Defence Force* retrieved on 20 May 2010 from the MINDEF Singapore Media Room at <http://www.mindef.gov.sg/imindef/resources/speeches/2008/18feb08_speech3.html>.

6   See *Literacy and Education, Key Annual Indicators* retrieved on 20 May 2010 from Singapore Statistics Office <http://www.singstat.gov.sg/stats/charts/lit-edu.html>.

7   Samuel P. Huntington, *The Soldier and the State: The Theory and Politics of Civil-Military Relations* (Cambridge, MA: Harvard University Press, 1957), 16-18.

8   Rupert Smith, *The Utility of Force: The Art of War in the Modern World* (New York: Alfred A Knopf Division Random House Inc, 2007), 323-325.

9   *NSmen Handbook 21ˢᵗ Edition* (Singapore: NS Admin Department, 2009), 14.

10   See *Section XIIA Chapter 295, the Singapore Armed Forces Act* (Republic of Singapore, 1970).

11   See *MINDEF News Release 16 Jan 2006, Ministerial Statement on NS Defaulters by Minister for Defence Teo Chee Hean* retrieved on 20 May 2010, MINDEF Singapore Media Room, at <http://www.mindef.gov.sg/imindef/news_and_events/nr/2006/jan/16jan06_nr.html>.

12   Male Permanent Residents in Singapore would be automatically offered citizenship if they served National Service.

13   Carl Skadian and Psalm B.C. Lew, *40 Years and 40 Stories of National Service* (Singapore: Landmark Books, 2007), 242.

14   *SAF Dictionary of Military Terms, Abbreviations and Acronyms* (Singapore: SAF Printing Centre, 1994).

15   Kim-Yin Chan and Psalm Lew, *The Challenge of Systematic Leadership Development in the Singapore Armed Forces*, Paper presented at the 40ᵗʰ International Applied Military Psychologists Symposium at Oslo, Norway, 24- 28 May 2004.

16   Skadian and Lew, *40 Years and 40 Stories of National Service*, 172-174.

17   The SAF Code of Conduct was introduced when the SAF was a fledgling Army and it was based on a need to establish professional efficacy and help frame an understanding of the relationship between the military and society. See also Kim-Yin Chan, Sukhmohinder Singh, Regena Ramaya and Kwee-Hoon Lim, *Spirit and Systems: Leadership Development for a Third Generation SAF* (Pointer Monograph No 4) (Singapore: SAFTI MI, 2005), 8.

18   The SAF initially printed the SAF Code of Conduct as little booklets with a red hard cover binding which the Soldiers were supposed to carry in their left breast pocket.

19   The SAF Code of Conduct was launched at a formal parade at the former Singapore Ministry of Interior and Defence on 14 Jul 1967. The late Dr. Goh Keng Swee, the then Minister signed this declaration which today is on display at the Army Museum of Singapore.

20   Louis Pojman, "Kantian and Deontological Systems," in George Lucas ed., *Ethics for Military Leaders*," 3rd Edition (Boston: Pearson Custom Publishing, 2000), 159.

21   This institute today is known as the SAFTI Military Institute.

22   See *The SAF Core Values: Our Common Identity* (Singapore: SAFTI MI, 1996).

23   Kim-Yin Chan, Sukhmohinder Singh, Regena Ramaya and Kwee-Hoon Lim, *Spirit and Systems: Leadership Development for a Third Generation SAF* (Pointer Monograph No 4) (Singapore: SAFTI MI, 2005), 73.

24   Aristotle, "The Moral Virtues" in George Lucas, ed., *Ethics for Military Leaders*, 3rd Edition (Boston: Pearson Custom Publishing, 2000), 289-291.

25   Chan et al., *Spirit and Systems: Leadership Development for a 3rd Generation SAF*, 17-22.

26   Ibid, 18.

27   *The SAF Core Values: Our Common Identity 2007 Edition* (Singapore: SAFTI MI, 2007), 41-44.

28   In clarifying Personal Values and how it is connected to the SAF Core Values, the SAF has largely adapted Kirschenbaum's concepts of Values Clarification. See Howard Kirschenbaum, "Clarifying Values Clarification: Some Theoretical Issues and a Review of Research," *Group & Organization Management*, Vol. 1 (1976), 99-116.

29   *The SAF Core Values: Our Common Identity 2007 Edition* (Singapore: SAFTI MI, 2007), 45.

30   Solomon E. Asch, "Opinions and Social Pressure," *Scientific American*, Vol. 193 (1955), 31-35.

31   David Gross, *Psychology: The Science of Mind and Behavior 3rd Edition* (London: Hodder and Stoughton, 1999), 688-693.

32   James Rest, *Moral Development in the Professions: Psychology and Applied Ethics*, (Hillsdale, New Jersey: L. Erlbaum Associates, 1994), 22-25.

33   Ibid, 23.

34   The SAF Definition of Ethical Reasoning includes a consideration of applying ethical reasoning principles and processes to all contexts. At present, the SAF Centre for Leadership Development is still developing a process model to describe how ethical decision making principles could be applied.

35   Chow-Hou Wee, *Sun Zi Art of War: An Illustrated Translation with Asian Perspectives and Insights* (Singapore: Prentice Hall, 2003), 299.

36   The SAF Definition of Care for Soldiers is the genuine concern that we have for the well-being of those in our command. This includes equipping, feeding and training both in peace and war.

37   Sun Zi argued that "When orders are regularly enforced, it is because of the mutual trust and confidence between the commander and his men." See also Wee (2003), 270.

38   Carl von Clausewitz, "On War" in Joseph I. Greene, ed., *The Essential Clausewitz* (Mineola, New York: Dover Publications, 2003), 26.

39   This quote was copied from Lieutenant General Ng Jui Ping's exhibit in the Chief of Army's Gallery Army Museum of Singapore on 07 May 2010.

40   Wee, *Sun Zi Art of War: An Illustrated Translation with Asian Perspectives and Insights*, 228.

41   In the Geneva Convention, this includes Prisoners of Wars and Non-combatants.

42   Skadian and Lew, *40 Years and 40 Stories of National Service*, 166-167.

43   Ibid, 192-193.

44   General (Ret) Charles Chandler Krulak, "The Strategic Corporal: Leadership in the 3 Block War", *Marines Magazine*, (January 1999).

45   Sun Zi says that a commander whose "concerns are always on protecting the welfare of the people and the upholding of the interests of the ruler… is a precious talent favoured by the nation." See also Wee (2003), 298.

46   Skadian and Lew, *40 Years and 40 Stories of National Service*, 274-275.

47   Ibid, 284-285.

48   See *Stories and Storytelling in the SAF Guidebook* (Singapore: SAFTI MI, 2010).

49   See *Reflection and Journaling Guidebook* (Singapore: SAFTI MI, 2010).

50   The philosophy behind Leadership Development and the SAF Core Values inculcation is adapted from Kolb's Theory of Experiential Learning. Hence, as a Leadership Development Process, the SAF Core Value inculcation is designed in terms of learning cycles. See Kim-Yin, Chan and Psalm Lew, *The Challenge of Systematic Leadership Development in the Singapore Armed Forces*, Paper presented the 40th International Applied Military Psychologists Symposium at Oslo, Norway 24- 28 May 2004.

51   Philip Zimbardo, *The Lucifer Effect: How Good People Turn Evil* (New York: Random House, 2008), 324-379.

52   Rest, *Moral Development in the Professions*, 4-9.

53   Gross, *The Science of Mind and Behavior*, 688-693.

54   Confucius, *The Analects* translated by Dim Cheuk Lau (Singapore: Penguin Classics, 1979), 43.

55   Paul Robinson, "Ethics Training and Development in the Military," *Parameters*, Vol. 37, (Spring 2007), 23.

56   Wee, *Sun Zi Art of War: An Illustrated Translation with Asian Perspectives and Insights*, 75.

CHAPTER 6

Developing Responsible Leaders – Ethics Education at the Swiss Military Academy

Dr. Stefan Seiler
*Andreas Fischer**

The importance of developing responsible leaders is obvious as recurrent misconduct among leaders continues to be an unfortunate reality. As such, military training at all levels, in general as well as during the preparation phase for operations, should focus on developing morally competent service personnel. This chapter starts with a definition of *leadership responsibility* and then shifts to the debate on how to develop responsible leaders. Dilemma training is explained and characterized as a comprehensive method to help achieve successful moral development. It is shown that dilemma training positively influences three major components in ethical decision-making: first, it raises one's personal moral competence such as one's level of moral sensitivity, accurate moral assessment and level of moral reasoning; second, the ethical climate of an organization will be positively influenced; and third, the quality of specific situational assessments will be enhanced. Additional conditions to help increase the probability of moral behaviour in military interventions are also discussed.

---

* The views expressed in this chapter are those of the authors and do not necessarily reflect the official policy of the Swiss Armed Forces.

INTRODUCTION

The Srebrenica massacres, the torture of prisoners in Abu Ghraib, the Guantanamo prison camp controversies, rumours of tortured and killed civilians in Iraq or the desecration of corpses in Afghanistan remind us that discussion on military and leadership ethics is not only a tempest in a teapot but that it strikes at the very heart of political and military leadership alike.

One could argue that prior to embarking on a concrete discussion of leadership ethics, consensus and clarity on the characterization of behaviour that is legally and morally right or wrong should be established. It is exactly this continuous ambiguity and discussion on moral behaviour, however, that builds the foundation for every development effort in the field of leadership ethics. It is also a practical reality that military leaders and soldiers are often confronted by moral conflicts that require them to make a decision under extremely stressful circumstances, with or without the consensus about what is right or wrong in the specific situation. Therefore, the goal should not be to transform military leaders into moral philosophers who are able to find the ultimate answer to all the ethical questions in military decision-making, but rather, to develop responsible leaders who act in accordance with high moral standards in their professional daily life.

This chapter focuses on a definition of leadership responsibility and highlights the type of training and other parameters that influence ethical decision-making in military leadership. The formulated recommendations are based on theoretical reflections and findings from an empirical study using 312 professional Swiss military officers based on situation-specific decision-making in interpersonal conflicts.

LEADERSHIP RESPONSIBILITY – A DEFINITION

Before entering the debate on how to develop responsible leaders, it is important to define the term *responsibility*. A problematic aspect in formulating a universally accepted definition of responsibility is the inherent normativity of the term.[1] For example, "If a word were ever to be described as a 'container concept', that word is 'responsibility'. […] Responsibility is a complex idea that has many equally plausible definitions, however, these definitions are rarely compatible. Responsibility or responsible are terms that express values, but the values they embody are not generally accepted and differ from time to time, place to place and speaker to speaker."[2] A description of the term is necessary, however, to ensure a common understanding of the concept, and at the same time, as an attempt to contribute to the formulation of a generally accepted definition. As such, we define responsible leadership as the endeavour of achieving set objectives by respecting fundamental values of human dignity and mission-specific rules in a particular situational context.[3] This definition encompasses four elements:

1.   Achieving objectives;

2.   Respecting fundamental values of human dignity;

3.   Following mission specific rules; and

4.   The situational context.

Achieving Objectives

Achieving objectives is the first element of *responsible leadership* that underlies the inseparability of determination and moral behaviour when it comes to critical ethical situations. Leaders have to focus on the mission; they have to be successful. This is the *instrumental rationality* of professional behaviour. At the same time, leaders must consider the moral implications of their actions and in order to be responsible, they have to behave morally right. This is the *ethical rationality* of professional behaviour. Not every professional decision has a moral dimension and the moral dimension within human interaction is not limited to the professional context. However, when the two dimensions *success* (instrumental rationality) and *ethics* (ethical rationality) come together, they have to be seen as intrinsically linked and of equal importance without neglecting their particular characteristics.[4] Therefore, any serious discussion about leadership ethics has to consider the existence of an instrumental rationality in leadership (the rationality of achieving objectives) AND the ethical rationality (see figure 1).

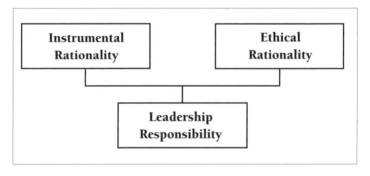

FIGURE 1: Instrumental and Ethical Rationality of *responsible leadership*[5]

The complex interaction of these two dimensions is best illustrated through a real life example. Consider the situation in which an aid convoy that is escorted by peacekeepers runs into a checkpoint manned by an adversarial party. The convoy is refused permission to pass unless half of the relief aid is left behind. Both the peacekeepers and the other party are heavily armed, including tanks.

In this example, the problematic nature of military decision-making when it comes to ethically critical situations is evident. The peacekeepers' mission is to provide relief aid to people in need, to protect the civilian drivers and convoy staff and at the same time, undertake every effort to de-escalate conflicts between the involved parties. In this situation, it is obvious that instrumental and ethical parameters will influence the decision of the military commander. The mission is to deliver the relief aid in time while protecting the civilian drivers. In addition to this complex situation, the commander should avoid any action that could result in the escalation of hostility in the region. How should the military commander respond? Should some of the relief aid be given to the other party with the remaining aid being delivered to the final destination? Should the commander turn around and find another route? Should force be used to pass through the checkpoint as the agreement signed in the convention by the conflict parties is not being respected? This example illustrates that the instrumental and ethical rationality components of leadership are intrinsically linked and cannot be separated when it comes to ethically critical situations. Is it more important to deliver the relief aid in time or to protect the civilian drivers? Both questions include instrumental as well as ethical aspects. If military force is used, the commander evaluates the instrumental responsibility of delivering on time and the ethical responsibility to provide the aid for those in need as higher than the instrumental and ethical responsibility for the civilian drivers. If some of the aid is handed over, the commander is valuing his/her responsibility for the drivers higher than the delivery of the aid. This example will be further discussed in a later section that illustrates the the importance of situational circumstances.

Respecting Fundamental Values of Human Dignity

The problematic nature of the second element of the definition of responsible behaviour lies in the definition and agreement of *fundamental values of human dignity*. The lowest common denominator should be the will to respect the Humanitarian Law and the Law of Armed Conflict. These laws are based on the assumption that every human being has an absolute and inherent worth that does not need to be acquired, cannot be lost or sold, and that precludes him/her from humiliation. Human dignity has been defined as the recognizable capacity to assert claims – "To respect a person, then, or to think of him as possessed of human dignity, simply is to think of him as a potential maker of claims."[6] In Immanuel Kant's philosophy, the postulate is made that rational beings have an intrinsic and absolute value, which is referred to as dignity. This supreme principle of morality must be an *a priori* proposition; it is a duty. This leads to the formulation of the categorical imperative: "Act only according to that maxim whereby you can at the same time will that it should become a universal law." Each individual agent regards itself as determining, by its decision to act in a certain way that everyone (including itself) will always act according to the same general rule in the future.[7] In asymmetric warfare, however, opponents often do not respect any fundamental laws nor do they treat their enemies in terms of the categorical imperative. Rather, they act in an unpredictable way whereby the right of genuine human dignity is not afforded to those that do not share the same ideology; the universality of the categorical imperative is not followed. This unpredictability of the opponent's reaction makes it extremely difficult for leaders to define an appropriate action (i.e., one does not know how the other party will react). Does this justify a violation of Humanitarian Law or the Law of Armed Conflict? The answer must be "no" since the nature of United Nations interventions is to bring or establish peace and to build structures and processes that ensure an ordered life for all people in a particular region. How should this goal be reached when the fundamental values of human dignity are not respected? Further, how do we give people a feeling of safety and freedom when they cannot be sure that the fundamental rules will be upheld?

Following Mission-Specific Rules

The third element pertains to following mission-specific rules. Each mission has specific rules of engagement (ROE) and rules of behaviour (ROB) that set the parameters within which the mission has to be achieved. These ROEs/ROBs must be clear and understandable for those involved in the mission. The lessons learned based on experiences such as the Srebrenica massacres,[8] serve as a clear indication that substantial improvements have been made in this domain. On the other hand, the vague and sometimes ambiguous wording of some new UN resolutions shows that political decision-making, at times, is driven by particular interests. Political decision-makers have to ensure that this ambiguity will not turn into unpredictable risk that puts military and civilian personnel in unnecessary danger. Therefore, clear mandates and rules of engagement for peacekeeping missions must be formulated. At the same time, they must insist that all parties involved agree on a clear mandate before sending troops into a conflict area. Otherwise, potential conditions for the next disaster to occur have been put in place.

The Situational Context

The fourth element of the definition of *responsible leadership* is the most complex. Whenever a decision is made, it is influenced by the situational context. As a result of changing situational parameters, a different course of action will generally have to be taken in each situation. This highlights the fact that the situational context plays a decisive role in defining the "best" alternative action. Therefore, there are no golden rules regarding the outcome of adequate situational decision-making.

In this context, the concept of *regulative control* and *guidance control*[9] are helpful models to categorize the different sources of control related to responsible behaviour. The assessment criterion for *regulative control* is the evaluation of the chosen action depending on the possible alternatives. The assessment criterion for *guidance control* is the evaluation of the free will and reflective decision of the acting individual. Based on this categorization, not only the action itself should be evaluated; the quality of the reflective consideration to act in a certain way should also be assessed. The importance of this second element of control is underlined by Martinelli-Fernandez[10] in her article about the Kantian contribution to ethics education in the military. She illustrated that students and soldiers on training should not only focus on "what to do" in a particular situation but also on questions of "why a particular action is carried out" and "what the motives behind a decision are". This will introduce students to the morality of rules and the nature of moral motivation that will help them to integrate an assessment of moral aspects in their decision-making process.[11]

In an empirical study with 312 professional Swiss military officers, Seiler[12] analyzed the impact of relatively stable basic moral beliefs (conception of men and moral efficacy belief) and the cognitive ability to analyze moral dilemmas (level of moral reasoning) in decision-making in bilateral leadership conflicts. Findings from the study illustrated that basic moral beliefs and the cognitive ability to analyze moral dilemmas have little impact on the decision as to how military officers will react in a specific bilateral conflict situation. Only 5% of the variance of the so-called situational decision-making could be explained by these variables. For none of the three concepts, a significant impact could be shown (see Figure 2).

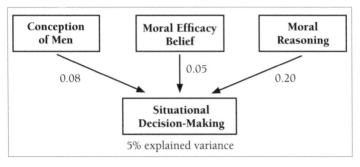

FIGURE 2: Causal effects on "Situational Decision-Making".

Only when basic moral beliefs (*Conception of Men* and *Moral Efficacy Belief*) and the level of moral reasoning were extremely low was a significant negative impact on the situational decision-making observed (i.e., people with very low values in basic moral beliefs and in moral reasoning showed significantly lower values in "situational decision-making" as compared to people with medium to high values in basic moral beliefs and moral reasoning. An additional observation was that people with medium to high values in moral believes and moral reasoning did not show very low values in "situational decision-making"; their scores ranged from medium to high. On the other hand, people with low values in moral beliefs and moral reasoning also showed very low values in "situational decision-making". These findings show that a minimal level of moral reasoning and a positive tendency in one's conception of men and moral efficacy beliefs serve as protection against completely inadequate decisions in conflict situations. In addition, the most important driving factor for decision-making in a specific situation was the interpretation of the situational circumstances itself (e.g., identifying the true intention and decisiveness of the opposite side, understanding their culture, analyzing own versus opposite resources and abilities are key elements in successful situational decision-making). These results are not surprising as a study of obedience illustrated, in an impressive way, the influential power of situational circumstances.[13]

The importance of the situational context can be illustrated by the previously mentioned example in which a relief aid convoy gets stopped by an adversary. What kind of armament does each side have? Did the adversary use force in previous situations or did they usually step back when confronted with force? How determined does the opposite commander appear? The series of relevant situation specific questions can continue. As such, an appropriate risk assessment is only possible by evaluating the relevant situational parameters.

MORAL DILEMMA TRAINING – THE WAY TO FOLLOW

The above reflections bring us closer to the question as to how to effectively train leaders in moral decision-making and leadership ethics. As the situational context is an important factor in moral decision-making, training interventions must focus on real life scenarios and not on general reflections about morally good or bad behaviour. Although general reflections may have an impact on general moral beliefs, Seiler found that basic moral beliefs do not have a significant impact on decision-making. A second criticism of situation-unspecific theoretical approaches is their lack of relevance to the real life of military leaders. Studies in the field of operational decision-making have clearly illustrated that situational assessments in real life scenarios are mainly based on previously gained experiences (in 87% of the cases) and involved *feature matching strategies*.[14] Only in a minority of the actions (in 12% of the cases) was decision-making related to theoretical reflections and explanations.[15] Klein observed decision-makers in their natural environments and concluded that in the majority of the cases, they spent a significant amount of time analyzing and understanding the situation to gain a thorough understanding of it.[16] They did not follow a traditional decision-making model to reach a solution (such as problem recognition, problem analysis, development of alternative solutions, decisions about the best solution). This research on naturalistic (the way people tend to solve their problems in an imminent situation) versus traditional decision-making (following a structured process when it comes to problem-solving), showed clear evidence that situational assessments in real life situations are more important than the reflective testing of different alternatives based on theoretical knowledge.

Mission-Specific Dilemma Training, where a group of people debate real moral conflicts, represents a promising way to develop "thinking patterns" (patterns of thoughts; engraved ways on how to approach moral conflicts), and feature strategies for future decision-making. At the Swiss Military Academy at ETH Zurich, the dilemma training method is applied in leadership ethics education. It starts with providing a group of professionals with a description of a concrete conflict situation. The closer the situation is to their natural environment, the more thinking patterns that can be developed. Therefore, the dilemmas should be presented and discussed under the rules of engagement of a concrete mission and be placed in a realistic context (i.e., the next deployment area). In the second phase, all participants are required to develop a personal solution to the dilemmas as well as provide justification for their proposed solutions. In the third phase, discussions about the different possible solutions take place. Participants are required to explain their point of view, listen to others, and integrate those reflections and arguments into their own situational analyses. If participants are open to this process, the learning curve is generally steep in this phase as they are evaluating their own reflections while at the same time, taking into consideration the reflections and conclusions of others. During this phase, new moral thinking patterns can be developed. The recommendation by Martinelli-Fernandez is to focus not only on the solution but also on the motives behind it, which should be integrated into the discussion.[17] The goal of this phase is to reach the best possible group solution. Figure 3 illustrates the dilemma training process.

FIGURE 3: Dilemma training process.

The dilemma training method offers a variety of learning opportunities for participants. First, military officers learn that the situational context is one of the most important factors in human decision-making. This helps them to develop increased sensitivity toward the problems related to this phenomenon. Behaviour is not only driven by cognitive reflection, but also by emotions, motives, and external parameters such as the actual situation.

Second, participants become more familiar with the context and the rules of engagements in peacekeeping missions. If the dilemmas are oriented toward a concrete future mission, they develop mission-specific thinking patterns and internalize the specifics of their mission. This leads to the third learning opportunity – the experiences gained from the dilemma discussions will provide a basis for situational assessments in real life. This helps officers understand the situational context faster. If a person repeatedly experiences the possibilities of having more than two solutions to a problem, he/she might immediately begin to look for different alternatives rather than the obvious black or white solution. This does not mean that the person will immediately know what to do, but that he/she will begin to automatically think of different alternatives. In this sense, dilemma training helps to develop new alternatives as a reference for situational decision-making.

A fourth learning opportunity provided by dilemma training is the positive influence it can have on moral reasoning and moral motivation. By dealing with realistic moral conflicts in group discussions, the ability to assess the moral dimension of leadership will improve. As research has demonstrated, this can serve to act as protection against completely inappropriate decisions in solving bilateral moral conflicts.[18] Future research will have to demonstrate if these results can be generalized from bilateral conflicts to different leadership contexts. In a military setting, the opportunity to develop moral reasoning through dilemma training is particularly important, as rigid hierarchical systems have been shown to have a significant negative impact on the level of moral reasoning. For example, research in the German armed forces Senger,[19] and results from a US Coast Guard study showed a significant negative relationship between rigidity of hierarchy and ethical decision-making.[20]

Dilemma training can have an added advantage if it is conducted with people that are going to be deployed to the same mission. This allows the group members to get to know each other's thoughts, values, emotions and understanding of the rules and regulations. Through several sessions of dilemma training, soldiers can begin to better predict each other's behaviour, understand the ways that others perceive moral aspects, and eventually, they come to a consensus in their decisions. This mutual understanding of each other's thinking and action and the anticipated uncertainty in the appraisal of the other's behaviour, helps to minimize frictions and tensions in the initial phase of a deployment. Dilemma training also helps to develop a common mutual moral understanding and/or a group culture in solving moral conflicts. This is important since a combination of the perceived wishes of others and the desire to comply with those wishes has been shown to be very good predictors of ethical behaviour.[21]

Peacekeeping missions and engagements in asymmetric warfare not only cause physical and emotional pressures but also affect moral decision-making. Every effort should be taken to train officers and soldiers as effectively as possible to be prepared to make the difficult and most appropriate decision. If dilemma training becomes an inherent part of military training, moral problem solving patterns can be developed that go beyond the normal course of thinking. As such, ongoing dilemma training throughout all military development programmes and mission specific dilemma training with the people involved in the same operation or deployment represent promising initiatives or steps in the right direction. In doing so, general thinking patterns and mission specific peculiarities become intrinsically linked. Ideally, soldiers should be able to develop automated moral problem-solving thinking patterns through training. This implies that dilemma training is not just a punctual short term intervention but an inherent and ongoing part of soldier development and training at all levels.

ADDITIONAL CONDITIONS TO INCREASE THE LIKELIHOOD OF MORAL BEHAVIOUR

In addition to dilemma training, other conditions exist that can help to increase the development of moral behaviour. Some of these conditions involve training/education, others centre on general circumstances under which service personnel are deployed. These aspects can complement successful preparation for peacekeeping operations from a moral point of view.

The first aspect is a general precondition: no operation should be carried out without clear rules of engagement, a clear mission, and adequately allocated resources. Although improvements in these areas have been made, recent UN resolutions have illustrated that constant attention has to be paid to this issue.

The second point focuses on general military education and training: each soldier has to know and understand the meaning and importance of the European Convention for the Protection of

Human Rights and Fundamental Freedoms, the Humanitarian Law and the Law of Armed Conflict. This is a precondition for soldiers and they should be committed to the application of these conventions and laws in their daily lives.

This leads to the third additional condition. As moral conflicts are unpredictable and every soldier is responsible for his/her own behaviour, a prevalent culture of discipline and self-control has to be established. The focus here should be on creating a zero-tolerance culture for unethical behaviour. This can only be achieved if the organization as a whole and each group is willing to include this in their governing statement. Dilemma training can help to sensitize the troops to the importance of this postulate.[22] It has been demonstrated that an organization's ethical climate is inversely related to the severity of ethical problems in the organization and is positively related to the ability to resolve ethical conflicts.[23] It has also been demonstrated that people tend to act in accordance with their perception of the average moral standards of others in the organization.[24] This also provides evidence for the importance of an organizations ethical climate.

A fourth important aspect is a deep understanding of the culture of the deployment area and the contextual circumstances. These two elements have an impact on the quality of the situational assessment. Understanding the cultural background, norms, rules and expectations are essential in situational decision-making. The same can be said about the current contextual circumstances. If the cultural background and current contextual circumstances are integrated into the dilemmas used during the training sessions, the training not only develops moral problem solving skills, but also serves to familiarize the participants with the particular circumstances of the upcoming deployment.

CONCLUSIONS

Developing responsible leaders for crisis situations is a crucial aspect for long-term success in military interventions. As such, military training should equally emphasize human behaviour in morally difficult situations as well as training on combat techniques. Dilemma training represents a promising approach for sustainable improvements in moral decision-making for military personnel. In conjunction with the additional conditions that influence moral behaviour, leaders can increase their ability to make the right decision and act accordingly when confronted with moral conflicts. The importance of considering the complex interaction of various personal, organizational, and situational influences when it comes to ethical leadership development is critical. Therefore, we emphasize in our leadership ethics education, individual as well as organizational aspects of leadership behaviour in ethically challenging situations, with a particular focus on mission-specific dilemma training. Future research is required to analyse optimal training conditions and the exact impact of dilemma training on soldiers' moral decision-making process and behaviour during deployments.

ENDNOTES

1   Mark Bovens, *The Quest for Responsibility. Accountability and Citizenship in Complex Organisations* (Cambridge: University Press, 1998).

2   Ibid, 22.

3   Adapted from Stefan Seiler, *Führungsverantwortung. Eine empirische Untersuchung zum Berufsethos von Führungskräften am Beispiel von Schweizer Berufsoffizieren* (Bern: Peter Lang, 2002), 33-39.

4   Fritz Oser, *Ethos - Die Vermenschlichung des Erfolgs* (Opladen: Leske + Budrich, 1998), 30-33.

5   Stefan Seiler, *Führungsverantwortung. Eine empirische Untersuchung zum Berufsethos von Führungskräften am Beispiel von Schweizer Berufsoffizieren* (Bern: Peter Lang, 2002); Stefan Seiler, "Führungsverantwortung - wenn Manager mehr als ihre Pflicht erfüllen", *Wirtschaftspsychologie* aktuell, Vol. 3 (2004), 54.

6   Joel Feinberg, "The Nature and Value of Rights", in Joel Feinberg, ed., *Rights, Justice, and the Bounds of Liberty* (Princeton: University Press, 1980), 3.

7   Immanuel Kant, *Grounding for the Metaphysics of Morals*, translated by James W. Ellington (Indianapolis: Hackett, 1993), 30.

8   The Srebrenica Massacre refers to the July 1995 killing of more than 7,000 Bosniak men in Srebrenica in Bosnia and Herzegovina, by units of the Army of Republika Srpska (VRS) under the command of General Ratko Mladi during the Bosnian War. Under the following link, a UN report about the Srebrenica Massacre and the lessons learned can be found: <http://daccess-dds-ny.un.org/doc/UNDOC/GEN/N99/348/76/IMG/N9934876.pdf?OpenElement>.

9   John Fischer and Mark Ravizza, *Responsibility and Control. A Theory of Moral Responsibility* (Cambridge: University Press, 1998).

10   Susan Martinelli-Fernandez, "Educating Honorable Warriors," *Journal of Military Ethics*, Vol. 1 (2006), 55-66.

11   Ibid, 61-62.

12   Seiler, *Führungsverantwortung. Eine empirische Untersuchung zum Berufsethos von Führungskräften am Beispiel von Schweizer Berufsoffizieren*, 247-298.

13   Stanley Milgram, "Behavioral Study of Obedience," *Journal of Abnormal and Social Psychology*, Vol. 67 (1963), 371-378.

14   *Feature matching strategies* refer to decision making strategies where individuals try to match characteristics (features) of a new situation with characteristics of a previously experienced situation. If a previous situation with similar features as the new situation is identified (features of experienced situation match with features of new situation), it is most likely

that the problem solving strategy of the previous situation will be applied to the new situation.

15   George L. Kaempf, Steve Wolf and Thomas E. Miller, *Decision making in the Aegis combat information centre*, Proceedings of the Human Factors and Ergonomics Society 37th Annual Meeting, (1993), 1107-1111; See also Jeffrey Morrison et al., *Tactical decision making under stress (TADMUS) decision support system*, (1997).

16   Gary Klein, *Sources of Power: How People Make Decisions* (Cambridge: University Press, 1998).

17   Martinelli-Fernandez, "Educating Honorable Warriors," 55-66.

18   Seiler, *Führungsverantwortung. Eine empirische Untersuchung zum Berufsethos von Führungskräften am Beispiel von Schweizer Berufsoffizieren*, 258-264.

19   Rainer Senger, "Segmentierung des moralischen Bewusstseins bei Soldaten", in G. Lind, H.A. Hartmann and R. Wakenhut, eds., *Moralisches Urteil und soziale Umwelt* (Weinheim: Beltz, 1983).

20   Richard White, *Ethics and Hierarchy: The Influence of a Rigidly Hierarchical Organization Design on Moral Reasoning* (Pennsylvania: Pennsylvania State University Press, 1997).

21   Man Kit Chang, "Predicting Unethical Behavior: A Comparison of the Theory of Reasoned Action and theTheory of Planned Behaviour," *Journal of Business Ethics*, Vol. 17 (1998), 1825-1834.

22   Stefan Seiler, "Organisationskultur und individ" uelle Verantwortungsübernahme – zur Schaffung eines stabilen Fundaments moralischen Handelns," in Oliver Dengg, ed., *Unternehmenskultur und soziales Handeln*, Band 2 (Wien: Schriftenreihe der Landesverteidigungsakademie, 2009).

23   Lynn Bartels, Edward Harrick, Kathryn Martell and Donald Strickland, "The Relationship about Ethical Climate and Ethical Problems within Human Resource Management," *Journal of Business Ethics*, Vol. 17 (1998), 799-804.

24   Thomas M. Jones and Lori Verstegen Ryan, "The Link Between Ethical Judgement and Actions in Organizations: A Moral Approbation Approach," *Organizational Science*, Vol. 8 (1997), 663-680.

CHAPTER 7

Analysis of Ethical Conduct within the Australian Defence Force

Brigadier Nick Jans
*Dr. Jamie Cullens**

INTRODUCTION: HOW "AT RISK"?

The issue of "ethics" is increasingly discussed in Australian Defence Force (ADF) leadership courses, and the ADF has yet to be dogged by a major ethical issue. Ostensibly, the Australian military institution seems to be performing satisfactorily in terms of its overall ethical conduct.

However, beyond such broad and indirect measures, there is little way of knowing just how "at risk" the ADF is in ethical terms. The same applies to all Western military institutions. There are simply no data on what kinds of ethical issues/dilemmas are encountered, how often they are encountered and by whom.

In an effort to establish an empirical basis for assessing the ethical conduct of the Australian military institution, the Centre for Defence Leadership Studies has been progressively gathering and cataloguing information on "ethical behaviour" from ADF officers. This report presents an analysis of the results.

---

* The views expressed in this paper are those of the authors and do not necessarily reflect those of the Australian Defence Force.

THE STUDY

Participants in various ADF ethics workshops in 2007 and 2008 were invited to provide brief details of any "ethical dilemmas" in which they were involved. This was done as part of the written evaluation of the workshop.[1] They were specifically asked to indicate:

- whether they had been confronted by an ethical dilemma on operations;

- whether they had been confronted by an ethical dilemma at home; and

- in each case, to briefly describe the details.

Figure 1 summarizes the responses by Service.

Most participants were at the O5 career level (i.e., Major and equivalent). A total of 286 incidents were generated, with 70% of all participants providing at least one incident (see Figure 1). Because more Army officers attended the ethics workshops, most responses came from Army officers. The tiny "Other" category was comprised of Australian Public Service officers at the Australian Command & Staff College (ACSC). What follows is therefore essentially an Army-based analysis.

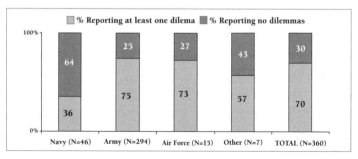

FIGURE 1: Responses within ethics workshops.

FINDINGS

As Figure 1 shows, three out of four Army officers reported at least one dilemma. The reporting rate for Navy officers was much lower, at only one of every three.

Details were provided for two-thirds of the 286 dilemmas generated (see Figure 2).

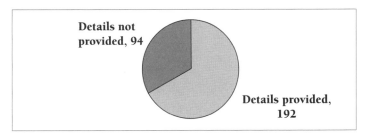

FIGURE 2: Extent to which details of the dilemmas were provided.

Respondents were much more likely to provide details for dilemmas that occurred on deployment than for incidents that had occurred at home (see Figure 3).

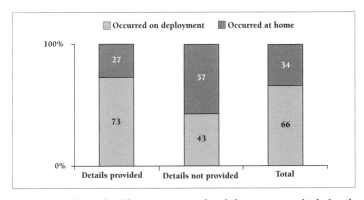

FIGURE 3: Where the dilemmas occurred and the extent to which details were provided.

After careful scrutiny of all the specified incidents, a coding frame was developed to cover the following combinations (see Figure 4):

- Who was behaving unethically, or was confronted with the ethical dilemma? Was it oneself or others?

- Where was the incident? Was it while deployed or at home/ashore?

- What was the broad nature of the incident? Did it involve a direct issue, i.e., involving oneself, or did it involve the matter of possibly ignoring someone else's transgressions?

- Did it involve a "soft" issue/transgression (i.e., no direct human or physical risk/damage)? Examples: Inappropriate/unprofessional behaviour; Lied or falsified/withheld information or reports.

- Or did it involve a "hard" issue/transgression (i.e., damaging/risking life & limb, health, well-being or safety)? Examples: Withheld aid/assistance to local population; Carelessly applied ROE.

KEY VARIABLE	POSSIBLE COMBINATIONS	
Who?	Oneself	Others
Where?	Deployment	At home/ashore
Level of involvement?	Direct, i.e., the officer transgressed	Indirect, i.e., the officer ignored others' transgressions
What?	"Soft", i.e., no direct human or physical risk or damage	"Hard", i.e., damaging or risking damage to life and limb, health, well-being, or safety

FIGURE 4: Coding frame.

This gave rise to eight possible combinations. Figure 5 shows the detail for one of these.

WHO	WHERE	DID WHAT	
Self	Deployed	Transgressed	**"Soft" transgressions (risking/resulting in not more than minor distress to others)** Showed favouritism Applied double standards Behaved inappropriately or unprofessionally Used position to advance personal/professional interests Misused privileges/resources Resisted/ignored superior direction/orders Gave inadequate support for whistleblowers Maintained inappropriate personal relations within the unit Lied or falsified/withheld information or reports **"Hard" transgressions (affecting/risking life, limb, health, well-being or safety)** Unnecessarily inconvenienced members or families Sanctioned willful damage to the environment Withheld aid/assistance to hostile locals/combatants Withheld aid/assistance to local population Carelessly applied ROE Sanctioned inappropriate behaviour, bullying, harassment, or harsh treatment of ADF members Sanctioned harsh treatment of or violence against prisoners Sanctioned violence against locals whose combatant status was unclear Committed bullying, harassment, or harsh treatment of ADF members Committed harsh treatment of or violence against prisoners Committed violence against locals/the environment Unnecessarily put military personnel in harm's way Deliberately killed prisoners Deliberately killed locals whose combatant status was unclear

FIGURE 5: Coding frame details (example).

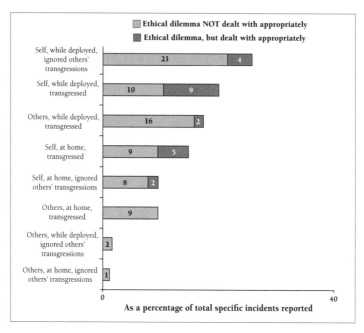

FIGURE 6: Type of ethical dilemma, for those for which details were provided. (Percentages may not total 100% because of rounding conventions.)

Figure 6 shows the distribution of dilemmas for which details were provided. The most frequent/common ethical dilemmas for which details were provided were encountered by oneself, on deployment, and were "indirect", in that they involve the dilemma of whether or not to ignore other people's or other agencies' transgressions. These comprise 25% of all dilemmas for which descriptions were provided.

About one-quarter of all such dilemmas were associated with a satisfactory outcome, i.e., the ethical dilemma was dealt with appropriately and presumably, the officer did eventually act in an ethical way (Figure 7). Perhaps not surprisingly, most such "satisfactory outcomes" involved a situation in which the individual officer was directly involved (see each of the "Self" categories in Figure 6).

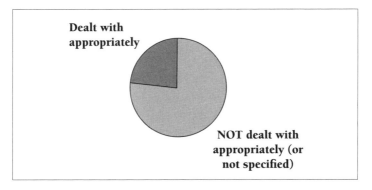

Dealt with appropriately

NOT dealt with appropriately (or not specified)

FIGURE 7: Extent to which a transgression was dealt with appropriately, for those dilemmas for which details were provided.

The most frequently cited type of ethical dilemma involved activities that were coded as "Inappropriate/unprofessional behaviour". These compromized 30% of the full set of the 191 incidents for which detail was provided. Incidents of "Inappropriate/unprofessional behaviour" were generally along the lines of having committed or observed conduct that was inappropriate or incorrect in professional terms and then failing to do something about it. The failure to act on something which was plainly inappropriate or unprofessional was the issue here. Other incidents could be readily categorized in terms of issues such as "showing favouritism", "applying double standards", "using one's position to advance personal or professional interests", and so on.

The "hard" incidents comprised 35% of the total 191 reported and detailed. Their distribution was more even. The most frequently cited were:

- "Withheld aid/assistance to local population" (9% of the total of 191 incidents, comprising 6% "not dealt with appropriately" and 3% "dealt with appropriately";

- "Carelessly applied ROE" (6% of the total of 191 incidents, comprising 4% not dealt with appropriately, 2% dealt with appropriately);

- "Sanctioned/Committed violence against locals/the environment" (6% of the total of 191 incidents, comprising 4% not dealt with appropriately and 2% dealt with appropriately); and

- "Unnecessarily put military personnel in harm's way" (3% of the total of 191 incidents, comprising 2% not dealt with appropriately and 1% dealt with appropriately)

Figure 8 shows that around two-thirds of the dilemmas for which details were provided involved a "soft" transgression.

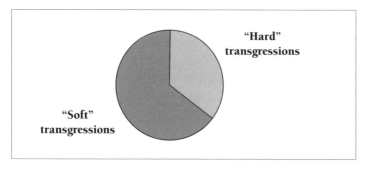

FIGURE 8: Nature of the transgression, for those dilemmas for which details were provided.

Figure 9 shows one example of the more detailed breakdown. This is the most frequently cited type of ethical dilemma: it concerns oneself, while deployed, and the ethical issue is whether or not to ignore others' transgressions.

It can be seen that most of these ethical dilemmas are of the "soft" transgression type, i.e., having no direct human or physical risk or damage.

Examples of "Inappropriate/unprofessional behaviour" include:

- alcohol being consumed within a unit beyond the ration allowed and no one doing anything about it;

- incompetence being tolerated, or reports of incompetence being ignored;

- "due process" not being applied within ship/unit procedures, but no one doing anything about it;

- issues of disloyalty;

- issues over what to do about dodgy business practices in the Middle East, such as the common use of bribery;

- and so on.

Figures 10 to 14 show the other five main categories of ethical dilemmas for which details were provided. This accounts for 97% of all such incidents (i.e., ethical dilemmas for which details were provided).

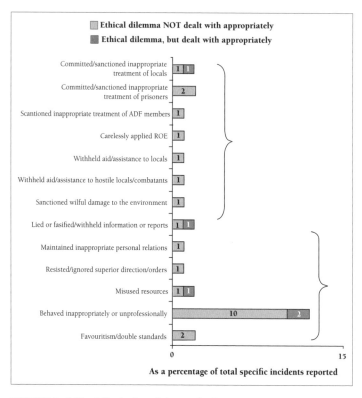

FIGURE 9: Self, while deployed, ignored others' transgressions.

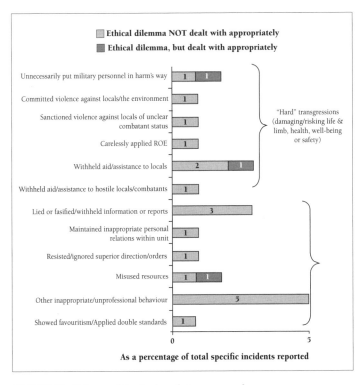

FIGURE 10: Others, while deployed, transgressed.

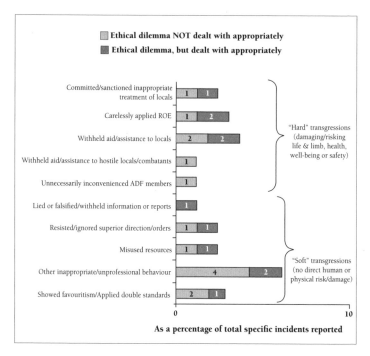

FIGURE 11: Self, while deployed, transgressed.

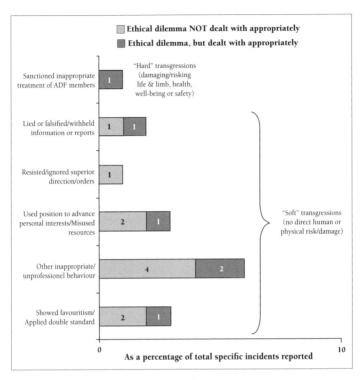

FIGURE 12: Self, at home, transgressed.

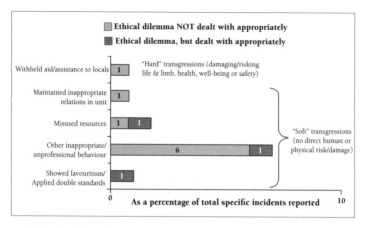

FIGURE 13: Self, at home, ignored others' transgressions.

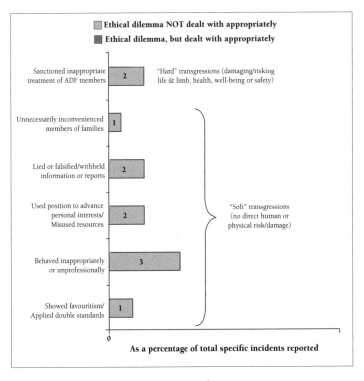

FIGURE 14: Others, at home, transgressed.

DISCUSSION

Is the sample representative?

It is reasonable to assume that the sample is representative for the Army, since it was sampled from all the officers who were attending a mandatory all-corps career course in a single year as well as from the sizable Army contingent at the ACSC course.

Although the Navy sample is not large, it can reasonably be assumed that the sample is representative of the Seaman Officer PQ.

All Seaman Officers who were destined for CO/XO roles in 2008 were involved in the ethics workshops.

The Air Force is plainly underrepresented. It included only those officers who were attending the ACSC (and then only a single ACSC course).

Why did a substantial minority of officers fail to provide details of their nominated dilemma?
And why was it much more likely that dilemmas seem to occur most frequently on deployment?

One officer in three did not provide details of their nominated dilemma. Why was this proportion so high? Why did some provide details and others did not?

To begin with, the indication that the officer had faced an ethical dilemma and the provision of the details of that dilemma, were voluntary. It is possible that a sizeable proportion of officers couldn't be bothered to provide such material. However, this explanation doesn't seem plausible, because the reception of every workshop was nothing short of enthusiastic.

Another reason could be that the space allowed in the questionnaire for the provision of details was too restricted for many to adequately provide a description. Perhaps respondents felt that they needed at least a minimum amount of space to do justice to the details of their dilemma, and they would have written more if they had had more space. This is more plausible as an explanation, although it still doesn't explain why such a large number of incidents were not detailed and why those that occurred on deployment were much more likely to be detailed. Many officers were sufficiently diligent to cram in an additional incident or two; and many provided contact details so that they could be followed up.

The most likely explanation for the reluctance to provide details for incidents that happened at home may be because those involved are somewhat "too close for comfort". On the face of it, this is the most likely explanation.

Why did the most frequent ethical dilemmas involve "Inappropriate or unprofessional behaviour"?

The most frequent reported ethical dilemmas involved "Inappropriate or unprofessional behaviour". That is, the ethical issue commonly is associated with behaviour which is inconsistent with professional codes of conduct, including unwritten/implicit codes of conduct. Examples of dilemmas were categorized under this heading include alcohol being consumed within the unit beyond the ration allowed and no one doing anything about it, incompetence being tolerated, disloyalty, etc: behaviour that, in other organisations, might be frowned upon but not necessarily be regarded as "unethical".

All this is a demonstration of the strong sense of professionalism that exists within the ADF officer corps.[2] So well ingrained are the implicit standards required of a member of the profession of arms that officers feel that an act which in another organization might be simply regarded as a drop in standards or evidence of lack of diligence is "unethical".

How can we explain the inter-Service differences?

Navy officers were significantly less likely to report on an ethical issue, when compared with their counterparts in the Army. Although the explanation for this might simply be that we don't have enough data from the Navy, it is more likely that the explanation lies in differences associated with the operational or cultural environments of the three Services.

Judging by these data, the Navy seems to be operating in a significantly different operational world than are their Army counterparts. This may be entirely reasonable as an explanation, with Navy operations largely confined to the relatively isolated and "hermetically sealed" shipboard environment. But there may be other, deeper explanations as well, such as might be associated with the acceptability of certain kinds of behaviour in certain units of certain Services.

Do the findings indicate that a situation of perpetual deployment is more ethically risky than one of prevailing peace?

The answer to this question is probably "yes". Not only is this what our data are telling us, with two-thirds of the ethical dilemmas cited occurring in deployment, but the explanation makes sense. In the considerably more chaotic environment of operations, the line between what is "right" and what is "not right" is much more likely to be blurred than in the more simple environment of peacetime exercises.

An alternative explanation, however, is that ethical dilemmas that are encountered on deployment are more likely to be in the forefront of people's minds, because of their greater severity and novelty – not to mention challenge.

All this indicates an issue that is worthy of further consideration.

Do the findings indicate a "comfortable" situation in respect to the ethical climate of the ADF?

On the one hand, we can point to the fact that two out of every three of the cited dilemmas were of the "soft" category: serious enough, but not of the degree of seriousness that might be associated with risk or damage to lives and material.

Moreover, a substantial number of the dilemmas were "satisfactorily resolved", in that they were accompanied by responsive and responsible action.

On the other hand, the presence of *any* significant level of ethical issues – and it is plain that, in the Army at any rate, there is a very high level of exposure to such issues – is cause for concern, even if the dilemmas themselves are comparatively minor. One of the more important reasons for this is that even minor ethical issues need to be dealt with promptly and appropriately. Apart from any other reason, to do otherwise contributes to a slackening of the ethical culture within the institution.

Minor misdemeanours in one year may encourage a climate in which further misdemeanours, of increasing severity, are likely to occur in subsequent years, because norms for tolerance have been progressively established.

The final and perhaps most telling point in regard to this particular question is that one-third of the respondents who indicated that they had dilemmas did not provide details. It must be assumed that a significant proportion of these un-detailed dilemmas were sufficiently serious to make the respondent reluctant to give any details at all.

CONCLUSIONS

An analysis of ethical dilemmas reported by ADF officers showed that most officers (70%) had faced an ethical dilemma in recent times. This was most likely to have occurred on deployment, rather than at home. Army officers were more likely to report an ethical dilemma than were Navy officers (the sample of Air Force officers was so small that it cannot be regarded as being statistically representative or even meaningful.)

This analysis has been a useful exercise, in that it has established an empirical framework by which ethical conduct on the organisational level can be measured.

Although it is somewhat reassuring to find that most of the ethical dilemmas that were reported were categorized as a "soft transgression", and that a substantial number of the dilemmas were "satisfactorily resolved", there is no reason for complacency. To begin with, minor misdemeanours in one year may encourage a climate in which further misdemeanours, of increasing severity, are likely to occur in subsequent years, because norms for tolerance have been progressively established. Moreover, one officer in three did not provide details of their nominated dilemma, and as mentioned above, it must be assumed that these un-detailed dilemmas were sufficiently serious to make the respondent reluctant to provide any details.

ENDNOTES

1   Workshops were conducted for the Navy CO/XO-designate course (O5 and O6), two Army O5 courses, and the 2008 ACSC course (O5).

2   Nick Jans, "Careers in Conflict 21C: The Dynamics of the Contemporary Military Career Experience," Centre for Defence Leadership Studies, Australian Defence College, interim report, December 2008.

CHAPTER 8

Morally Challenging Situations: Potential Sources of Moral Stress in a Military Context

Sofia Nilsson[*]

INTRODUCTION – THE DUAL DILEMMA OF MILITARY ETHICS

Armed Forces possess weapons. As such, military ethics concerns the overarching question of when the use of armed force is legitimate. Military ethics is a matter of extreme importance, partly because of the military's power to cause destruction and death, and partly due to the built-in dualism, or "main paradox", as verbalized by Verweij and Värri "How is it possible to maintain one's ethical consistency and be an ethical subject by justifying killing and respecting human dignity at the same time?"[1]

In recent years, the scale, complexity, and scope of military operations have been said to create new moral dilemmas. Some scholars claim that future operations will require more "ethical sophistication" on the part of military personnel as the nature of operations has been altered to include aspects "other than war".[2] The concept of "moral fitness" emphasizes individual responsibility by introducing an attitude of alertness and responsibility on a moral

---

[*] The views expressed in this chapter are those of the author and do not necessarily reflect those of the Swedish Armed Forces.

level.[3] Some scholars talk about the need for a peacekeeper ethos to motivate soldiers and officers, a core element being the protection of human life.[4] From a theoretical perspective, the phenomenon of moral fitness appears to ascribe to individuals the ability to discern right from wrong during military operations. However, put in the perspective of military ethics, the perception of what is "right" appears complicated by comprising both:

1. the protection of human life, and

2. the use of violence/killing with the ultimate aim of protecting human life.

Since military personnel (officers and soldiers) are assumed to make morally tough decisions for which there is no right or wrong per se, the ethical duality or dilemma stated above is suggested to inflict high psychological demands on them as individuals. One is prompted to ask if there is a rational way to uphold personal ethical consistency while simultaneously being an ethical subject executing military tasks that might include the lawful killing of others. It can be assumed that individuals possessing moral fitness are psychologically worse off in situations where they are expected to justify violent means to a morally-correct end, and refraining from doing what they find ethically appropriate as a first choice of action.

In keeping with military ethics, officers and soldiers are continuously faced with morally difficult situations, where there is much at stake, in which they have to choose between "right" and "wrong" courses of action. Scholars of military ethics are, first and foremost, concerned with issues of the principle of humanity, humanitarian intervention, just war, ethical decision-making, ethical behaviour, etc. The author of this chapter, however, also sees a need for perspectives that emphasize the individual officer or soldier confronting morally difficult situations in the field in addition to any psychological constraints arising from not always being able to act in accordance with one's own moral conscience.

MORAL STRESS IN A MILITARY CONTEXT

It has been argued that any decision with a potential to harm or benefit people is a decision that has ethical dimensions.[5] In turn, ethical decision-making presumes an individual recognizes a moral dimension to a potential problem. The decision-making process is moral on the basis of the existence of moral considerations and not because the resulting decision is necessarily consistent with ethical principles and norms.[6] The excerpt below illustrates the individual as a moral agent during ethical decision-making.

> *In a crisis, a truly thinking person will not look for rules and laws but will say, 'I must be true to myself, I must not do anything that I cannot live with, that I cannot remember.'*[7]

Are soldiers and officers in a position to always act in accordance with their own moral conscience? Taking military ethics as a starting point, it can be concluded that reality is not that simple. Rather, perceptions of right and wrong are likely to differ from one situation to another. Morally tough situations are likely to result in a specific kind of personal stress reaction labelled moral stress, that might affect operative abilities negatively.[8]

Moral stress is a phenomenon that has almost exclusively been studied in a nursing context[9] and refers to painful feelings on a personal level that tend to arise in two specific kinds of situations:

1.   situations that are characterized by more than one right course of action, where the choice to act on one decision will necessarily preclude the possibility of acting on the other;[10] and

2.   situations in which the individual is conscious of the morally appropriate action a situation requires, but cannot carry it out due to institutional obstacles such as lack of time, supervisory support, etc.[11]

Officers and soldiers are bound to face morally challenging situations during international operations and are therefore at high risk of being affected by moral stress. Upon examining the nursing literature, one finds that psychological detachment is highlighted as a potential coping strategy applied during difficult ethical decision-making. However, by psychologically detaching themselves, individuals face the risk of becoming cynical toward the assignment.[12] Consequently, by not paying attention to the consequences of moral constraints, there is a risk that military personnel might experience a lose of moral awareness and moral sensitivity.[13] Bearing in mind that military power can cause death and destruction, such individuals could become dangerous and counterproductive. As moral stress has not previously been studied in relation to military task completion, there is a great need for further research in order to find the right measures to cope with moral constraints to secure high operative performance. As such, the key issue of this chapter is to gain a deeper understanding of the potential sources of moral stress in a military context. From a moral stress perspective, morally problematic situations are suggested to be moral stressors. Consequently, these situations are interesting in terms of being the very phenomenon causing moral stress reactions. Efforts to find ways of coping with moral stress should begin with an understanding of the underlying moral mechanisms in military service that tend to evoke moral stress reactions.

SOURCES OF MORAL STRESS AS PERCEIVED BY SWEDISH CADETS: THE SWEDISH MILITARY CONTEXT

According to classical stress theory, there are no stressful events *per se*. Rather, stress is defined as a subjective phenomenon or as a psychological or physiological response to a situation that can be interpreted as challenging, threatening or overwhelming. Accordingly, the same event is prone to be appraised in different ways, depending on individual experience and life situation.[14] These stipulations should likewise hold water in the case of moral stress. Bearing in mind the different experiences of various countries Armed Forces, there is a need to understand potential sources of moral stress in light of their national history. Sweden, for example, has not been at war for two hundred years. Its last battle was a "minor struggle" taking place in Norway in 1814 that claimed the life of three Swedish soldiers.[15] The appraisal process of Swedish military personnel is therefore likely to differ from that of other countries. Nevertheless, the Swedish military's commitment to peace support operations, which comprises both peacekeeping and peace-enforcement, has recently increased. Peace support is now one of the main tasks of the Swedish Armed Forces.[16] Even though Sweden has had a relatively peaceful history, it has participated in many difficult operations in countries such as Afghanistan, Bosnia, Congo, Liberia, Chad, Somalia, and the former Yugoslavia. This in mind, it should be noted that the results of this study may be of greater relevance to countries with a national military history that resembles that of the Swedish Armed Forces (SAF).

For our purposes, 112 Swedish cadets (101 men/11 women), in their twenties or early thirties, were asked to describe *the worst morally/ethically difficult situation they could see themselves facing during international service*. Flanagan's critical incident technique was used to construct the open-ended question that was part of a larger leadership survey.[17] It was assumed that knowledge of the worst morally challenging situation would illicit indicators of high-risk moral stressors. Data were analyzed using cluster analysis.[18]

Of the Swedish cadets, 20.5% possessed international experience (7.1 % had completed more than one mission). Their apprehension of morally stressful situations may therefore reflect both their military education and international experience. All moral stressors, as described by the Swedish cadets, consistently appeared to override the morals and standards of the individual and are thus expected to evoke moral stress reactions. There seems to be a mutual understanding among the informants that the kind of ethical decision-making that is emphasized often involves risking the lives of others. Such discussions are made rapidly and on the basis of insufficient and uncertain basic data and require individuals to deal with the consequences of their own decisions. Potential sources of moral stress as perceived by the Swedish cadets are described and discussed below.

HAVING TO COMPROMISE ON PERSONAL MORALS AND STANDARDS: RELATED TO CONCEPTIONS OF LIFE

The Swedish cadets reported how potential sources of moral stress are associated with situations where one is forced to compromise personal morals and standards concerning conceptions of life.

This type of moral stressor is, according to the data analysis, was related to *Immoral attitudes and behaviours* and the *Maltreatment of children.*

IMMORAL ATTITUDES AND BEHAVIOURS

According to the study of Swedish cadets, stressors that compromise an individual's morals and standards are often related to issues rooted deep within personal moral value systems. These tend to surface when individuals are exposed to attitudes and behaviours that diverge from their own perceptions of how things "ought to be." An example of this emerges when the Swedish cadets refer to the *foreign cultures and unfamiliar norms* of civilians and military colleagues from other countries regarding their view of women:

> When it comes to other cultures, like for example, Afghanistan…
> Islam forces women to cover themselves. If I saw someone
> adversely affected by such a degrading practice, I would have
> a hard time keeping my mouth shut and respecting it.

Several informants also indicated that it is morally difficult to experience oppression and abusive behaviours that are related to other countries' religious practices. The very existence of behaviours related to subjugation tends to evoke strong emotions, with individuals perceiving themselves powerless to "correct" what they think is wrong. By trying to correct or interfere, they believe that they might impair or harm good international relations.

Culture has been defined as "aquired knowledge that people use to interpret, experience and generate social behavior."[19] Theoretically, this kind of knowledge is assumed to shape values and attitudes, and affect behaviour. One explanatory factor to perceiving immoral attitudes and behaviours as morally strenuous might be ethnocentric perceptions of what is right and wrong. Ethnocetrism is the technical name "for the view of things in which one's own group is the centre of everything, and all others are scaled and rated with reference to it".[20] This means that individuals appraise the world from their own point of view and experience, making them inclined to see their own personal positions as all-embracing, and assuming that everybody else shares the same cultural norms and attitudes.[21] When this proves not to be the case, anyone departing from the individual's own perceptions of right and wrong is perceived as "different".[22] Since, from a western perspective, the subjugation of women is negative and involves immoral attitudes and abusive behaviour, ethnocentric perceptions in this regard are suggested to evoke strong moral stress reactions.

Additionally, informants described *dubious morals and standards* among military personnel from other cultures and civilians in the host country as potential sources of moral stress. According to the open-ended question, dubious morals and standards include racism, torture, oppression, indiscriminate violence, and disrespectful behaviour. These morals and standards contradict those of the SAF. Even so, dubious morals and standards are also sometimes reported to be associated with the behaviour of Swedish compatriots, including failure to adhere to military values, group ridicule of the civil population, sexist comments, and lack of cultural or political sensitivity to the host country. As described previously, individuals reported how they would find their inability to "put things right" as morally strenuous. Further, one might suggest that the presence of dubious morals and standards among Swedish compatriots highlights the incongruence, at times, between individual values and those of the Swedish military organisation. This presents a moral dimension in itself.

MALTREATMENT OF CHILDREN

Another reported conception of life related moral stressor concerned the maltreatment of children. From a wider perspective, this moral stressor may be seen to be an explicit example of previously mentioned sources of moral stress, stemming from a combination of foreign culture/norms and dubious morals and standards. As an example, moral aspects of the maltreatment of children included having to witness *child abuse* without intervening for fear of further aggravating the situation. In some cultures, physical punishment may be a "normal" aspect of disciplining children. Questioning this may cause personal offence or, in a broader longer term context, negatively impact international cooperation and the completion of military tasks. Moral stress arises not only from witnessing abusive behaviour, but also from the notion that it is ok to hurt someone who is exposed and vulnerable. Here one might discern cultural underlying differences at the core of the issue, especially when considering the Swedish (western) outlook on moral norms on abusive behaviour in relation to children. Tolerance for the physical punishment of children is extremely low in Sweden due in part to the statutory ban that affects public attitudes towards the use of this form of parental discipline.[23]

Further considering the maltreatment of children as a potential source of moral stress, many informants reported the worst moral stressor to stem from military service in war zones where child soldiers could be confronted and ultimately have *to be fought or shot*. They expressed anxiety over their own potential actions in such a situation.

In conclusion, life-related perceptions of right and wrong can be assumed to expose individual value systems in general. Ethnocentric perceptions of right and wrong might also serve as a basis of individual appraisal and provide some explanation for the moral stressors to be discussed, although in a more implicit manner. Potential moral stressors (i.e., the moral dilemmas and situations where the individual is prevented from taking necessary action) are presented below.

HAVING TO COMPROMISE ON PERSONAL MORALS AND STANDARDS: BEING PREVENTED FROM TAKING NECESSARY ACTION

One situation that the Swedish cadets reported as a source of moral stress involved *organization* and *leadership-related* factors that prevent the individual from taking necessary action. In these situations, someone or something else appears to have made the "morally right" decision on behalf of the individual.

ORGANISATION-RELATED FACTORS

Many informants refer to a *lack of juridical support* in conventions such as the Rules of Engagement, politics, laws and regulations as morally trying when such conventions prevent an individual from combating ethnic cleansing, stopping sexual or violent abuse and crime, or from helping the local population. The same moral dilemma arises in situations where the individual wishes to execute tasks that have not been approved by the SAF. Here, having to "let things happen" or "watch innocent people suffer" with the individual being prevented from taking human responsibility appears to be the common denominator. The core aspect seems to be that individuals know they could have made a difference, had it not been for legal restraints.

The same kind of reasoning may be applicable to situations in which a *lack of resources*, in terms of both staff and materials, hinders individuals from taking what is perceived to be necessary action. The inability to take the necessary action appears to evoke feelings of failing the ones trusting them. Lack of resources tends to become a moral issue in situations where the individual is not able to help people who are suffering. This moral stressor appears more salient in situations where the resources that do exist are instead set aside for the benefit or use by the military unit. Another dimension of this stressor reported by the Swedish cadets was the lack of sufficient resources to provide safety for its military members.

LEADERSHIP-RELATED FACTORS

Leadership or *superior order* is also described as a factor that is likely to hinder the individual from taking the necessary action in the field and at the political level. *Lack of leader support* is morally strenuous when it overrides ones own "moral compass" or perception of what is morally right in a specific situation. One informant expressed this as:

> When the management and one's own 'inner moral compass' are in conflict, like in [name of country, author's remark], when troops, because of a superior order, were forced to abandon people who were about to get murdered… ethnic cleansing…

Another leader-related example that was reported to be a probable source of moral stress was concern over being expected to take "innocent lives" on the basis of a superior order. Superior orders might thus inflict moral stress by both forcing personnel to act contrary to their own morals and standards (active form) while at the same time causing them to refrain from doing what they perceive to be the "morally right thing" (passive form).

The moral stressors that appear to stem from a conflict between leader-subordinate relations, need to be discussed in the light of military culture. Many studies have focused on the consequences of incongruence between the personal characteristics of employees and the attributes of the organization where they are employed.[24] In military organizations, however, the opposite mechanisms are also likely to be at play since principles of moral obligations in terms of organizational loyalty and obedience are central. This is illustrated by David L. Perry:

> The military places a premium on hierarchy, and inculcates strong habits of obedience to superior officers in those who enter the profession. Obedience is often fully consensual: soldiers and officers can feel tremendous trust in and respect for their commanders. But soldiers must also be encouraged and trained to refuse to obey clearly unethical or illegal orders, and enabled to do so without retribution.[25]

The excerpt above serves as an illustration of potential conceptions of right and wrong in the military. The perception of what constitutes the "moral" course of action tends to be situational and defined by the military task and/or superior orders. Johnson talks about "the loyalty syndrome" and refers to situations where right and wrong is subordinate to the overriding value of loyalty to the leader.[26] Johnson states that:

> Loyalty, an admirable and necessary quality within limits, can become all-consuming. It also becomes dangerous when a genuine wholesome loyalty to the boss degenerates into

covering up for him, hiding things from him, or not differing with him when he is wrong.[27]

In the aftermath of the Second World War, the term "banality of evil" described those individuals who were perceived to be incapable of telling right from wrong or who were unable to distinguish obedience from morality.[28] Nevertheless, considering military organizational loyalty, obedience might well be what constitutes the individual's actual way of understanding what is morally correct. During such circumstances, moral constraints could be assumed to arise if the individual is forced to act contrary to superior orders, even with the utmost aim to uphold human dignity. Is disloyalty to be understood then as morally correct in such conditions? Situations might also be characterized by the opposite mechanisms; a superior order might inflict moral stress by preventing individuals from acting in the way they perceive to be morally correct. Would disloyalty be correct in this case? The issue is twofold.

HAVING TO COMPROMISE PERSONAL MORALS AND STANDARDS: MORAL DILEMMAS

The Swedish cadets also highlighted moral dilemmas as potential underlying causes of moral stress. These potential stressors are described as being related to *leadership factors* as well as questions of *life and death* associated with completing tasks on an international level. As previously stated, moral dilemmas refer to situations in which the individual has to choose one course of action and that this choice will necessarily preclude another. Several informants stated a fear of making the wrong decision when handling a moral dilemma as a potential stressor, this fear appearing to be strong due to the perception that as military personnel, they rarely had enough information to make well-reasoned decisions. Lack of information in itself was also reported to constitute a moral dilemma.

> *Making the wrong decision or being afraid of not choosing the right thing to act on or the right course of action.*

LEADERSHIP-RELATED FACTORS

The Swedish cadets described providing *moral guidance to subordinates* as a potential moral stressor. This would involve, for example, providing subordinates with information on how to handle ethically challenging situations. Such a leader task is reported to be made difficult by the omnipresent uncertainty of what is *de facto* the "right" or "wrong" way to go about handling a problem. Leaders might be worse off psychologically in these kinds of situations as such conditions are apt to obstruct leader responsibility.

> *How to act appropriately when situations arise that are extremely unclear and diffuse and where a decision is needed.*

According to the study participants, moral ambiguity appears to complicate the guidance of subordinates' moral behaviour. Thus, providing moral guidance is suggested to be a moral dilemma in itself as such guidance presumes knowledge of what is in fact morally right or wrong. Do we possess the moral right to guide someone else if we lack the "right" answer ourselves? Relating the problems associated with moral guidance (leader's perspective) to a lack of leader support/superior order inflicted on subordinate actions (subordinate perspective) is sometimes assumed to negatively impact on leader-subordinate relations by breeding conflicts. Grundstein-Amado suggests that professionals at different hierarchical levels tend to enact different values, motivations, and expectations.[29] In this case, however, moral ambiguity and confusion on both sides appears to be a concern.

According to one of the open-ended questions, many informants found *having to report* or *reprimand departures from laws and regulations* as a potential moral stressor.

> *When a group member does something that is inappropriate or illegal, it must be reported. Should you report it or not? Consider the best interests of the group or follow the rules?*

Underlying explanatory factors for this moral dilemma appear to comprise moral ambiguity – what is "right" or "wrong" in a specific situation – combined with leader responsibility versus loyalty towards subordinates. Moral ambiguity is sometimes assumed to be the reason for leaders favouring a departure from the rules, as they find it to be the most morally sound solution to a problematic situation. This is suggested to result in feelings of disloyalty toward the military system, which in turn might also give rise to moral stress. In contrast, reporting subordinates might induce feelings of disloyalty, not towards the military system, but toward the reported individuals and subordinates as a group.

LIFE AND DEATH RELATED FACTORS

The far greatest numbers of situations involving moral dilemmas, as described by the Swedish cadets, are ones that relate to life and death. These moral dilemmas can be divided into three categories:

1. having to prioritize between safety and the military task;
2. having to prioritize between individuals; and
3. issues concerning the right to inflict injury or death.

Prioritizing between safety and the military task

Prioritizing between safety and the military task concerns whether or not an individual executes assignments that will inevitably put the safety of others at risk – that at worst, could result in military and/or civilian losses. A central element of this moral stressor appears related to being the one who actually gives an order, which, in the long term, will negatively impact on human life. An example of such a situation occurs when one is required to calculate the risk of collateral damage which can be difficult as targets are often unidentified.

> It is really tough participating in real-time combat action in a complex setting where civilians and civilian property are part of the battlefield.

This moral dilemma probably arises fairly often and primarily concerns the tangible choice of acting on a military task versus keeping subordinates or civilians out of harms way. Acting on a military task is assumed to be associated with military loyalty and as such, obedience to the military system. Doing the opposite and not acting according to the military task might thus constitute a moral dilemma. In the long term, completing the task would probably help other civilians in the area. At the same time, keeping civilians or subordinates out of risk might refer to the loyalty of group members and ultimately to the principle of humanity. This was illustrated by an informant as follows:

> Choosing between the assignment and the group. It's very important that the group feels good. At the same time, you have to be committed to the task.

The excerpt above provides an illustrative example of the dual dilemma in military ethics faced by officers and soldiers who are expected to complete a military task that might involve the loss of human life. At times, as in this case, the completion of the task presumes actions that might contradict human dignity for a party in the short term. Another informant described the dilemma as:

> *On international service, I think decision-making connected to the safety of civilians will be very difficult. Utilitarian decisions might work well on paper when you're sitting at your school desk, but I think it will be very hard to work that way during operations.*

According to the informants, the morally worst-case scenario would be a situation where their own decision-making would have a bad result for either party, irrespective of whether that decision was based on personal morals or superior orders.

Prioritizing between individuals

Another dilemma that is reported as potentially morally demanding is having to prioritize, not between military tasks and safety, but between individuals in life and death related situations. Having to prioritize between military colleagues and civilians and to decide whose life to save first, has been addressed as a moral challenge.

The first ethical dimension when it comes to prioritizing between individuals involves deciding *who to help in the first place*. One informant stressed that while many are in need of help, it is impossible to provide for everyone. The moral dilemma is reported to being forced to decide which minority to help, who to help when resources are scarce, and having to choose which civilians will be provided with a slightly better living condition.

Another moral dilemma, as reported by the Swedish cadets occurs in circumstances where military personnel have to decide whose safety is priority number one – *the military unit or civilians*. A further challenge may be that the military unit consists of military comrades. Tripodi notes the risk of not being prepared to take extra risks or feeling morally responsible for people with whom you have nothing in common.[30] Moreover, since doing the right thing often involves personal sacrifice, the moral motivation or will power to do so tends to be overridden by personal interests.[31] In light of the data presented, military comrades are assumed to have priority over civilians.

Another concern reported was the *selection of individuals or groups to send off to difficult operations* where an imminent risk of getting wounded or killed may result.

> *Do I choose between a huge risk to me and my comrades or do I stay passive? For example, in [name of country, author's remark], when soldiers had to watch comrades being shot at in a tin shed by a superior enemy.*

The dilemma of having to prioritize between the lives of individuals also concerns situations where individuals must leave a comrade behind in order to look after civilians, save their own lives or those of the group. In this case, the matter involves *prioritizing between individuals that are wounded*.

Issues Concerning the Right to Inflict Injury or Death

The philosophy of the moral right to inflict injury or death appears to lie implicitly in many of the dilemmas that have been presented. The moral dilemma – the right to inflict injury or death – appears to bring up the ultimate question. The individual's starting point, at times, is whether or not to kill or get killed, whether to live or die.

The first aspect reported to be a moral concern is whether or not military personnel have *the moral right to make use of violence or fire power*, for example, their right to order an attack formation or bombing assignment. This leads to the next issue reported as potentially being morally strenuous: having to calculate the *level of violence* in a specific situation, where the ultimate stage might entail deadly force. Some informants also mentioned the risk of friendly fire.

> *Whether or not to use fire power? Is the situation that serious that I have to open fire?*

Having to make a decision about the level of violence appears most stressful when fire for effect was not part of the initial plan. Perhaps this points to the human difficulty of changing one's own ethical mindset and should be the subject of future research.

Making the actual *choice to injure or kill* someone is a source of moral stress most commonly highlighted by participants in the study and as the one they are likely to face during international service, apart from having to fight or shoot a child soldier. This moral dilemma refers to making a conscious decision to take someone else's life.

CONCLUSIONS

In Need of an Ethical Code and Moral Guidance

Taking the dual dilemma of military ethics as a starting point for understanding potential moral stressors during military international service, it appears fair to conclude that there is an ambiguity, or lack of clarity in ethical decision-making and of moral ideals inherent in military task completion. The contradictions that might arise between the principle of humanity, military tasks and superior order are not unproblematic, as unravelling the nature of what is right and wrong in the military appears highly complex. Ambiguity has been brought forward as a relevant factor within most research fields concerning questions of morality.[32] In the military, the ambiguity of what is morally correct – the military task, obedience/loyalty, human dignity – is suggested to put the individual officer or soldier in a rather strenuous position because there is no clear moral guidance. This can result in moral confusion and a high risk of being inflicted by moral stress reactions. Moral dilemmas might even involve having to grade human dignity in terms of prioritizing between human lives. Even so, military personnel are expected to possess moral fitness as well as being able to alternate between two diametrically different ethical mindsets: the protection of human dignity while at times relying on the use of violence/killing in the process of protecting human dignity. Tripodi asks for an ethical code that would provide peacekeepers with clear guidance when confronted with situations in which their decisions can determine life or death.[33] The author of this chapter suggests that the same kind of guidance is necessary for morally difficult situations faced by the SAF. Such moral guidance, however, must be flexible enough to fit the nature of morally tough military situations. Thus, moral ambiguity and the need for flexibility in handling ethical decision-making complicate straightforward plans of action. This paves the way for moral education and well-organized stress-relieving measures to ensure healthy and strong operative abilities. Moreover, there is a great need to further explore aspects of moral stress within the military.

Further research efforts on moral stress should consider cultural differences. If emotional detachment proves to be a coping strategy when handling morally challenging situations, it could be assumed that the most experienced Armed Forces will be at greater risk of developing cynical individuals who, in the long term, run the risk of being deprived of their moral awareness. However, in relation to the SAF or other Armed Forces lacking the same military experience, individuals are instead likely to be at a greater risk of being affected by moral stress reactions. Obviously, there are pitfalls related to both contexts.

Individual and Organizational (shared) Moral Responsibility

It appears as if there is an enormous responsibility put on military personnel when it comes to ethical decision-making, both in terms of ensuring a successful task outcome and maintaining moral fitness. This might seem extraordinary, bearing in mind the difficulties that appear inherent to providing moral guidance. Military organizations might want to alleviate some of the psychological constraints put on their personnel to lessen the risk of them being affected by moral stress reactions. One must also keep in mind that moral motivation or will power to do the right thing is often overridden by personal interests, as doing the right thing often involves personal sacrifice.[34] This means that individuals are apt to refrain from doing what they believe to be morally right. Are such theoretical standpoints also applicable to the military field? If so, how will this affect military task completion and respect of human dignity? If an officer or soldier refrains from following their own conscience during international military service, the practical consequences might be devastating (the individuals themselves are at high risk of being affected by moral stress). The moral ambiguity and moral confusion of "right" and "wrong" needs to be addressed, as moral stress might result in negative effects on the individual's general health and by inflicting, so called, moral injury.[35] Incentives for evoking such negative effects on human performance must be further examined.

Limitations of the Study

The author of this chapter does not claim to have captured all the relevant components of potential sources of moral stress in the Swedish military context. This study also lacks some degree of representativeness, which is inherent to the chosen qualitative method used. The author chose to focus on the worst-case scenario that Swedish cadets fear facing. Also within this area, there may be many contextual variations. A more thorough study of ethical decision-making from a moral stress perspective is underway that will hopefully provide more insight into this research area.

ENDNOTES

1   Veli-Matti Värri, "Some Problems of Ethics in Military Education. The question of ethics in the military space" in J. Toiskallio, ed., *Ethical Education in the Military* (Helsinki: Finnish National Defence University Press, 2007), 31-42; Desiree Verweij, "Military ethics: A contradiction in terms?" in J. Toiskallio, ed., *Ethical Education in the Military* (Helsinki: Finnish National Defence University Press, 2007), 43-62.

2   Rudy Richardson, Desiree Verweij and Donna Winslow, "Moral Fitness for Peace Operations," *Journal of Political and Military Sociology*, (Summer 2004), 99-113.

3   Ibid.

4   See for example, Paolo Tripodi, "Peacekeeper of the Twenty-first Century: A Comparison Between Professional Soldiers and Draftees in Peace Support Operation," *Small Wars & Insurgencies*, Vol. 14, No. 2, (2003), 71-86.

5   Tomas Jones, "Ethical Decision-making by Individuals in Organizations: An issue-contingent Model," *Academy of Management Review*, Vol. 16, No. 2 (1991), 366-395.

6   Ibid.

7   Elisabeth Young-Bruehl, *Why Arendt Matters* (New Haven & London: Yale University. Press, 2006), 200.

8   Andrew Jameton, *Nursing practice: The Ethical Issues* (Englewood Cliffs, NJ: Prentice Hall, 1984).

9   Wendy J. Austin, Leon Kagan, Marlene Rankel and Vangie Bergum, "The balancing act: Psychiatrists' Experience of Moral Distress," *Medicine, Health Care and Philosophy*, Vol. 11, No. 1 (2007), 367-371; Mary Corley, "Nurse Moral Distress: A Proposed Theory and Research Agenda," *Nursing Ethics*, Vol. 9, No. 6 (2002), 636-650; Ellen Elpern, Barbara Covert and Ruth Kleinpell, "Moral Distress of Staff Nurses in a Medical Intensive Care Unit," *American Journal of Critical Care*, Vol. 14, (2005), 523-530; Jean-Jacques Georges and Mieke Grypdonck, "Moral Problems Experienced by Nurses When Caring for Terminally Ill People: A Literature Review," *Nursing Ethics*, Vol. 9 (2002), 155-178; Ann Hamric and Leslie Blackhall, "Nurse-Physician Perspectives on the Care of Dying Patients in Intensive Care Units: Collaboration, Moral Distress, and Ethical Climate," *Critical Care Medicine*, Vol. 35, No. 2 (2007), 422-429; Christopher Johns, "Unravelling the Dilemmas Within Everyday Nursing Practice," *Nursing Ethics*, Vol. 6, (1999), 288-298; Kim Lützen, Agneta Cronqvist, Annabella Magnusson and Lars Andersson, "Moral Stress: Synthesis of a Concept," *Nursing Ethics*, Vol. 10, No. 3 (2003), 312-322; Melinda Mobley, Mohamed Rady, Joseph Verheijde, Bhavesh Patel and Joel Larson, "The Relationship Between Moral Distress and Perception of Futile Care in the Critical Care Unit," *Intensive and Critical Care Nursing*, Vol. 23, (2007), 256-263; Patricia Pendry, "Moral distress: Recognizing it to Retain Nurses," *Nursing Economics*, Vol. 25, (2007), 217-221; Tineke Schoot, Ireen Proot, Marja Legius, Ruud ter Meulen and Luc de Witte, "Client-centered Home Care: Balancing Between Competing Responsibilities," *Clinical Nursing Research*, Vol. 15, (2006), 231-254; Arie J.G. Van der Arend and Corine H.M. Remmers-van den Hurk, "Moral Problems Among Dutch Nurses: A Survey,"

Nursing Ethics, Vol. 6, (1999), 468-482; Zane Robinson Wolf and Patti Rager Zuzelo, "Never Again" Stories of Nurses: Dilemmas in Nursing Practice," *Qualitative Health Research*, Vol. 16, No. 9 (2006), 1191-1206; and, Patti Rager Zuzelo, "Exploring the Moral Distress of Registered Nurses," *Nursing Ethics*, Vol. 14, No. 3 (2007), 344-359.

10   Mary C. Corley, "Nurse Moral Distress: A Proposed Theory and Research Agenda," *Nursing Ethics*, Vol. 9, No. 6 (2002), 636-650.

11   Andrew Jameton, *Nursing Practice: The Ethical Issues* (Englewood Cliffs, NJ: Prentice Hall, 1984).

12   Verena Tschudin and Christine Schmitz, "The Impact of Conflict and War on International Nursing and Ethics," *Nursing Ethics*, Vol. 10, (2003), 354-367.

13   **Moral awareness** refers to "an interpretive process wherein the individual recognizes that a moral problem exists in a situation or that a moral standard or principle is relevant to some set of circumstances," (James Rest, *Moral development: Advances in Research and Theory* (New York: Praeger Publishers, 1986). Moral sensitivity is instead referred to as "the ability to recognize a moral conflict, show a contextual and intuitive understanding of the patient's vulnerable situation, and have insight into the ethical consequences of decision on behalf of the person", 521 (Kim Lützén, Agneta Johansson and Gun Nordström, "Moral Sensitivity: Some Differences Between Nurses and Physicians," *Nursing Ethics*, Vol. 7, (2000), 521–530.

14   Richard Lazarus, *Psychological Stress and the Coping Process* (New York: McGraw Hill, 1966); Richard Lazarus, *Emotions and Adaption* (New York: Oxford University Press, 1991); Richard Lazarus, *Stress and Emotion: A New Synthesis* (London: Free Association Books, 1999).

15   Eva Johansson, *The UNknown Soldier: A Portrait of the Swedish Peacekeeper at the Threshold of the 21st Century* (Karlstad: Klaria Tryckeri AB, 2001).

16   Ibid.

17   The critical incident technique is a systematic inductive "open-ended" procedure to gain verbal or written information by focusing on critical behaviors. For more information, see John Flanagan, "The Critical Incident Technique," *Psychological Bulletin*, Vol. 51, No. 4 (1954), 327-358.

18   Matthew Miles and Michael Huberman, *Qualitative Data Analysis: A Sourcebook of New Methods* (London: SAGE Publications, 1984).

MILITARY ETHICS: INTERNATIONAL PERSPECTIVES

19   Richard Hodgetts, Fred Luthans and Jonathan Doh, *International Management: Culture, Strategy and Behavior* (New York: McGraw-Hill Irwin, 2006), 93.

20   William Graham Sumner, *Folkways* (Boston: Ginn, 1906), 12-13.

21   Ibid.

22   Vittorio Lanternari, "Ethnocentrism and Ideology," *Ethnic and Racial Studies*, Vol. 3, No. 4, (1980), 52-66.

23   Julian Roberts, "Changing Public Attitudes Towards Corporal Punishment: The Effects of Statutory Reform in Sweden," *Child Abuse and Neglect*, Vol. 24, No. 8 (2000), 1027-1035.

24   Daniel Cable and Timothy Judge, "Person-Organization Fit, Job Choice Decisions, and Organizational Entry," *Organizational Behavior and Human Decision Processes*, Vol. 67, No. 3 (1996), 294-311.

25   David Perry, "Military Ethics and Business Ethics," The keynote address to Conference on Corporate Social Responsibility and Value-Based Management, Roskilde, Denmark, December, 2003.

26   Kermit Johnson, "Ethical Issues of Military Leadership," in L.J. Matthews & D.E. Brown, eds., *The Parameters of Military Ethics* (Virginia: Pergamon-Brassey's International Defense publishers, Inc., 1989).

27   Ibid, p. 75.

28   Young-Bruehl, *Why Arendt Matters*, 59.

29   Rivka Grundstein-Amado, "Differences in Ethical Decision-making Processes Among Nurses and Doctors," *Journal of Advanced Nursing*, Vol. 17, No. 2 (1992), 129-137.

30   Paolo Tripodi, "Peacekeepers, Moral Autonomy and the Use of Force," *Journal of Military Ethics*, Vol. 5, No. 3, (2006), 214-232.

31   J. Peter Bradley, "Why People Make the Wrong Choices: The Psychology of Ethical Failure," in Ted van Baarda and Desiree Verweij, eds., *The Moral Dimension of Asymmetrical Warfare: Counter-Terrorism, Democratic Values and Military Ethics* (Boston: Martinus Nijhoff Publishers, 2009), 279-311.

32   See for example, for discussions on moral ambiguity in a military context. Martin Cook, "Moral Foundations of Military Service," *Parameters*,

(Spring 2000), 117-129, and Sidney Axinn, *A Moral Military* (Philadelphia: Temple University Press, 2009).

33   Paolo Tripodi, (2008). "Soldier's Moral Responsibility in Peace Support Operations," *International Journal on World Peace*, (March 2008), 7-26.

34   Bradley, "Why People Make the Wrong Choices: The Psychology of Ethical Failure," 279-311.

35   Brett Litz, Nathan Stein, Eileen Delaney, Leslie Lebowitz, William Nash, Caroline Silva and Shira Maguen, "Moral Injury and Moral Repair in War Veterans: A preliminary Model and Intervention Strategy," *Clinical Psychology Review*, Vol. 29, No. 8 (2009), 695-706.

CHAPTER 9

Some Ethical Challenges in Military Personnel Research

Craig Leslie Mantle
*Justin C. Wright**

> *After going through what I did, a lot of times people ask, "Aren't you mentally screwed up?" or "Have you had any stress injuries?" and things like that. I don't think so. I think I'm perfectly fine. I'm a stronger person for it I think. Certainly, after I came back from Afghanistan, I definitely went through a bit of a transitional period, which is completely normal. But you work through that and you carry on. … Not everybody who goes into a war zone comes back screwed up – it's actually a small percentage. Sure, everybody comes back different, but you would come back different from any experience.*

> *Master Corporal Christopher Lorne Harding, MMV, CD*

Since the mid-1990s, the Canadian Forces (CF) has placed an increased emphasis on: 1) rigorous, social scientific research in order to better understand the "human factor" in operations; and 2) the impact of operations on the mental health of military members. Concurrently, and within the context of both a quick operational tempo and an ever changing security environment, awareness and diagnoses of operational stress injuries (OSIs), such as post-traumatic stress disorder (PTSD), have increased markedly. As

---

* The views expressed in this chapter are those of the authors and do not necessarily reflect the official policy of the Canadian Forces or the Department of National Defence.

simple evidence, contemporary national newspapers frequently include articles dealing with such illnesses, attributing onset to the difficult mission that is Afghanistan, describing the military's reaction and assessing the impact on families.[1] As a result, civilian and military researchers, and the broader military community itself, have become increasingly concerned with the potential adverse impact of legitimate research on military members and with the development of parallel strategies to mitigate risk to participants.

The need for timely, rigorous and innovative research in order to facilitate mission success, however defined, has assumed an even greater importance in a complex security environment characterized by counter-insurgency, whole of government operations and multi-national coalitions.[2] In particular, the CF has recognized that much more attention and resources must be directed towards the rigorous examination of personnel in order to ensure their ultimate success in the field and, of course, the maintenance of their overall physical and mental health. Military personnel researchers are, in fact, one of the fastest growing segments of the civilian research community within Canada's Department of National Defence (DND) today. Current personnel research ranges from issues of quality of life for serving members and their families, to the effects of increased and prolonged operational tempo, to issues impacting on training, professional development, socialization and retention. Such a list is inexhaustible. *Yet how can such research, important as it is, be conducted in a safe manner that minimizes risk to the subjects of that research?*

A recent, multi-year book project undertaken by the Canadian Forces Leadership Institute (CFLI) provided the impetus for this chapter; it also serves as a starting point from which the above question might possibly be answered, if only partially. Very briefly, the larger initiative involved the collection of first-person accounts, as told by decorated veterans, of the circumstances under which they earned one of Canada's highest honours for their actions in Afghanistan, usually during high-intensity combat operations. For this project, entitled *In Their Own Words: Canadian Stories of Valour and Bravery from Afghanistan, 2001-2007*,[3] researchers interviewed 23 members or former members of the CF, face-to-face, in order to collect their powerful, and at times, harrowing narratives. The collected "stories" were then condensed into 14 separate chapters (on occasion, more than one soldier was decorated for a particular engagement and it only made sense to combine their individual narratives into one meta-narrative). This publication will be forthcoming in late-2010 or very early-2011 in both English and French. Owing to the many constraints with which researchers are constantly faced (time, available personnel, limited financial resources, other academic commitments, and so on), it was duly decided to focus exclusively on those soldiers that had received a specific decoration in a specific locale during a specific time period.[4] In all fairness, however, any grouping of personnel that had served overseas would admittedly have been appropriate for this project, all no doubt possessing instructive and insightful stories.

The purpose of this groundbreaking project was not to glorify war in any respect whatsoever or to place this select group of individuals upon an even higher pedestal, that is to say, to hero-worship. Rather, CFLI endeavoured to capture the first-hand accounts of the circumstances under which certain personnel earned their prestigious decorations in order to accrue positive examples of the four military values that the CF expects its members to both possess and exemplify daily: Duty, Loyalty, Integrity, Courage.[5] Being told in the recipient's own words, moreover, ensured that each individual story was more powerful and illuminating than anything CFLI could ever write on its own. Although not a stated aim *per se*, such stories, given their highly emotive content, ultimately provided a degree of insight into such important operational factors as leadership, cohesion, teamwork, morale, casualty management, and discipline. Finally, to a very limited extent, and as a completely unintended consequence, *In Their Own Words* also helped in understanding "the mind of the soldier" – why certain perceptions are the way that they are, why they acted in a particular manner when safer options were clearly available, why they did the things that they did.

By discussing some of the ethical challenges that confronted the CFLI research team as it moved *In Their Own Words* from concept to manuscript, this chapter will endeavour to answer the above italicized question, considering in the process, in no particular order:

- participants' rights in a military context, including informed consent, confidentiality and their degree of involvement in the editorial process;

- access to participants and considerations of power in relation to their chain of command;

- researchers' obligations, especially in terms of their awareness of OSIs and the mitigation of associated risk; and,

- the broader issue of risk with respect to military members' contract of unlimited liability.

Taken on the whole, this chapter will raise and explore a number of pertinent issues that, it seems, *all* researchers dealing with *any* military population must at the very least consider when framing their methodological approach. As will quickly become apparent, the following content is primarily intended for new and junior research personnel, yet the pages of this chapter should provide something of value to every reader.

A few caveats. This chapter is not intended in any way as a policy statement on research with potentially vulnerable groups[6] within or outside the CF, nor is it meant to provide a comprehensive list of "dos" and "don'ts" when conducting research within the defence community. Furthermore, the following discussion is not meant to apply to every possible research scenario for the variety of circumstances in which researchers might possibly find themselves enmeshed could never be accurately, even wholly, anticipated. Rather, the pages that follow raise a number of important and relevant issues that were encountered by the present authors during their sustained work in the field, all of which should be considered further. To be sure, the commentary that appears below is intended only to contribute to the larger discussion of defence ethics and, perhaps, to engender a degree of debate, not only in Canada, but internationally as well. As can be surmised, the primary purpose of this chapter is to raise awareness of particular issues within the broader defence community in order to ensure that military members (both active and retired, including veterans of past conflicts of whatever vintage) are in no way harmed by well-meaning research, research that is intended to ensure that the CF and other allied militaries succeed professionally in their many missions, both at home and abroad, wherever that may be.

Every stage of the larger book project presented its own unique dilemmas and problems, the vast majority of which revolved around the implementation of an interview protocol that was capable of both collecting the required information and, most important of all, protecting the participants' well-being. Researchers had to be at all times respectful, courteous, non-judgemental, sympathetic, patient and accommodating. While such requirements are neither new nor novel – after all, researchers have always had to be like this – these attributes were absolutely essential in a project of this type that had the very real potential, at least theoretically, to seriously impact the well-being of CF members (that is, of course, by asking them to recount particularly trying episodes during which, in some cases, fellow soldiers were injured or killed and they themselves were called upon to take life). There was no perfect solution to every difficulty that presented itself since every choice had its own benefits and costs, some more significant than others. The entire project team, from the Director CFLI to the CFLI staff members that conducted the actual interviews (a combination of both senior military members and junior civilian public servants), did what was thought to be most appropriate, most ethically-sound and in the best interest of the participants' well-being. Ultimately, the methodology adopted by the CFLI research team, as outlined in Figure 1 below and elsewhere described in considerable detail,[7] represents one specific attempt to grapple with and respond to a number of difficult ethical questions and dilemmas related to conducting defence research with a potentially vulnerable population.

The research methodology employed by CFLI for *In Their Own Words* was always within the prescribed boundaries as articulated in various policy guidelines. Several key ethical considerations were hotly debated and discussed throughout the entire project, and where appropriate, specific measures were taken in response in order to mitigate risk and harm. Although not necessarily required by any policy guideline *per se*, some measures were adopted simply because it was the "right thing to do" under the prevailing circumstances. The CFLI research team often felt that a certain step simply had to be taken in the interest of the participants, regardless of time and resource implications; such considerations extended the timeline of the project considerably. It was better to delay publication and ensure a safe experience for the participants than possibly compromise their well-being through a less than rigorous methodology simply to ensure quick project completion.

Canada's current mission in Afghanistan was the sole impetus behind CFLI's larger book project, yet the issues raised herein are more broadly applicable. Stated differently, personnel that have served in Afghanistan must not be the only members of the military that are approached in the manner suggested below. Personnel engaged in any type of military operation, from the domestic to the deployed – think here the recovery of non-contiguous human remains after the 1998 Swissair Flight 111 disaster off the coast of Nova Scotia to various peace support missions the world over – run the risk of incurring both physical and mental trauma. Without doubt, the fact that military members may have been subjected to trauma of whatever sort while performing their various duties in whatever location is what is most important when researchers begin to frame, and eventually implement, their protocols.

ETHICAL STANDARDS IN CANADIAN DEFENCE RESEARCH

In Canada, the overarching policy governing research involving human subjects is the Tri-Council Policy Statement (TCPS).[8] A joint declaration representing the fields of health sciences, social sciences, and natural and engineering sciences, the TCPS articulates the legal and ethical guidelines to which all legitimate research involving human subjects must absolutely adhere. To ensure that Canadian research involving human subjects meets the ethical standards of the TCPS, research institutions and communities of practitioners (for instance, universities and medical research laboratories) are required to submit all proposed research to research ethics boards (REBs) for review. It is, therefore, the function of REBs to uphold the principles of the TCPS.

In the introductory section of the TCPS, two essential components for ethical research involving humans are identified as: 1) the selection and achievement of morally acceptable ends; and 2) the morally acceptable means to those ends. The TCPS ultimately stipulates that these two components are essential to ensuring that research involving humans adheres to the Canadian moral imperative of respect for human dignity. More specifically, these two components establish a requirement that the well-being and integrity of the individual must remain the highest priority in research involving humans. Within Canada, DND has officially adopted the TCPS as the ethical standard to which all Canadian military personnel research must conform. In this way, all research involving military members, whether serving or retired, must place the well-being of those individuals above all other considerations, including the potential usefulness of the research itself.

As articulated in the TCPS, the ethical conduct of research is an ever-evolving enterprise. Changes in socio-cultural context and political sentiment (both domestic and international), advances in technology, and the increasing sophistication and complexity of the scientific endeavour itself mean that the ethical guidelines enunciated in the TCPS must remain flexible and responsive to new and emerging circumstances of research involving human

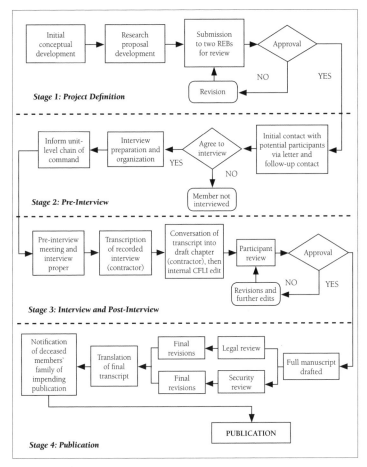

FIGURE 1: Research and Publication Process for *In Their Own Words*.

subjects. In short, the conduct of ethical research, or doing what is judged to be "the right thing," often means having to go "above and beyond" what is minimally or legally required. With respect to *In Their Own Words*, CFLI experienced just such a circumstance in which additional steps were added to the protocol because it was simply felt to be proper. Many researchers, moreover, face challenges that have no clear "right" solution. Confronted with such ethical dilemmas, researchers must consider carefully their approach and strive to respond to the dilemma with due diligence and with the participant's well-being foremost in mind; a most difficult challenge it most certainly can be, but one that must be met regardless.

LESSONS LEARNED FROM RECENT DND RESEARCH

As can be gleaned from Figure 1, the research process for *In Their Own Words* was rigorous and complex, involving several stages of review, approval and revision. Such a protocol required the committal of a good deal of both financial and human resources, and a good deal of patience on the part of the participants (for which CFLI is exceedingly grateful). It would certainly have been cheaper and faster to implement a more streamlined protocol, yet that would not have been ethical and may, in fact, have jeopardized the well-being of participants. In light of the nature of this project, the many obligations demanded by Canadian research ethics policy and, more important, the moral obligation owed to the military and ex-military members who consented to an interview, the present authors strongly assert that the adopted protocol, time- and resource-intensive as it was, was simply the "right thing to do," perhaps the only thing to do.

In many respects, the individual steps that were eventually implemented were not immediately apparent and often required the research team to expend considerable effort in grappling with difficult ethical dilemmas. In other words, the solutions to each dilemma influenced the protocol's final construction and form. Every stage of the research protocol, as illustrated in Figure 1, was consciously evaluated by the research team for both positive and negative consequences, and if the latter ever outweighed the former, a new approach was immediately developed. The remainder of this chapter will therefore describe and discuss a number of the ethical dilemmas that the CFLI research team faced while designing its research methodology; the following discussion will outline the various considerations given to these issues and the strategies ultimately adopted in response.

* * *

Ethical Consideration # 1 – How do researchers define "undue risk" in relation to participants in a military context where risk and danger are constants?

As articulated in the TCPS, the definition of "undue risk" (usually qualified as more than what research subjects would typically experience in their "normal" daily lives) is meant to protect humans from participation in research that goes above and beyond what is commonly understood to be "normal" or "acceptable" risk of harm. In other words, the research should pose no more risk than that which the participant would normally encounter in the areas of their daily lives related to the research. In a military context, a literal interpretation of the TCPS raises an important ethical question, namely, "What constitutes 'undue risk' for a soldier whose primary purpose is combat, and by extension, what is considered 'normal' or 'acceptable' risk of harm for such individuals?" Shall "undue risk" be defined in relation to combat operations (which are generally the exception) or in relation to activities that cannot be classified as combat operations (which are generally the norm)?

In the researchers' opinion, it is not appropriate to assume that soldiers are immune to harm when participating in research just because of the degree of risk that they faced in combat operations in the past, that is, if they can handle the latter, then they can certainly handle the former. The same can also be said of the passage of time. It seems likewise inappropriate to assume that time diminishes the impact of traumatic experiences, that an event some 70 years ago, say during the Second World War (1939-1945) or the Korean War (1950-1953), cannot have a detrimental impact on health in the present. Regardless of when an event occurred, the same concern for minimizing harm and maximizing well-being must always be observed.

The potential for these incorrect assumptions to inform military personnel research is an important concern that the defence research community must acknowledge, especially given the absolute primacy that the CF places on protecting members' well-being as a crucial prerequisite to achieving mission success. With respect to *In Their Own Words*, CFLI, in partnership with DND's ethics review process, succeeded in ensuring that "undue risk" for combat soldiers participating in the research project was appropriately interpreted and addressed. In the end, the participants were afforded every reasonable protection, *regardless* of their military service or the nature of the circumstances for which they were formally recognized. Stated somewhat differently, the research participants' past experiences, no matter how traumatic or benign, in no way absolved researchers from ensuring their complete safety and comfort during the research process; their recent experiences only reinforced the need for concern.

Ethical Consideration # 2 – In the event that it is reasonable to assume that potential research participants are at risk for OSIs, such as PTSD, is it appropriate for researchers themselves to pre-screen for such medical conditions?

In the course of developing the interview protocol, the research team was faced with the difficult question of how to react in a worst-case scenario in which an interviewee was adversely affected during an interview, that is to say, that the interview itself, because of its purpose, triggered a medical crisis. The principle of due diligence suggests that researchers must know how to react to such a situation and to ensure that the risk of harm to the participant is minimized in the first place.[9] At one point, with the idea of due diligence in mind, the suggestion was raised that pre-screening potential participants was one method of ensuring that only those soldiers in good mental health would be subjected to a line of questioning that had the very real potential of exacerbating any possible underlying medical conditions. After deeper reflection, and based upon the informed advice of a military medical practitioner, a subject matter expert (SME) in the field of OSIs, the research team questioned whether this suggested approach would lead to more negative than positive consequences in terms of the participants' well-being. In light of the fact that the researchers were not trained clinicians, selecting, implementing and interpreting the results of such a pre-screening tool would be beyond their ability (and, indeed, what was ethical). It was also reasonable to assume, when evaluating the merits of this suggestion, that participants would perceive such a request as overly invasive and offensive, thus jeopardizing the quality of their contributions or even their participation entirely. Who would really want to participate in a project after being judged to have an OSI by a civilian with no military or medical experience? In this particular instance, it was the decision to *not* follow a suggested course of action that best served the participants' well-being and was thus felt to be "the right thing to do."

Recognizing that they were not medical experts and that attempting anything approaching a psychological assessment of the participants prior to the interview was not the preferred way forward, the research team instead did their level best to prepare themselves for the most likely eventualities. The end result of this preparation was to raise the research team's awareness of OSIs, namely their origins, triggers and manifestations, and how the ill should be dealt with should an episode unfortunately occur during an interview. In turn, such preparation informed the manner in which the interviews were conducted, affecting such considerations as seating arrangements, the number and timing of breaks, the provisioning of ample opportunities both before and during the interview to withdraw from participation, and so forth; such preparation also helped formulate the content of an information package in which the appropriate local resources available to each participant to help cope with OSIs were outlined should they eventually need assistance. The military medical SME believed that such preparation was indeed sufficient and ensured that the principle of due diligence was entirely satisfied. By developing a robust and flexible protocol, the participants' well-being was at all times protected to the best of the researchers' ability.

Ethical Consideration # 3 – How can researchers ensure voluntary participation when participants live and work within a chain of command or an organizational hierarchy and thus may perceive research requests as obligatory service?

One of the unique challenges of conducting military personnel research is striking an appropriate balance between research that is ethically "right" and responsible and research that respects organizational protocol, including the military chain of command. In Canada, the Social Science Research Review Board (SSRRB), DND's REB, first secures approval from an appropriate level of leadership before issuing formal authorization for research projects. With respect to *In Their Own Words*, since the pool of potential participants was located within the army exclusively, the SSRRB secured authorization for the study from the Chief of the Land Staff, as well as the Chief of Military Personnel, a lieutenant-general and major-general, respectively. Receiving approval at higher levels, however, does not necessarily mean that researchers can ignore unit-level leadership when engaging unit personnel; such lower-level leadership should be kept "in the loop" as to researcher intentions and should be informed when, where and by whom their personnel will be interviewed, and of course, for what purpose.

Although researchers cannot ignore the military chain of command when conducting personnel research, there is also a fundamental ethical obligation (one of the most important, in fact) to ensure that potential participants have the ability to make a free, informed and voluntary decision as to participation. Amid the social scientific and qualitative methodological literature, the impact of power dynamics and relationships among various actors in the research process, including their impact on voluntary participation, has been widely discussed. In this light, participants were initially approached privately, thus affording them the opportunity to make a decision to participate without the risk of perceived or real pressure from their superiors (and, it could be argued, from their peers and subordinates as well). If members agreed to an interview, their immediate chain of command was then informed so that specific individuals within could make arrangements for their personnel to be excused from duty during the time of the interview. If potential participants declined to participate, their decision would in no way be detrimental as their superiors (and their peers and subordinates) would not have been aware of the original invitation in the first place, thereby eliminating the fear of reprisal or adverse comment. The chain of command was circumvented at the outset in the interest of ensuring participant well-being, yet it was "brought up to speed" *when, and only when*, the participant had agreed to an interview. To be absolutely clear, the above comments are in no way meant to suggest that unit-level leadership would exert pressure on a decorated member to participate in a research initiative that might compromise their well-being, only that the potential for such a dynamic theoretically existed, thus compelling researchers to mitigate that theoretical possibility in turn.

Ethical Consideration # 4 – What are the implications of a (sometimes wide) disparity in rank between military research participants and military researchers?

To repeat, the issue of power dynamics and relationships among various actors in the research process has been widely discussed in the social scientific and qualitative methodological literature. As it relates to military personnel research, the presence of rank creates a very explicit and overt power dynamic between uniformed participant and uniformed researcher. (A different dynamic altogether prevails between uniformed participant and civilian researcher.) Such influences as formal authority and hierarchical position cannot easily be dismissed in a research context, especially if they hold the potential to influence participants, either positively or negatively, or to elicit a perception of obligation to participate on the part of the participants. It is also important to consider whether or not the participants perceive themselves in a position to answer freely or if the presence of a more senior-ranking member causes them to alter or withhold their views and responses.

Although the potential to influence is always there in a research situation involving power dynamics such as rank disparity, the research team did not observe any explicit negative impact during the course of the interviews. Throughout the interviewing phase of *In Their Own Words*, the military members posted to CFLI who helped conduct the interviews were either senior officers (the most junior being a major, the most senior being a lieutenant-colonel) and a non-commissioned chief petty officer second class. By comparison, the interviewees tended to be more junior in rank, in the case of officers, majors or captains, and in the case of NCMs, privates to warrant officers. All in all however, the participants seemed comfortable and at ease with the research team, freely offering their insights into the specific events for which they were decorated, as well as their very private personal reactions to some very emotional events. That they were at ease is a testament to the uniformed researchers' savvy and ability to approach the interview in an informal and unceremonious manner. Such statements are not meant to suggest that appropriate respect for military rank and custom was not observed, but rather that formality was largely suspended during the course of the interview itself so that the participants could feel at liberty to speak freely and candidly. With that being said, however, military protocol was duly observed at both the beginning and conclusion of each interview, with the participants all acknowledging their superior with appropriate forms of address, such as "sir" or their actual rank and surname.

It is also worth noting that, despite not wearing a uniform or sharing an insider's perspective, the rapport between civilian researchers and military participants (largely established over time through e-mail correspondence and upon first introductions in person) likely impacted the course of the interview as well. It can reasonably be assumed that differences in experience, organizational culture and education (or a variety of other factors) all had some degree of impact on the participants' degree of comfort and the information that they elected to share.

Ultimately, researchers can never know with absolute certainty whether the participants withheld information or certain details due to the various dynamics operating during the interview. After conducting several interviews for this project however, the researchers felt confident that participants engaged freely and openly in the entire process. While some information may have been withheld (undoubtedly certain things were), the sheer emotive power of each individual interview and resulting chapter testifies to the participants' willingness to share much, if not most, of their experience.

Although the civilian staff members brought to the project specific expertise in project management and academic research (both civilians possessed a master's degree in either history or sociology), the inclusion of military members on the research team had several important methodological advantages:

- First, including CFLI's military members allowed the research team to leverage the notions of "familial" community and professional identity within the military, that is to say, including CFLI's military members in the interview process allowed the participants to tell their stories to someone with whom they could easily identify. Speaking to an individual with military experience allowed the participant to use operational language, cultural expressions and "jargon," while remaining confident that the interviewing team would understand their meaning, both literally and culturally.

- Second, the presence of a CFLI military member gave the project an additional degree of credibility, not only in the eyes of the participant, but also in the estimation of the participant's chain of command, an important element in terms of gaining access to the participant in the first place (as will be recalled, the chain of command was informed of CFLI's impending visit once the participant had agreed to an interview, yet regardless of the participant's wishes, the chain of command ultimately controlled access to personnel).

- Third, given the operational experience held by CFLI's military members, they were arguably more sensitized and thus better positioned to monitor the participants during the course of the interview for signs of distress and discomfort; they were similarly prepared to take subsequent action, such as redirecting the course of the dialogue or pausing for a break. The inclusion of CFLI's military members in the interview process thus added to the measures taken to ensure the well-being of participants.

- Finally, inclusion of CFLI's military members in the research team allowed specific questions to be asked that might not have occurred to civilians given their lack of military experience, such questions ultimately adding to the richness of the finished product.

The inclusion of CFLI's uniformed members as part of the research team unquestionably enhanced the quality of the data collected. More important, however, it ensured the participants' well-being by creating an environment in which they could safely tell their story to a knowledgeable and sympathetic ear. Such advantages seem, on balance, to have outweighed any negative consequences stemming from a disparity in rank. Relying on the few military members posted to CFLI was felt to be the "right thing to do" overall.

Ethical Consideration # 5 – How much confidentiality can actually be promised to individuals in an organization that is meant to be accountable to the public?

One of the cornerstones of ethical research outlined in the TCPS is the protection of participants' confidentiality. In military personnel research, the norm is survey participation in which respondents remain entirely anonymous. For obvious reasons, participation was not anonymous in In *Their Own Words*, nor was it at all desired. Confidentiality was nevertheless extended in the form of participants retaining a veto, that is, having a final say as to what was actually published. As a condition of informed consent, the researchers allowed the participants to vet all drafts and ultimately decide what comments could be disseminated and which ones had to be severed. Some comments were made during the heat of the moment, during the interview, that upon reflection may not have been entirely suitable for public consumption (relating exclusively to the manner in which certain Canadian soldiers were killed). To protect the confidential nature of all material provided by the participants, whether or not it had been deemed inappropriate for publication or was simply awaiting publication, the researchers restricted accessibility to the raw interview data to only those individuals directly on, or supervised by, the CFLI research team. The two contractors employed at different stages of this project (see Figure 1 above) were instructed, in no uncertain terms, that the material that they were handling was confidential and was not to be disseminated under any circumstances. Extending such confidentiality to the participants was, in the terms used in this chapter, the "right thing to do."

Such an arrangement, however, raises the question of how much confidentiality can actually be promised? Working in a time when Access to Information (ATI) requests are an ever-present reality, and belonging to an organization that is accountable to the public – the Government of Canada in general and DND in particular – researchers must be cognizant of the fact that their raw data may have to be released, regardless of any promises made to participants. Public servants are naturally subject to the laws of Canada and the research data that they collect while employed as a public servant is technically not theirs personally, but rather the Crown's.

In retrospect, the CFLI research team could have approached the issue of confidentiality somewhat differently; the methodology could have been improved. Although nothing would have changed with respect to ensuring the highest degree of participant privacy – they would still have the veto, all drafts would be kept under lock-and-key, the number of individuals granted access to such material would be minimized – interviewees could have been made aware at the outset that the interview was subject to ATI and would have to be turned over should a request ever be forthcoming. That the research team did not consider this potential eventuality until it was too late only underscores the point that is being made throughout this entire chapter, namely that defence researchers must be aware of larger issues and such larger issues must be openly discussed within the broader defence community. Such a discussion, as but one example, might possibly begin with a consideration of the impact of potential ATI requests on interview participation, dynamics and results.

CONCLUDING REMARKS

In sum, the overarching purpose of this chapter has been to illustrate a *few* of the ethical challenges that investigators might possibly face when conducting research with military personnel, especially with individuals for whom participation in a research program may adversely affect their health by exacerbating a pre-existing mental illness (in this case, some form of OSI). The difficulties discussed above are by no means comprehensive as each project will present its own unique challenges. The solutions ultimately adopted by the CFLI research team worked well for the project at hand. Although such strategies were effective in this particular case, it is not suggested that they will work in all scenarios. By offering the above perspective, however, it is hoped that a possible way forward has at least been suggested that other researchers might possibly employ, either in whole or in part, when confronted with similar challenges. It is also hoped that this chapter will encourage such issues as have been raised herein to be debated and discussed, both within and outside the defence research community, both in Canada and internationally.

With respect to defence research, the onus for ensuring that the well-being of participants is not jeopardized through meeting operational requirements and achieving mission success quite clearly lies on the organization itself and any researchers working with the organization. What must be remembered is that, in an environment that values constant achievement of an exceedingly high order, proper ethical conduct must not be allowed to fall by the wayside in the interest of task completion. Participants must at all times be protected, whatever the cost.

ENDNOTES

1   Some representative examples include: "Hidden scars," *Toronto Star*, 14 June 2008, ID1, ID4-5; "Afghan war takes its toll," *Toronto Star*, 29 October 2007, A2; and, "Bracing for war's hidden fallout," *Toronto Star*, 13 July 2009, A3.

2   CFLI has studied some aspects of whole of government operations and multi-national coalitions. See Craig Leslie Mantle, *"How do we go about building peace while we're still at war?" Canada, Afghanistan and the Whole of Government Concept* (Kingston, Ontario: Canadian Forces Leadership Institute Technical Report 2008-02), and, CFLI Project Team, *Broadsword or Rapier? The Canadian Forces' Involvement in 21ˢᵗ Century Coalition Operations* (Kingston, Ontario: Canadian Forces Leadership Institute Technical Report 2008-01). Both reports are available to interested parties without charge, by contacting CFLI.

3   *In Their Own Words* is a component of CFLI's much larger Strategic Leadership Writing Project, an initiative that seeks to create a uniquely Canadian body of leadership knowledge, to stimulate thought and debate on a variety of leadership topics, to aid in professional military development, and to increase general public awareness of some of the unique challenges faced by CF personnel.

4   Only military personnel that had received the Star of Military Valour (SMV), the Star of Courage (SC), the Medal of Military Valour (MMV) or the Medal of Bravery (MB) were considered for inclusion in this project.

5   As described in Canada, Department of National Defence, *Duty with Honour: The Profession of Arms in Canada* (Ottawa: 2003). In an updated edition, published in 2010, the four Canadian military values remain central and unchanged.

6   "Potentially vulnerable groups" are here taken to mean those military members that *may have* an OSI owing to their service, that is, that their service in Afghanistan was possibly traumatic enough to negatively impact mental health. Given the circumstances under which participants earned their decorations – high-intensity combat operations or other highly dangerous situations – the CFLI research team thought best to collectively consider the participants a potentially vulnerable group and proceed accordingly, a complex methodology being the end result. A research protocol for investigating less vulnerable groups would surely look entirely different. Researchers must therefore constantly evaluate the degree of risk posed to participants by their investigations and incorporate sufficient and appropriate safeguards into their methodology. In light of research participants' diversity of experience, there are no "one-size-fits-all" or "cookie-cutter" solutions when formulating research protocols.

7   Justin C. Wright and Craig Leslie Mantle, *Researching Potentially Vulnerable Groups in the Canadian Forces: Methodological Considerations for Military Personnel Research* (Kingston, Ontario: Canadian Forces Leadership Institute Technical Note 2010-01).

8   Canada, Canadian Institutes of Health Research, Natural Sciences and Engineering Research Council of Canada, Social Sciences and Humanities Research Council of Canada, *Tri-Council Policy Statement: Ethical Conduct for Research Involving Humans* (1998, with 2000, 2002 and 2005 amendments). See <http://www.pre.ethics.gc.ca/eng/policy-politique/tcps-eptc> for further detail.

9   Due diligence is here taken to mean, taking every reasonable precaution to prevent harm or injury that a reasonable person could reasonably be expected to take.

CHAPTER 10

Sapta Marga: The Indonesian Armed Forces' Code of Conduct and its Implementation in the Post-New Order Era

Colonel Imam Edy Mulyono
*Lieutenant-Colonel Eri Radityawara Hidayat**

> *"Remember ! Our soldiers are not mercenaries,*
> *nor soldiers who can easily digress.*
> *We join the military because of our own free will,*
> *and we stand ready to give the ultimate sacrifice,*
> *for the nation and the state"*
>
> *General Sudirman – TNI Commander*
> *Armed Forces Day, October 5, 1949[1]*

INTRODUCTION

Most writings on military ethics dwell on the question of how should a soldier fight a war? For example, should a soldier always obey a direct military order in combat even though he/she knows that the order contravenes military laws such as the Geneva and the Hague Conventions? Since one can find plentiful writings on ethical dilemmas in combat, this chapter attempted to discuss

* The views expressed in this chapter are those of the authors and do not necessarily reflect the official policy of the TNI or the TNI AD.

military ethics from a distinctively Indonesian experience by trying to find the answer to the following ethical dilemma: What should the leadership of an armed forces do when a direct order is received that contradicts the country's constitution (i.e., the Armed Forces were asked to become a military ruler)?

In the case of the Indonesian National Defence Forces or the *Tentara Nasional Indonesia* (TNI) and the Indonesian National Army or the *Tentara National Indonesia Angkatan Darat* (TNI AD), there were suspicions both at home and abroad, that the military reform of 1998 was only lip service, disguised as a tool to soften the criticism and that the TNI would eventually return to the authoritarian era of the New Order government when the time and situation permitted them to do so. Two very significant events related to military ethical dilemmas occurred during the transition era from the authoritarian New Order government to the democratic Reformation government. The first was the decision by the TNI Commander, General Wiranto, to not use the extraordinary power given by President Suharto on May 18th 1998, to become a military ruler of Indonesia. The second was the sophisticated message sent by the Army high command that was intended to prevent President Abdurrahman Wahid from issuing a presidential decree to dissolve the parliament, declare a state of emergency, and then use the military and police forces to neutralize his political opponents.

This chapter will attempt to explain the concept of military ethics from the perspective of the TNI during the critical events in the early post New Order era that presented an ethical dilemma for the TNI leadership.

MILITARY ETHICS DEFINED

The word ethics, which has its origin from the Greek word *ethikos*, later translated by the Romans into the Latin word, *morale*, concerns itself with the moral choices that an individual must make; in other words, a moral philosophical question about what a person should do when confronted with a moral dilemma.[2] It was Socrates (371), the classical Greek philosopher, who argued that the most important question people should strive to answer is not the scientific understanding of nature, but the quest for true happiness through knowing the ethical principles of life.[3] Modern philosophical discourses on ethics can be traced back to the treatise *Ethica* (1677), a *magnum opus* by the Dutch-Jewish philosopher Baruch Spinoza, who in not a very different fashion from Socrates, attempted to demonstrate that the way to human happiness in a deterministic world can only be achieved through living the ethical life according to the guidance of reasonable moral values.[4] Later on, the German philosopher Immanuel Kant (1795), in his philosophical essay, wrote "In an objective sense, morals are a practical science, as the sum of laws exacting unconditional obedience, in accordance with which we ought to act."[5] Therefore, according to this Kantian view, societies needed a practical moral code to guide its members on what can and cannot be done and that must be followed by its members.

However, it was French sociologist Emile Durkheim, the father of modern social science, who at the end of the 19th century first talked about the need for a system of professional codes as a way to provide moral restraint in a complex society characterized by a modern economy.[6] Durkheim stated that every profession should establish some sort of moral rules based on the profession's ethical principles so that whenever a member of the profession experienced a contradictory moral choice, he/she can always refer to the value system of the profession. This is in line with the view that professionals have traditionally been viewed as acting in the spirit of public service.[7]

The modern military can certainly be considered a profession. In his famous book, *The Soldier and the State*, Samuel Huntington stated that it is military professionalism, especially the profession of the officers' corps that distinguishes the modern military officer from the ancient warrior and its civilian counterparts.[8] According to Huntington, the distinctive feature of this professionalism is the competencies related to the "management of violence", in which an officer has a responsibility to organize, equip and train his soldiers, plan its activities and direct its operations in and out of combat.

Huntington argued that an officer must follow a strict code of conduct that will guide his behaviour toward his fellow soldiers (especially his subordinates who must obey him), toward the state which he serves, and to the society that approved the use of his competencies for the good of the people. Since officers are trusted by society to lead soldiers who will use lethal power to "manage the violence", it is inevitable that there will be officers who abuse their powers in order to achieve personal ends. History has demonstrated that this abuse of power has happened in every major conflict and battleground known to men. Therefore, the perennial military ethical question that one can always ask is, "Should a soldier ever disobey a direct military order?"

Huntington elaborated this dilemma further when he contrasted military obedience versus professional competence and military obedience versus non-military values.[9] According to Huntington, the conflict between military obedience and professional competence pertains to the relation of a military subordinate to a military superior in relation to various issues, from operational to doctrinal aspects. While the former is concerned with the implementation of a military order from a superior officer, which according to the judgement of the subordinate will result in a military disaster, the later can take the form of a demand by a superior officer for a rigid and inflexible obedience to established tactics and technology, so that the subordinate might consider it to be a dangerous routine that will stifle military progress. On the other hand, Huntington suggested that the conflict between military obedience versus non-military values happens when an officer is ordered by a civilian authority to support a cause which he knows will lead to national disaster or which he believes will violate the law of the land.

This chapter will try to address the military ethical dilemmas presented by Huntington, especially in relation to the conflict between military obedience versus non-military values in the Indonesian context. Therefore it is imperative that the discussion touch upon the TNI's code of conduct.

THE TNI'S CODE OF CONDUCT

The 220 million people who live in the South East Asian archipelago called Indonesia come from more than 19,000 islands, have descended from over 200 native ethnic groups and races who speak distinctly different languages and worship a variety of religions.[10] Historically, Indonesia was very much influenced by Indic culture, in which the *Srivijaya*, Hindu Buddhist naval kingdom was established on the island of Sumatra, while the agricultural Buddhist *Syailendra* and the Hindu *Mataram* dynasties were established on the island of Java in the 7th century.[11] Indonesia's past glory reached its zenith when the Hindu kingdom *Majapahit* was established in the 13th century and covered much of modern day Indonesia, including Siam (Thailand), the Philippines, Indochina, Brunei, Singapore and Malaysia.[12] Later on, Indian and Chinese traders brought Islam to Indonesia through peaceful means. Islam became the dominant religion in Sumatra and Java by the 16th century, mostly mixed with existing cultural and religious influences from the Hindu Buddhist tradition.[13] At about the same time, the Dutch, and to a lesser extent the Portuguese, arrived, seeking to monopolize nutmeg, cloves, and pepper in the Moluccas. Western cultural influences came with them and they eventually became the colonizer of modern day Indonesia for 300 years.[14] In 1942, Japan invaded Indonesia, driving out the Dutch occupational forces, until Sukarno declared independence on the 17th of August 1945, and soon after, the War of Independence broke out for about four years, when Dutch forces along with allied troops, tried to reclaim their tropical colony.[15]

Although there were occasional conflicts, on the whole, the different social groups that form modern day Indonesia live side by side harmoniously.[16] While many people take this for granted, Indonesian dynamics are actually a recipe for disaster. Consider the fact that not only is Indonesia the fourth largest country in the world in terms of population, it also has the most Muslims, much more than even the many officially Islamic Middle Eastern countries combined.[17] Yet at the same time, it has more Christians than the entire population of "Christian" Australia plus New Zealand;[18] there are more than three times the Hindus on the island of Bali than all of the Hindus in Sri Lanka.[19] The Indonesian part of the island of Borneo alone is more than two times larger than the British isles.[20] Far more people in Indonesia have mother tongues other than Indonesian, compared to all of the inhabitants of

Belgium, which has conflicts due to language differences.[21] Further, there are more Indonesians of Chinese descent than the whole population of Singapore, the overseas Chinese bastion of South East Asia.[22] It is of no wonder that Colin Brown said Indonesia is "an unlikely nation", while Adam Schwarz said Indonesia is a "nation in waiting".[23] It is therefore imperative to ask the existential question: What is the glue that has held this very diverse archipelagic nation together for so long and that has prevented it from falling apart?

The Five Principles

Basically, the foundation of the Unitary State of the Republic of Indonesia is the state ideology called the "Five Principles" or *Pancasila*, which is represented in the national Coat of Arms that can be seen in the following figure.

FIGURE 1: The Indonesian Coat of Arms

The Garuda bird, a mythical golden eagle, is common to both Hindu and Buddhist mythology which symbolizes the preservation of cosmic order. The shield represents the *Pancasila* ideology. The star represents the "Belief in one God" and the chain represents "A just and civilized humanity". The Banyan tree represents the "Unity of Indonesia" and the Javanese wild bull represents "Democracy by consensus". The paddy and cotton represents "Social justice for all Indonesians."[24] The scroll bears the national motto of Indonesia "*Bhinneka Tunggal Ika*", or "Unity in diversity", while the number of feathers represents the 17-8-1945 constitution, which defined the nation and how it is governed.[25]

With *Pancasila* as state ideology, all the religious groupings in Indonesia are accommodated in the first principle which acknowledges the existence of a Supreme Being and reflects the religious nature of Indonesians, without referring or favouring any one religion. At the same time, the third principle recognizes that Indonesia is a multi-ethnic, multi-religion, multi-racial, multi-cultural, multi-lingual state, hence, the national motto *Bhinneka Tunggal Ika*. The fourth principle, acknowledges the collective nature of Indonesian society. Unlike Western liberal democracies, in the Indonesian democratic system, consensus is preferable to voting. This does not mean, however, that voting is not allowed in the decision-making process, but it should only be considered as a last resort, after all avenues to accommodate the different views have been exhausted.

It is the genius of the founding father of Indonesia, that with *Pancasila* as the state ideology, Indonesian society has "a balanced, well-matched harmonious set of principles very much in keeping with the high value ascribed in the Indonesian culture to balance, harmony and unity," so much that every social, racial and religious grouping can relate to it, and feel that they live in the same house called Indonesia.[26] Although often dismissed by Westerners as a collection of "motherhood statements", and despite the fact that from time to time, communal, ethnic and religious conflicts do happen, the national consensus generally holds and *Pancasila* is able to represent a grand political compromise that recognizes the religious nature of the majority of Indonesians, yet, could also provide a modern non-partisan ideological basis for Indonesia's plural society.[27] Not surprisingly, *Pancasila* has become one of the cornerstones of the TNI's code of conduct.

The Core Identity of the TNI

The other foundation of TNI's code of conduct is what is known as the *Core Identity (Jati Diri)*. As a direct descendant of the various militias that fought the Japanese and Dutch occupying forces during Indonesia's struggle for independence, the TNI was not formed by the government. In fact, it was initiated by the people who wanted to liberate themselves from colonial powers.[28] The heroism and sacrifice of the people at that time to achieve a common goal, eventually resulted in the formulation of the *Jati Diri* of the TNI.[29] First, the TNI is the People's Armed Forces (*Tentara Rakyat*), meaning that the TNI is not a distinct entity, but very much part of the society that it serves. Second, the TNI is a Patriotic Armed Forces (*Tentara Pejuang*), an armed forces that will keep the spirit of the struggle for independence and will never surrender to the enemy or to any adverse circumstance it may encounter. Third, the TNI is a National Armed Forces (*Tentara Nasional*), which belongs to all of the ethnic, racial and religious groups that formed Indonesia. After the enactment of the TNI's Bill of Law in 2004, however, the TNI accepted another identity as a Professional Armed Forces (*Tentara Profesional*), reflecting the demands of a modern society.[30]

The Seven Pledges and the Soldier's Oath of the TNI

The Seven Pledges of the TNI or *Sapta Marga* as it is known in Indonesia was officially proclaimed by the Chief of Staff of the TNI on October the 5th 1951 during Indonesia's Armed Forces Day.[31] The pledges of the *Sapta Marga* (as a code of conduct for Indonesian soldiers) are: (1) We are citizens of the Unitary State of the Republic of Indonesia, which is based upon Pancasila; (2) We are Indonesian patriots, supporters and defenders of the ideology of the state, who are responsible and will never surrender; (3) We are knights of Indonesia, who worship one God, and defend honesty, the truth and justice; (4) We are soldiers of the TNI, guardian of the Indonesian state and nation; (5) We are soldiers of the TNI, will uphold discipline, loyal to the leadership and safeguard military honor; (6) We are soldiers of the TNI, emphasizing knightliness in duty, and are always ready to dedicate ourselves to the state and the nation; and, (7) We are soldiers of the TNI, faithful and committed to the Soldier's Oath.[32]

The Soldier's Oath is as follows: In the name of God, I swear that: (1) I will be faithful to the Unitary State of the Republic of Indonesia which is based on *Pancasila* and the 1945 Constitution; (2) I will abide by the law of the land and uphold military discipline; (3) I will be loyal to my superior officer, without disobeying order or decisions; (4) I will carry out my duties with a full sense of responsibility to the TNI and the Republic of Indonesia; and, (5) I will keep firmly all military secrets.[33]

The first three pledges of *Sapta Marga* reflect the core identity of the TNI as a people's armed forces, a national armed forces and a patriotic armed forces as well as the fact that TNI soldiers are also citizens of a country that is based on *Pancasila* and its principles.

The other four pledges reflect the fact that apart from a professional force which is responsible for the country's defence, the TNI is the defender of *Pancasila* that will support the government of the day and that is also loyal to the state ideology and the 1945 Constitution. Since all TNI soldiers must pledge their loyalty to the *Sapta Marga* and the Soldier's Oath, the question to be asked is what would happen if the TNI is ordered to do something that it deems is contrary to *Pancasila* as the state ideology and the 1945 constitution? One way to predict the answer to this question would be to understand the history of the *Sapta Marga* itself.

Sapta Marga as a code of conduct for the Indonesian military was not born in a vacuum. After the War of Independence (from 1950 onwards), Indonesia's civilian government was progressively weakened by ideological sentiments.[34] The political climate was so unstable that approximately 100 different political parties emerged with the average cabinets lasting for only 15 months each. Even worse for the TNI, however, was that various political parties made efforts to recruit soldiers into their ranks.[35] The growth of the communist party, regional separatist threats to the integrity of the state, especially the South Moluccan Republic (*Republik Maluku Selatan*), attempts to form a theocracy through the formation of armed Islamic groups such as the *Darul Islam*, and the military disgust at the failure of liberal, Western style parliamentary democracy, reinforced the perceptions in the officers' corps that the TNI was the only genuine "national" institution, who would defend the *Pancasila* state as a non-communist, non-secular, non-theological, non-liberal Western style democracy, unitary state.[36]

Against this background, the Joint Chief of Staffs established a committee headed by Colonel R. Djoko Bambang Supeno, to formulate pledges for Indonesian soldiers.[37] At that time,

Colonel Supeno was Second in Command of the TNI AD.[38]
With *Sapta Marga*, the TNI reaffirmed its role as the defender
of *Pancasila* and the 1945 Constitution. It further pledged its
commitment to maintain the integrity of the Unitary State of the
Republic of Indonesia as a *Pancasila* state, and promised not to
surrender to any forces that might try to change it.[39] With *Sapta
Marga*, TNI officers and enlisted soldiers have a code of conduct that not only reflects the core identity of the TNI and the
Pancasila ideology, but also provides the guidelines on how to
behave as Indonesian citizens, fighters and soldiers who have a
sacred duty to maintain national security and create a prosperous
society based on *Pancasila* and the 1945 Constitution.

The Eight Military Obligations

Apart from *Sapta Marga* and the Soldier's Oath, there is another
code of conduct for Indonesian soldiers that provides a general
guideline on how a soldier should behave toward civilians. It is
called the Eight Military Obligations or *Delapan Wajib TNI* and
its contents are as follows: (1) Be friendly and courteous to the
people; (2) Be polite to the people; (3) Treat women with respect;
(4) Maintain honour and dignity in front of the public; (5) Be a
role model in behaviour and humility; (6) Never take advantage of
the people; (7) Never intimidate and hurt the people's hearts and
minds; and, (8) Take the lead in attempting to solve the people's
problem in the surrounding area.[40] These obligations are basically
derived from the TNI's Core Identity as the People's Armed Forces.

A CONTEMPORARY MILITARY ETHICAL DILEMMA FACED BY THE TNI

The first military ethical dilemma faced by the TNI leadership occurred when the Dutch occupational forces attacked the fledging republican armed forces in Yogyakarta on the 19th of December 1948 with superior forces and firearms.[41] President Sukarno decided to wait in the Yogyakarta presidential palace and attempted to solve the conflict diplomatically. For the TNI leadership, however, this action was considered the same as surrendering to the Dutch. General Sudirman, the legendary TNI commander reported to the president that he disagreed with the president's decision. General Sudirman asked his permission to continue the struggle as a leader of a guerrilla army because he believed the main task of the TNI was to defend the country. General Sudirman did not deny the position of the armed forces as a tool of the government, but at the same time, he also felt the military should be a freedom fighter, just like many other groups outside of the formal forces.[42] This experience became the embryo for the values that were embedded in the TNI's code of conduct.

The most significant military ethical dilemma in the contemporary history of the TNI occurred when the Asian financial crisis started in the middle of 1997.[43] For Indonesia, the crisis not only touched the monetary sector, but became a full blown multidimensional crisis that ultimately led to the downfall of President Suharto and the "New Order" regime that had ruled Indonesia for more than three decades.[44] During the tumultuous period prior to the resignation of President Suharto on the 21st of May 1998, General Wiranto, the TNI Commander, received Presidential Instruction No 16. dated May 18th 1998, which designated him as the Commander of the National Restoration for Stability and

Order Command (*Komando Operasi Pemulihan Keamanan dan Ketertiban Nasional – KOPKKN*), with General Subagyo, the Chief of Staff of the TNI AD as the Vice Commander.[45]

This Presidential Instruction would have provided General Wiranto with extraordinary and sweeping powers to become the *de jure* and *de facto* military ruler of Indonesia with control over intelligence agencies, commando units and conventional forces, the territorial commands, and more legal and operational authority than an armed forces commander would have. Not only did General Wiranto choose not to use this power, General Subagyo also declined this offer.[46] In fact General Wiranto considered the decision that he made was a "true test of loyalty to the nation ... the mandate was passed on to me. I could have pressed the government (at that time) to impose an "SOB" (*Staat van Oorlog en Beleg* or state of war and siege), to declare a state of emergency and take over power ... that would have been the easiest way ... We could have taken over ... I myself could have done that ...".[47]

One of the most important reasons that the TNI chose not to seize power was, as stated by General Wiranto, the Indonesian military officers were loyal to the state. "We are loyal to the system, not to individuals. If we were faithful to Suharto it was because at that time he was a true, legal and constitutional president. The same thing goes for Habibie. Well ... the person (holding the presidency) may change but the TNI's loyalty to the constitution is consistent."[48] He also added that another reason for not taking power was the belief that using the presidential instruction to gain power and suppress the wishes of the Indonesian people would have resulted in violence on the street, which certainly would be against the Core Identity of the TNI as a People's Armed Forces.[49]

General Wiranto realized that even though he could have easily seized power, securing this power without constitutional legitimacy was meaningless.[50] In fact, although the military had pressured presidents in the past, there was no precedent in Indonesia for an outright military coup. Unlike many other developing countries, the TNI did not enter into politics by way of *coup d'état* but in an orderly and legal fashion.[51] Presumably, even if the commander of the TNI chooses to do so, there would be no guarantee that the officer corps would be willing to follow.[52]

When describing the New Order government, John Hasseman, an expert on the TNI asserted "Indonesia can be said to have a government with a powerful military, but not a military government".[53] In fact, it can be said that the issue has been more centred on civilian politicians and the government of the day who were tempted at times to seek support from the military to further their own political agenda.[54] It is of no wonder that General Wiranto preferred to consult with constitutional lawyers on the legality of his action, rather than rushing to take over the president's job.[55] And, according to General Wiranto, Admiral Joseph Prueher, Commander of the United States Pacific Command (USPACOM), praised him for his willingness to support the transfer of power in accordance with the Indonesian constitution, considering that many people initially doubted his intention to do so.[56]

If we look at the seven pledges of *Sapta Marga*, General Wiranto's action is actually consistent with the fourth pledge, which states that he should become the *guardian of the Indonesian state and nation*. Certainly he had an ethical dilemma. As an officer, he was obliged to follow the order of the President as the Commander in Chief as stated in the fifth pledge of *Sapta Marga* and the Soldier's Oath. But as a senior military leader, he knew that if he obeyed the president's order, his action would lead to national disasters such as a constitutional crisis and public resistance which would have eventually caused bloodshed. Some experts suggested that the TNI should abandon its traditional ethos such as loyalty to *Sapta Marga*, *Pancasila*, and the 1945 Constitution, and instead reorient its loyalty to the government of the day so that it can fully disengage from politics.[57] This dilemma is consistent with Huntington's view as presented earlier in this chapter. From this point of view, it can be argued that the TNI's leadership at that time could be categorized as professional soldiers rather than praetorian ones.

General Ryamizard Ryacudu and the Presidential Decree

On Saturday morning the 19th of May 2001, seventy panzers, thirty tanks, and a thousand combat ready soldiers were assembled at the headquarter of the TNI AD's Strategic Reserve Command (*Komando Cadangan Strategis Angkatan Darat* – KOSTRAD), which is the most prominent Army Command located near the presidential palace. These forces were there to attend a loyalty pledge ceremony led by its commander, Lieutenant-General Ryamizard Ryacudu.[58] It was widely expected that President Abdurrahman Wahid would announce a Presidential Decree that would declare a state of emergency, dissolve parliament, and replace the leadership of the TNI.[59]

During the ceremony, rumors spread that the TNI would not support the implementation of the decree. As a consequence, the TNI was accused in the media of trying to stage a coup. The TNI AD Vice Chief of Staff, Lieutenant-General Kiki Syahnakri countered this by declaring that at least 95 % of TNI's soldiers were not interested in politics and that they only wanted to improve their professionalism. The TNI AD Chief of Staff, General Endriartono Sutarto then conveyed to the press that under no circumstance would the TNI take over power – the TNI will always be on the side of the people.[60] In fact, the military countered the speculations by declaring that they were still loyal to the President of the Republic of Indonesia as long as the President upheld the 1945 Constitution (this is the TNI's highest mandate).[61] The presence of military forces so close to the palace, however, was interpreted as the TNI's rejection for the planned decree.

It was unfortunate that President Abdurrahman Wahid, who was well known as the champion of human rights and democracy, in the last days of his presidency, resorted to authoritarianism. By declaring a state of emergency, he threatened to use the security forces to execute his orders and muzzle his opponents.[62] Yet, President Wahid's intention to use force provided the TNI with an opportunity to prove that the TNI was already transformed from a force that could be used as an instrument of power during the New Order era, into a responsible armed forces that respected the democratically elected parliament. This was consistent with the TNI's New Paradigm of neutrality and non-involvement in day-to-day partisan politics.[63]

In this case, the subtle conflict between the military and its political superior showed that when the TNI leadership was forced to choose between political manoeuvring by the civilian leadership and upholding the TNI's code of conduct, they chose their military values. The TNI maintained its position as the protector of the democratic process that was mandated by the 1945 Constitution and the *Pancasila* state ideology because it believed members of parliament were democratically elected by the people. For the TNI leadership, this is why it would be illegal and unconstitutional to dissolve the parliament, even though at that time, the parliament was planning to impeach the president.

The refusal of senior military figures to accept the post of TNI commander as long as they support the decree, such as Lieutenant-General Johnny Josephus Lumintang and Lieutenant-General Djaja Suparman, confirmed their loyalty to the TNI's code of conduct. Cynics might question why the military chose not to support President Wahid in 2001, yet they essentially became the protector of President Suharto during the New Order era up until 1998, supporting all of his policies. However, one can say that despite his strong arm tactics, during President Suharto's reign of power, the president never once tried to dissolve the parliament and use the military to enforce it, which would have been in violation of the 1945 constitution and the state ideology of *Pancasila*.

If we relate the above discussion to Huntington's civil-military relations, it is clearly shown that in the case of General Ryacudu, there was a conflict between military obedience and political wisdom.[64] In addition, it can also be noted that there was a conflict between military obedience and the legal status of the President's intention. The TNI only serves the legitimate constituted authorities of the state. When President Wahid claimed that his intention was legal, although it was considered illegal by parliament, the TNI followed the parliament's judgement. Eventually, the TNI's consideration to follow the parliament's decision was supported by the parliament's firm decision to convene a special session to censure the president. The military was not trying to show that it was not loyal to the president; rather, it was sending a message of its commitment to the state and the nation, and not to any individual.

MILITARY ETHICS: INTERNATIONAL PERSPECTIVES

CONCLUSION

It has been more than ten years since the TNI's internal reformation was launched, most important of which was its retreat from day-to-day politics.[65] Time has proven that the impact of this effort has truly transformed civil-military relations in the country, making Indonesia an emerging democratic country, successful in its transition from authoritarian rule.[66] The TNI's transformation in this regard, has been considered as a role model for military change in terms of civil-military relations.[67]

The suggestion that the TNI should abandon its traditional ethos such as loyalty to *Sapta Marga*, *Pancasila*, and the 1945 Constitution, and pledge its loyalty merely to the government of the day, was not obeyed by the TNI. On the contrary, it was proven that the TNI's code of conduct was relevant as a guideline to solve the ethical military dilemma on military obedience versus non-military values, as put forward by Huntington. This fact was also supported by the insignificant political roles that the TNI plays in today's Indonesia. This shows the precious values of the *Sapta Marga* as the code of conduct for the TNI's leadership. This is the most significant reason behind the TNIs leadership decision when confronted with an ethical dilemma of becoming a military ruler or using the power at their disposal to support an authoritarian decree that was not supported by parliament. They instead chose to be loyal to their values.

The fact is that these value systems, which were passed down by TNI's founding fathers, are imprinted in the minds of every TNI soldier. Whenever the TNI leadership has had disagreement with the civilian authority, whenever the fate of Indonesia was at stake, whenever the military has had the opportunity to seize power, it did not. The TNI leadership always maintained its code of conduct to remain above politics and with the people.[68]

> *"The government may change every day;*
> *The military remains the same."*

General Sudirman – Commander-in-Chief
1947, Yogyakarta.[69]

ENDNOTES

1   Agus Pribadi, *Mengikuti Jejak Panglima Besar Jenderal Soedirman, Pahlawan Pembela Kemerdekaan 1916-1950* [Following the footsteps of Great Commander General Soedirman, Freedom Fighter Hero 1916-1950] (Jakarta: Prenada Media, 2009).

2   Joanne Ciulla, *Ethics, the Heart of Leadership* (Westport, CT: Praeger Publishers, 2004), xvi.

3   Edgar Marchant and Otis Todd (Editors and translators), *Xenophon's Memorabilia. Oeconomicus, Symposium, Apology* (Cambridge, MA: Harvard University Press, 1997), 9-13.

4   Steven Nadler, *Spinoza's Ethics: An Introduction* (New York, NY: Cambridge University Press, 2006), x, 243.

5   Immanuel Kant, *Perpetual Peace: A Philosophical Essay*, translated by M. Campbell Smith (London: George Allen & Unwin, 1917), 161.

6   Émile Durkheim, *Professional Ethics and Civic Morals* (New York, NY: Routledge, 2003), 14-15.

7   Daryl Koehn, *The Ground of Professional Ethics* (New York: Taylor & Francis, 2001), 2, 182.

8   Samuel P. Huntington, *The Soldier and the State: The Theory and Politics of Civil-Military Relations* (Cambridge, MA: Harvard University Press, 1957), 7-8.

9   Ibid, 74-76.

10   Adrian Vickers, *A History of Modern Indonesia* (Cambridge: Cambridge University Press, 2005), 1.

11   Steven Drakeley, *The History of Indonesia* (Wesport, CT: Greenwood Press, 2005), 14-16.

12   Merle Calvin Ricklefs, *A History of Modern Indonesia Since c. 1300, 2ⁿᵈ Edition* (Stanford: Stanford University Press, 1991), 19.

13   Cliford Geertz, "The Javanese Kijaji: The Changing Role of a Cultural Broker," *Comparative Studies in Society and History*, Vol. 2, No. 2 (1960), 228-249. See also Tan Ta Sen, *Cheng Ho and Islam in Southeast Asia* (Singapore: Institute of Southeast Asian Studies, 2009), 195-196; and, Greg Barton, *Abdurrahman Wahid: Muslim Democrat, Indonesian President* (Sydney, Australia: University of New South Wales Press Ltd., 2002), 65 -67.

14   Anthony Reid, *Southeast Asia in the Age of Commerce 1450-1680. Volume Two: Expansion and Crisis* (New Haven: Yale University Press, 1993), 2-5.

15   Sadao Oba, "My Recollections of Java during the Pacific War and Merdeka," *Indonesia and the Malay World*, Vol. 8, No. 21 (1980), 6-14.

16   Douglas Ramage, *Politics in Indonesia: Democracy, Islam and the Ideology of Tolerance* (London: Taylor & Francis, 2005), 135.

17   Indonesia's population in 2009 was estimated to be around 242 million [with about 200 million Muslims]. The Islamic Republic of Iran has 66 million people, the Kingdom of Saudi Arabia has 28 million and the Islamic Republic of Afghanistan has 33 million. See *GeoHive: Global Statistics*, retrieved 2 March 2010 from <http://www.geohive.com>.

18   The Indonesian Ministry of Religious Affairs estimated that there were about 19 million Protestants and 8 million Catholics living in the country in 2009, while the population of Australia in 2009 was estimated at 21 million and New Zealand at 4 million. See *GeoHive: Global Statistics on Australia and New Zealand and US Department of State, International Religious Freedom: 2009 Report on International Religious Freedom, East Asia and Pacific, Indonesia*, retrieved 2 March 2010 from <http://www.state.gov/g/drl/rls/irf/2009/127271.htm>.

19   The Indonesian Ministry of Religious Affairs estimated that about 10 million Hindus live in the country, the majority in Bali, while Sri Lanka has about 3 million Hindus. See *US Department of State, International Religious*

Freedom: 2009 Report on International Religious Freedom, South and Central Asia, Sri Lanka, retrieved 2 March 2010 from <http://www.state.gov/g/drl/rls/irf/2009/127371.htm>.

20   The Indonesian part of Kalimantan has a total area of 547,891 sq km, while the total area of the United Kingdom, including Northern Ireland, is 242,910 sq km. See *GeoHive: Global Statistics on Indonesia and the United Kingdom*, retrieved 2 March 2010 from <http://www.geohive.com>.

21   The Indonesian language, Bahasa Indonesia, was derived from Malay, the language spoken by traders. Malays however, constituted a mere 3.5 % of the total Indonesian population. The dominant language group in Indonesia is Javanese, spoken by about 41% of the people, followed by Sundanese (15 % of the population). The Indonesian founding fathers wisely chose Bahasa Indonesia, instead of the dominant Javanese language for the sake of national unity, so that no ethic grouping could complain that they have to learn the language spoken by the dominant group. Unlike many other multilingual countries, by and large, there has not been a single conflict in Indonesia that was based on language differences. Belgium, with about 6 million Flemish and 3.5 million French speaking Walloons, has not been able to solve it's problems on language differences in relation to its national identity. See the Permanent Committee on Geographical Names, *Indonesia, Population and Administrative Divisions*, retrieved 2 March 2010 from <http://www.pcgn.org.uk/Indonesia-%20Population&AdminDivs-%202003.pdf>, Gloria Poedjosoedarmo, "The Effect of Bahasa Indonesia as a Lingua Franca on the Javanese System of Speech Levels and their Functions," *International Journal of the Sociology of Language,* No. 177 (2006), 111-121; and, Jaak Billiet, Bart Maddens, and André-Paul Frognier. "Does Belgium (Still) Exist? Differences in Political Culture between Flemings and Walloons," *West European Politics*, Vol. 29, No. 5 (2006), 912-932.

22   The estimated population of Singapore in 2009 was around 4 million, while it was estimated in the early 1990s that the total number of people of Chinese descent in Indonesia was about 7.3 million. See D.L. Poston Jr, M.X. Mao, M.Y. Yu, "The Global Distribution of the Overseas Chinese Around 1990, *Population and Development Review*, Vol. 20, No. 3 (1994), 631-645 and GeoHive: *Global Statistics on Singapore*, retrieved 2 March 2010 from <http://www.geohive.com>.

23   Colin Brown, *A Short History of Indonesia: The Unlikely Nation?* (Crows Nest, Australia: Allen & Unwin, 2003). See also Adam Schwarz, *A Nation in Waiting: Indonesia's Search for Stability* (Boulder, CO: Westview Press, 2000).

24 Department of Information, Republic of Indonesia, *Indonesia 1999: An Official Handbook* (Jakarta: Department of Information, Republic of Indonesia, 1999).

25 Sally Heinrich, *Key to Indonesia* (Carlton South, Australia: Curriculum Corporation, 2005), 10.

26 Eka Darmaputera, *Pancasila and the Search for Identity and Modernity in Indonesian Society* (Unpublished PhD Dissertation, Boston: Boston College, 1982), 330.

27 Barton, *Abdurrahman Wahid: Muslim Democrat, Indonesian President*, op. cit., 14.

28 Barry Turner, *Nasution: Total People's Resistance and Organicist Thinking in Indonesia* (Unpublished PhD Dissertation, Melbourne: Swinburne University of Technology, 2005), 70.

29 Lieutenant-Colonels Eri Hidayat and Gunawan (2008). "People's Army, Patriotic Army, National Army and Professional Army: History, Challenges and the Development of Core Identity in the Indonesian National Army," in *Professional Ideology and Development: International Perspectives*, Lieutenant-Colonel Jeff Stouffer & Justin C. Wright, eds., (Kingston, Ontario: Canadian Defence Academy Press, 2008), 47.

30 Letkol Inf Imam Santosa, *TNI Sudah Berusia 62 Tahun, lalu Bagaimana?* [TNI is Already 62 Years Old, Then What?] May 2008 <http://www.tni.mil.id/news>.

31 Bilveer Singh, *Civil-military Relations in Democratising Indonesia: The Potentials and Limits to Change* (Canberra: Strategic and Defence Studies Centre, Australian National University, 2001), 64.

32 Lieutenant-Colonel Eddy S. Harisanto, *The Dual Function of The Indonesian Armed Forces* (Dwi Fungsi ABRI), Master of Science in Management Thesis (Monterey CA: US Naval Postgraduate School, 1993), 43-44. There are many translations of the Seven Pledges. This translation is an adaptation of the translation by Colonel Harisanto of the Indonesian Air Force. The writers found his translation to be closest in meaning to the original version of *Sapta Marga*.

33 Ibid, 44.

34   Seskoad, Dharma Pusaka 45: *Hasil seminar TNI-AD ke III, tanggal 13 s/d 18 Maret 1972* [Sacred Duties 45: Result of the 3rd TNI AD Seminar, 13 to 18 March 1972] (Bandung, Indonesia: Seskoad, 1972).

35   Mabes ABRI, *Pengantar Sishankamrata* [Introduction to The People's Security and Defense System – Sishankamrata] (Bandung: Sekolah Staf dan Komando ABRI, 1993).

36   Douglas Ramage, *Politics in Indonesia: Democracy, Islam and the Ideology of Tolerance* (London: Taylor & Francis, 2005), 8-9.

37   Tahi Bonar Simatupang and Peter Suwarno, *The Fallacy of a Myth* (Jakarta: Pustaka Sinar Harapan, 1996), 133.

38   Ernst Utrecht, *The Indonesian Army: A Socio-political Study of an Armed, Privileged Group in the Developing Countries* (Townsville, Australia: Southeast Asian Studies Committee, James Cook University, 1979), 9.

39   Katharine McGregor, *History in Uniform: Military Ideology and the Construction of Indonesia's Past* (Singapore: National University of Singapore Press, 2007), 124.

40   Mabesad, *Profile of the Indonesian Army* (Jakarta: Mabesad, 2007), 19.

41   Himawan Soetanto, *Yogyakarta 19 Desember 1948: Jenderal Spoor* (Operatie Kraai) versus Jenderal Sudirman (Perintah Siasat No. 1) [Yogyakarta December 19 1948: General Spoor (Operations Kraai) versus General Sudirman (Operations Order No. 1)] (Jakarta: Gramedia Pustaka Utama, 2006), 290.

42   Salim Said, *Soeharto's Armed Forces: Problems of Civil Military Relations in Indonesia* (Jakarta: Pustaka Sinar Harapan, 2006), 40.

43   William Hunter, George Kaufman, Thomas Krueger, eds., *The Asian Financial Crisis: Origins, Implications and Solutions* (Norwell, MA: Kluwer Academic Publishers, 2000), 48.

44   Kevin O'Rourke, *Reformasi: The Struggle for Power in Post-Soeharto Indonesia* (Crows Nest, NSW: Allen & Unwin, 2002), 64.

45   Wiranto, *Dari Catatan Wiranto, Jenderal Purnawirawan: Bersaksi Di Tengah Badai* [From the notes of Wiranto, Retired General: Witnessing in the Midst of a Storm] (Jakarta: Ide Indonesia, 2003), 82.

MILITARY ETHICS: INTERNATIONAL PERSPECTIVES

46 Marcus Mietzner, "From Soeharto to Habibie: The Indonesian Armed Forces and Political Islam During the Transition," in Geoff Forrester, ed., *Post-Soeharto Indonesia: Renewal or Chaos?* (Singapore: Research School of Pacific and Asian Studies/Institute of Southeast Asian Studies, 1999), 81. See also Barton (2002), op. cit., 240-241.

47 Anonymous, "Wiranto Says He Already Passed Up Chance For Power," *Jakarta Post*, March 5, 1999, 2.

48 Ibid.

49 Ibid.

50 O'Rourke, *Reformasi: The Struggle for Power in Post-Soeharto Indonesia,* op.cit., 153.

51 Salim Said, *Legitimizing Military Rule: Indonesian Armed Forces Ideology* (Jakarta: Pustaka Sinar Harapan, 2006).

52 O'Rourke, *Reformasi: The Struggle for Power in Post-Soeharto Indonesia*, op.cit., 162.

53 John Hasseman, "To Change a Military – The Indonesian Experience," *Joint Force Quarterly*, Vol. 29, (2000), 23-30.

54 Marcus Mietzner, *The Politics of Military Reform in Post-Suharto Indonesia: Elite Conflict, Nationalism, and Institutional Resistance* (Washington: East-West Center, 2006), 16.

55 Adam Schwarz, *A Nation in Waiting: Indonesia's Search for Stability* (Boulder, CO: Westview Press, 2000), 364.

56 Wiranto, *Dari Catatan Wiranto Jenderal Purnawirawan: Bersaksi Di Tengah Badai*, op.cit., vii.

57 Terence Lee, "Indonesian military taking the slow road to reform," *The Straits Times*, December 18, 2004, review section.

58 Hidayat Tantan, Koesworo Setiawan, and Kholis Bakri, "Pergeseran di Tubuh Angkatan Darat: Rayuan Dekrit Jenderal Politik," [Rotation in the Army: Seduction of Presidential Decree for Political Generals] *Gatra*, May 21, 2001.

59   Robin Bush, *Nahdlatul Ulama and the Struggle for Power within Islam and Politics in Indonesia* (Singapore: Institute of Southeast Asian Studies, 2009), 138.

60   Michael Malley, "Indonesia in 2001: Restoring Stability in Jakarta," *Asian Survey*, Vol. 42, No. 1 (2002), 124-132.

61   Syahrir, "TNI kembali unjuk gigi dengan menolak pilihan Gus Dur untuk jabatan KSAD," [TNI again showed its teeth by rejecting Gus Dur's choice for Army Chief of Staff] *Radio Nederland*, May 21, 2001.

62   Mietzner, "From Soeharto to Habibie: The Indonesian Armed Forces and Political Islam During the Transition," op.cit., 29.

63   Markas Besar Tentara Nasional Indonesia, *Implementasi Paradigma Baru TNI dalam berbagai keadaan mutakhir* [Implementation of TNI's New Paradigm in the latest situations] (Jakarta: Mabes TNI, 2001), 57.

64   Huntington, *The Soldier and the State: The Theory and Politics of Civil-Military Relations*, op.cit., 77.

65   Leonard Sebastian, *Realpolitik ideology: Indonesia's Use of Military Force* (Singapore: Institute of Southeast Asian Studies, 2006), 334.

66   Tim Huxley, *Security Sector Reform, Proceeding of the International Seminar: Indonesia 2025: Geopolitical and security challenges*, Indonesian Defense University, Jakarta March 11-12, 2009 (Jakarta: Department of Defence of the Republic of Indonesia, 2009), 66.

67   Hasseman, "To Change a Military – The Indonesian Experience," op.cit., 29 & 23.

68   Michael Vatikiotis, *Indonesian Politics Under Suharto: The Rise and Fall of the New Order, Third edition* (New York: Routledge, 1998), 229.

69   Ibid, 64.

MILITARY ETHICS: INTERNATIONAL PERSPECTIVES

CHAPTER 11

Command During Air Combat Operations: The Confluence of Command, Law, and Ethics

Brigadier-General Dwight Davies[*]

Operational command of a fighting force in combat presents the ultimate challenge to an officer and is normally the pinnacle of an officers career. It is here that the commander will face the greatest personal and professional challenges, at a time when most stressed, fatigued, and alone more than ever likely experienced. The extensive professional training and experiences of a career normally present commanders with the opportunity to acquire the requisite knowledge and skills required to succeed. In many respects, command in combat represents the confluence of three powerful streams: the institution of command, the law of armed conflict, and personal ethics. For the most part, the waters of each of these merge without conflict or ripple, each of the currents reinforcing the others. Yet in some specific cases, the merging results in cross-currents that produce rough water that must be successfully navigated by the commander. I believe that a commander that has faced, or considered, such turbulence prior to finding himself/herself in action is far better equipped to succeed in the most demanding role of his/her career.

---

[*] The views expressed in this chapter are those of the author and do not necessarily reflect the official policy of the Canadian Forces or the Department of National Defence.

Within the professional development of officers, significant emphasis is placed on the study of the art and science of command as well as the examination of law as it pertains to the use of force. It is noteworthy that the subject of ethics is not addressed with a similar level of effort; officers are not routinely provided with the time, mentoring, and thought-provoking material to cause them to sharpen their abilities in this important area.

I had the great fortune to experience a number of significant ethical challenges in the earlier portion of my career and the very great luck to have selected an elective on military ethics while attending the Air War College. While the article that follows attempts to illustrate the effects of all three influences, command, law, and ethics, it is heavily weighted to the latter as this is an area that I consider crucial to success, and potentially an area in which the Canadian Forces has not invested the same level of attention as the other two. In my opening paragraph, the significance of a combat command to an officer was emphasized; I was fortunate enough to have been selected to command a combat force of CF-18 fighter aircraft in the lead up and execution of the combat operations against the armed forces of the Former Republic of Yugoslavia, OPERATION ALLIED FORCE. Many of the points are made by providing personal examples from this intense combat operation. In doing so, I hope that it will better illustrate the points that I am trying to make.[1]

THE BASICS: COMMAND, LAW, AND ETHICS

Command: Leadership

While command is not unique or specific to fighter combat operations, command in combat does require a fundamental personal expertise with the capabilities and effects of the force under command. Throughout my early flying years, I honed my personal skills as a fighter pilot, but I also absorbed a number of lessons on leadership and command that were to pay off in the crucible of combat.

While I served under a variety of commanders and witnessed a variety of different approaches to leadership, one particular event left an indelible impression. I was a very junior member of a fighter squadron equipped with 18 CF-5 aircraft.[2] While this aircraft was not renowned for high levels of serviceability, we could routinely count on 9 or 10 to be available for flying on any given day. During one spell, we suffered a dramatic decrease in aircraft serviceability, to the point where only two or three would be available on the line each day. Each morning, the Captain in charge of aircraft repair would brief on the long list of major malfunctions of the many broken aircraft, complete with explanations as to why they would not be flyable for a protracted period. He would then return to the helm of his maintenance group. This "dry" spell continued for weeks, with no apparent hope for improvement, and with continual erosion in the combat capability of the squadron. The Captain happened to be sent for a week-long period of duty at a distant location. The following Monday morning, the Lieutenant acting in his place arrived at the morning briefing and proceeded to inform a stunned squadron that 14 of the 18 aircraft were ready to fly! This turned out to be the low point of the week, as the men managed to put more and more aircraft in the sky. The following Monday the Captain was back, and with some embarrassment, he briefed the bad news that there were only a couple of aircraft repaired and flyable. The squadron commander rapidly moved to replace the maintenance officer, and things returned to an even keel with the sustainable rate of 9 to 10 aircraft per day on the line. The obvious lesson was that the Captain had created such a poor working environment that his demoralized personnel were in failure. I drew a less obvious and much more important lesson: inspired people are capable of accomplishing miraculous performance. With the temporary absence of the maintenance officer, they did not simply work to achieve the 9 to 10 aircraft that was the best that could be reasonable accomplished, they pressed way beyond that. They were inspired to great accomplishment.

While I was to see this effect in other situations during my career, nowhere was it as evident as in the performance of the task force in combat operations. To a person, they rose to the challenges of combat, each feeling that sense of "I wonder if I am good enough", and "this is what I have dedicated my professional life to do". From extraordinary levels of aircraft serviceability (only one mission lost in the entire period), to solving issues with armament, there was nothing that they could not accomplish. As their commander, I found that my few concerns were of holding them back and ensuring that they took adequate time away from tasks to rest; to enable them to effectively perform at a high level for a protracted period. They were inspired from within; this makes command remarkably easier than if this was not the case.

Command: Life and Death

Air Force officers are not strangers to violent death. In the course of a career, particularly by the time one reaches senior enough rank to be placed in a combat command, you have faced the death of friends and learned to deal with it. That having been said, these were accidental deaths resulting from the inherent risks of air operations. Most of us will have also faced and succeeded in a variety of command positions, surmounting the many and varied challenges that are an inherent part of normal command. However, it is only in the crucible of combat that the command accountability truly imparts the greatest of human responsibilities: the power of life and death.

Combat clearly implies the deliberate use of lethal force and the expectation of a lethal response from the enemy. Thus, the first of the life and death responsibilities becomes clear; how to balance the achievement of the mission versus the risk to the lives of those under your command. Obviously, equipment, training, and tactics have all been developed to minimize the risks involved, but once the shooting starts, the risks faced by the aircrew are dramatic. A commander cannot expect to accomplish the mission without placing people at risk; yet no responsible commander can order them into harm's way without the conviction that the risks are essential to accomplishing the mission and that all possible measures have been taken to mitigate the risks.

Second, any bombing campaign will inevitably lead to situations in which important targets are located in proximity to non-combatants. The Law of Armed Conflict extensively addresses such attacks; however, the fundamental reality is that Commander's will face decisions to attack targets with the high likelihood that these attacks will result in the death or injury to non-combatants. This too is a weighty responsibility that is unique to combat operations.

Finally, there is the aspect of killing the enemy. While it is obvious that many attacks are deliberately intended to cause death and injury to enemy forces, and all military training is geared to prepare our forces to perform this mission, it remains a sobering decision to order the deliberate killing of other humans. This too, represents a commander accountability that is unique to combat operations.

Command: The Way You Fight Matters

It is easy to remain tightly focused on combat operations; however, commanders must not lose sight of the fact that combat operations represent only one aspect of the entire undertaking. Combat is rarely undertaken prior to the exhaustion of all other diplomatic and economic pressures to cause the opposing leadership to acquiesce. Once the combat phase has been won, some form of peace, cooperation, and co-existence will resume. How the combat phase is conducted will influence the start conditions for the ensuing peace. The destruction of some targets may bring about significant military advantage during the combat phase and thus may even hasten victory. It can also, however, significantly hamper the resumption of peaceful coexistence in the aftermath. This could include the destruction of transportation and electric grids or other infrastructure that is important to everyday life. From another point of view, collateral non-combatant deaths that have resulted from legitimate attacks on important targets could poison future relationships and thus, render the resumption of normalized relations, post-conflict, extremely difficult. I would therefore argue that a commander must be cognizant of the potential impacts of his actions and decisions over the longer term and avoid simply focusing on an expedient military victory. The application of military force is but one of the potential phases in the continuum of relations that will continue well after the immediate issue is resolved.

The Law of Armed Conflict (LOAC)

Our current officer professional development program provides a solid foundation on the Law of Armed Conflict. Moreover, the laws themselves are written in operational language that makes them relatively easy to understand and apply. Finally, the underlying theme that is evident in these laws, that of reducing some of the suffering and protecting certain people and objects, helps to make the application of these laws more straight forward for the operational commander. This is not evident in our training, as we are accustomed to requesting and applying Rules of Engagement (ROE) which have a significant role to play when the application of force is either highly undesirable or unlikely. These rules are very detailed, complex, restrictive and challenging to apply. Once the use of force is intended, as a deliberate act during a mission, the impact of ROEs diminish dramatically. In the case of bombing attacks during an Air Campaign, ROEs have an extremely diminished role with the LOAC coming to the fore and assuming the pre-eminent importance.

Added to the professional education that a commander would have received during his career, he/she can count on additional training in LOAC prior to a deployment and can expect the assistance and advice of a legal team from the Judge Advocate General (JAG). These extremely professional lawyers have reach-back that permits them to tap into the entirety of the experience and knowledge of the JAG branch. Thus, I would say that an operational commander is extremely well served in this regard.

In many respects, if the conduct of air combat operations could be likened to a roadway, the LOAC represents the ditches on the two sides. The training and education helps in identifying the ditches, lawyers act as the rumble strips to let you know when you are approaching the shoulder of the road or to help point out the drop-off where the grass starts. That having been said, the roadway that remains is still quite wide, and permits for a variety of lanes and speeds to be selected.

In my experience, the lawyers that were deployed were extremely dedicated, focused on mission accomplishment and were imbued with the warrior spirit. They integrated into the combat team at a variety of levels, specifically including the mission planning phase where they had access to details from weapons and weapons effects to attack geometry. They were an enabler that allowed me to make decisions with a greater sense of confidence with respect to the legality of our undertakings. I would, however, sound a note of caution. Lawyers are accountable for the quality of their advice and will be judged and dealt with by their peers and superiors. Commanders are accountable for their decisions and will be judged by a wide spectrum of venues, including a variety of courts. In short, lawyers advise, commanders decide. It is important in combat that there can be no confusion as to the two distinct roles as well as the distinct accountabilities.

Finally, virtually all possible scenarios will see Canadians fighting as part of a coalition. The coalition command structure will likely have the preponderance of control over the campaign plan and the conduct of operations, including targeting. It is crucial for any national commander to consider that coalition organizations may have a very limited accountability. It was very clear to me that I was answerable for the actions and conduct of the force under my command and that I could not duck this by insisting that NATO had issued the orders. NATO wouldn't go to jail; as the Canadian commander, the same was not necessarily true for me.

Ethics

In the mid- to late-nineties, the Canadian Forces emphasized enhanced ethical training. This was the direct result of a number of scandals that arose in the early 1990s, culminating in the fallout from the Somalia mission. In many cases, the ethics training focused on complex situational issues in which individuals were faced with impossibly demanding choices that involved negative consequences for any decision. While I support this type of intellectual exercise on the basis that it is stimulating and can cause us to reflect on our core values, it is not truly reflective of the types of situations one necessarily faces in a combat command.

I was fortunate enough to have had the opportunity to study the theory and practice of ethics as an elective while attending the Air War College as a Lieutenant-Colonel. This permitted me to critically examine my own fundamental values, to examine my experiences, and to develop a personal understanding and confidence in my abilities. I would highly commend this as a professional development activity for all officers.

There are a number of ways of categorizing approaches to ethical decision-making. To permit a practical examination, I propose dividing decision-making into three categories based on the following underlying philosophies:

1. Rule-based: act in accordance with the rules, laws, published procedures, etc.

2. Consequence based: act according to the probable result (i.e., if good will be the result of the act, then the act is good or right).

3. Situational: act after considering all factors, including the current situation, rules, likely outcomes, and other factors.

Clearly, any ethics system that was uniquely based on either of the first two quantifications would have significant shortcomings in application. Rule-based ethics may ensure that you don't falsify claims or break laws, but they will leave you adrift when faced with circumstances not covered by rules or situations for which the various sets of rules are in conflict. Consequence-based ethics on the other hand, could be used to justify clearly immoral acts, based solely on the "good" outcomes expected. Accordingly, each of these two structures over-simplifies ethics, yet contributes in part to a better understanding.

The final proposed characterization, that of situational ethics, incorporates aspects of the previous two, rules and consequences, as well as an examination of all other pertinent factors. The relative weighting of each of the many varied aspects of the situation would be rather individual in nature and the resulting decisions would be fundamentally dependent on the individual's sense of the relative weight of each factor, his/her inherent sense of right, and the level of moral courage to act in accordance with ones convictions. The key to this level of ethical structure is thus seen to be the individual. In the proposed metaphor of combat being a roadway, with the LOAC being the ditches, I would now add that the application of ethical command is like a force that helps steer towards the centreline. I would posit that a commander should be sufficiently educated and confident in his/her personal ethical judgement and courage to act and to be able to succeed in the application of the "situational" approach to ethical consideration. To enable this level of behaviour, dedicated education including assisted introspective self-examination is appropriate.

Two basic assumptions regarding the foundation of moral values can be identified: that we are all born with a basic set of morals, or that we develop our values through exposure to society. In that laws vary dramatically from one society to another, and that religious beliefs also come in a wide spectrum, it is significant that, despite the differences in circumstances, there is a remarkable similarity in the basic moral values. Despite this relatively common set of values, history has continued to confirm that there exists a wide spectrum of behaviour, from ethical to decidedly unethical. In fact, many of the scandals of the Canadian Forces of the early 90's, particularly those involving officers of high rank and accountability, would lead one to believe that the individual concerned lacked any sense of right and wrong. What made these individuals err? How could they corrupt or ignore their values to this extent? How can anyone be confident that "this could not have been me"? Answering this fundamental question is the essence of defining one's own touchstone.[3]

Ethics: Finding My Touchstone

Perhaps the truest test of oneself is an examination of past actions. How did you react in past circumstances? Had you ever faced an ethical challenge in the past? For me, this reflection began the development of my personal touchstone. The more I reflected, the more I was able to identify circumstances in which I had been tested. In each case, I felt that my decisions and actions had demonstrated a clear standard of high integrity and the result in each case was positive. This seemed to further reinforce the "rightness" of my actions. From this arose my confidence that, if faced with a challenge, I would choose the "right" thing. While I had a number of experiences in my early career in which I had felt conflicted – labouring under pressure to act contrary to my sense of "right things". There was one formative event that made a lifelong impression and gave me the courage to do the "right thing" in the future; it became my touchstone event.

I was a Lieutenant-Colonel in an operations staff assignment at our operational headquarters. My Colonel had been absent for a period and the Operations General summoned me with an urgent task. I was to assemble a team and produce an estimate on the viability of deploying a contingent of twin-engined transport training aircraft from the Air Force to augment our deployed forces in Bosnia. This was to be a command and liaison transport function. Accordingly, I assembled a team and spent two incredibly intense days evaluating and solving the many challenges associated with such a deployment. The analysis clearly led me to believe that the deployment should not proceed for two reasons: the aircraft had no self-protection equipment, tactics, or techniques which would be essential in the face of a hostile threat; and second, the crews had no training or experience with the flight procedures required to operate in this demanding and unforgiving theatre. My estimate concluded with a strong recommendation against the proposed deployment. Shortly after submitting the estimate to the General, I received some higher-level, subtle feedback on the content and wording. As I sat at the computer and finalized the minor changes, I was struck with a sudden and disconcerting thought; what if the General wanted the recommendation changed? I felt nauseous; I didn't know what I would do.

In fighter aircraft of the 1970s and 1980s, most of the important systems had a "BIT" check, or built in test system. To test the system, the pilot pressed the "BIT" light in and waited to see if the bulb would light, indicating a successful test, or if it would not, indicating failure. My ethical BIT check was about to be performed. When I returned to the General's office with the amended estimate, he immediately "pressed to test". He indicated that he was not happy with the estimate's recommendations and that the commander of the Air Force and the Chief of the Defence Staff also wanted the recommendation to support the deployment. I stood there, palms sweaty, heart racing, sick to my stomach. Would my "BIT" check light illuminate or not? Suddenly, my way became clear; I agreed to completely rewrite the estimate, so as to strongly support a deployment recommendation, *for the General's signature*. He quickly rejected this proposal, telling me that this was to be my estimate. I responded that if the estimate was to be under my signature, then it stood as written. I was dismissed.

You cannot imagine my distress in the following weeks. As strange as it seems, six weeks later a light twin transport aircraft of another nation rapidly deployed to Bosnia to fill that very same role. It crashed into a mountain, killing all onboard, including a US Secretary of State. The resulting investigation revealed not only the manifest lack of preparation for these crews to operate in this area, but also showed dramatic levels of inappropriate pressure by the senior command chain to deploy this aircraft and push the ill-prepared crew to undertake the mission.

In the course of my studies at the Air War College, I selected an elective called "Command and Conscience", given by Dr. Toner. As part of the course I was required to read the book *The Nightingale's Song*,[4] which is set in the Iran-Contra scandal era and follows the lives of five US officers as they progress through the US Naval Academy, face combat in Vietnam and subsequently rise to powerful positions. Despite their courage, determination, and dedication, each is flawed in his own way by the experiences of life and each stumbles when put to the test. While I thoroughly enjoyed the book, the further I read, the more I was filled with a sense of unease that I couldn't identify at first. Then it came to me: as a fighter pilot I frequently had cause to read the findings of flight safety accident investigations involving other pilots; in every case I knew something horrible happened in the end, but I didn't know why up front. As I read the investigation report, my initial reaction was "this could have been me". Yet as I continued to read, the accident pilot's decisions or actions became increasingly out of sync with what I believed I would have done and the feelings of "this could have been me" faded, in most cases, to be replaced by a growing certainty that "this would not have happened to me". Similarly, as I read this book and remarked on the many similarities between my early career and those of the subjects, I faced a growing sense of dread that "this could have been me." Just as with the accident reports; however, this unease was dispelled as I progressed further into the book and grew increasingly certain that I would have acted differently. What made me so confident? In that early 1990s era of military scandals, how could I be sure? I had my touchstone. My period of ethical reflection had shown me that I had successfully withstood many situations where I had experienced pressure of one sort or another to act against my better judgement and in each case I had decided to do what was "right".

Ethical Challenge: How To Know It When You See It

Finally, how do I define an operational ethical challenge? I define this as a situation in which one is facing internal turmoil over a decision to act. In essence, the turmoil represents the internal debate over doing what one knows or feels to be "the right thing", while feeling pressure to act against this value. The source of conflict may be temptation (personal gain, pleasure), orders from a superior, rules, or any other source of influence over your actions. I can generally tell when I am facing such a situation, as I find myself returning to the problem over and over again. In the shower, in bed before trying to sleep, on the way to work, while running, the issue continues to haunt. Having been there before,

I now have the confidence to apply my touchstone, to identify the fundamental pressure that is making me conflicted, and to then confidently reach a decision and act.

CONFLUENCE IN COMBAT: OPERATION ALLIED FORCE

Having briefly covered some discussion of the basics of Command, Law, and Ethics, I will now endeavour to illustrate their interplay in an air combat environment. In that the mission importance and the conditions under which the mission are undertaken will vary and every individual will bring his/her own distinct ethical abilities to the battle, no two circumstances will ever be identical. That said, I am hopeful that the following vignettes will help to illustrate the interplay between the three major influences on a commander and will provide sufficient impetuous to cause the reader to reflect on their own values and reactions to situations.

The focus is on those difficult decisions that I undertook, where it was not evident as to how to proceed, and where there existed some pressure or influence to act counter to my values, thus requiring me to resist, or alter course. These represent but a tiny fraction of the multitude of decisions that were a part of every day in combat; however, they represent the most interesting of cases and should provide the best vantage point from which to observe.

Setting the Stage: The Lead-Up

The conflict in the Balkans demanded much attention and significant military commitments throughout the decade of the 1990s. By 1998, a certain stability had been reached in the region; however, the president of the Former Republic of Yugoslavia (FRY),

President Milosevic, was fomenting a crisis within his country in an effort to fuel a resurgence of Serbian nationalism, and thus buttress support for his vision of a greater Serbia. He seized upon the growing population of Muslim Albanian Kosovars within the province of Kosovo to launch his campaign. In that this province was widely viewed as the birthplace of the Serbian people, he was able to create relatively widespread support for his campaign against these "intruders" and was able to bring a significant unity to the largely Serbian population of FRY. As he continued to fuel the crisis, the persecution and abuse of the Kosovars became more and more open and increasingly supported by the military forces of FRY. Predictably, these actions became increasingly known and visible outside the borders of the country as reports of abuses and refugees began to flow out of the province. The growing international concern over the situation, in view of the potential for a significant humanitarian disaster or worse, led to diplomatic engagements with the FRY government. All manner of diplomatic tools were used, including embargos, blockades and other forms of pressure. By February 1999, it became apparent that Milosevic would not be swayed by any measure short of military force. Accordingly, in March 1999, NATO commenced an intensive Air Campaign against the Former Republic of Yugoslavia as a last resort to force Serbian President Milosevic to acquiesce to international demands to cease the open persecution of Kosovars. The campaign lasted three months and was the most significant aerial combat operation by the Canadian Air Force since the Second World War. The Canadian commitment rapidly rose from an initial six to a peak of eighteen CF-18 fighter aircraft along with 350 personnel. This potent fighting force was capable of and tasked to perform both Air Superiority and Air Attack missions with the preponderance of the missions being bombing sorties.

In the course of the operation, the Canadian task force flew over 500 bombing sorties, 200 Air Superiority sorties and dropped over 200 tons of bombs. Only one mission was cancelled due to a mechanical malfunction of the aircraft. There were no significant safety occurrences and no notable incident of collateral damage. In view of the significant experience and qualifications of the Canadian fighter pilots, they were tasked to lead a vastly disproportionate number of the missions in which they flew, fully half of all of their missions; this normally implied planning and leading missions of over 40 attack aircraft, of which four would be Canadian. In all, the Canadian bombing effort represented in the order of ten percent of the NATO attacks. By any measure, this was a dramatically successful performance in the crucible of combat operations.

Having been chosen to command the task force commencing in January of 1999, I was in the professionally challenging position of commanding the force during its theatre workups prior to the outset of hostilities and for the first seven weeks of combat. I experienced firsthand the frustrations, challenges, and satisfactions that come from such a perspective. While my experience under combat conditions led me to conclude that my military career had prepared me extraordinarily well to face the challenges of command, it is in the interplay of command responsibilities, personal ethical convictions and the law of armed conflict that I experienced which led to the most significant personal challenges and present the best opportunity to provoke some thought for future combat commanders.

In the interests of providing a better understanding of the circumstances of command I faced, it is important to understand a few fundamental aspects that were extant at the time. First, as a task force that was under the operational control (OPCON) to NATO,

I had little influence over the overall conduct of the campaign and thus, over target selection. I could and did express my reservations with respect to certain aspects, but was largely excluded from the larger direction of the campaign. Second, Canada had not yet instituted any national process for the oversight and approval of targets. While this is no longer the case, during my command I held the responsibility and authority to reject NATO-assigned missions on behalf of Canada.

THE CONFLUENCE: SMOOTH WATER, EDDIES, AND SOME TURBULENCE

Vignette: First Ripples: Pilot Aid Books

One of the results from the aftermath of the Somalia incident was the publication of orders concerning the approval of "soldier cards".[5] In order to retain higher control over the publication and wording or interpretation of ROE, approval of the wording of soldier cards was retained at the national headquarters level. Soldier cards were intended to provide a ready reference for soldiers, enabling review and study of the rules of engagement during the various lulls that naturally occur as a part of the ebb and flow of an operation. The restriction on the approval levels for such cards was done to ensure that the wording on these cards did not inadvertently give rise to erroneous or unintended interpretations and to also ensure that the deployed commander did not "interpret" his/her approved ROE in an undesired fashion.

Fighter aircraft operations are governed by an unimaginable stack of orders, instructions, and regulations. This is magnified dramatically under combat conditions, where tasking orders, airspace control orders, special instructions, etc. are all applicable, bulky, and subject to rapid amendment. That said, the portion of this morass of directives that applies to any specific unit, or mission, is but a small proportion. Of that, some is critical during mission planning, whereas some other portions must be available to the pilot throughout the mission. Accordingly, air forces all over the world have developed the same solution: they extract the relevant information for the mission and the unit and produce a much smaller, condensed version that can be referred to during mission planning and execution. These "pilot aids" are carried in the cockpit.

In our case, weeks before the commencement of combat, a determination had been made by the JAG branch that these extracts constituted an air force version of a "soldier card" and were therefore subject to national approval. I duly forwarded the proposed book to Canada for approval. As the days passed and the outset of combat operations neared, I could not obtain the required approval. In that it is essential that pilots train with these books in order to facilitate their locating the relevant information rapidly, either during planning or in-flight, this was a matter of increasing concern to me; how could I ask these young men to risk their lives in combat, without having given them the tools and the time to prepare themselves as well as they could? I returned to the issue over and over; I was conflicted. The reason was clear; my orders prohibited me from doing what I knew to be essential. Finally, with only a few days remaining before the likely onset of combat operations, I ordered the issuance of the booklets to my pilots. My AJAG immediately appeared in my office; stating that I was in violation of my orders. I agreed and showed her the FLASH message that I had sent to national headquarters which started out with "in violation of my orders at ref, I have ordered the issuance of the pilot aid books...". I could not countenance further delay and thus, had placed the onus on my commander to support me or take alternative action. In the case in point, I immediately received a message approving the action I had taken.

Vignette: Some Splashing: Cluster Munitions

From the very start of the campaign, the Supreme Allied Commander Europe (SACEUR) placed inordinate priority on the destruction of the Serbian army in Kosovo. In that cluster munitions are highly effective against assembled ground forces, they were obviously a weapon to be considered. Accordingly, I was approached and asked if my forces could employ this weapon. On the face of it the answer was technically simple; our aircraft could drop these weapons, our pilots were trained and Canada did have the weapons. I examined the question further, however, as these weapons (as they existed at the time) had a relatively high "dud" rate; that is, a significant portion of the smaller bomblets would not explode and thus would remain on the ground as a danger to personnel.

I concluded a couple of things. First, we were at war for the benefit of the Kosovars. As such, it seemed inconsistent with our overall objective to take action in combat that would require extensive clean up operations to make their land safe for their use afterward. Second, such a weapon choice would obviously represent an enduring danger to our own troops who would surely be called upon to patrol and even to clean up the province after the successful completion of the combat campaign. Finally, from a weapons effectiveness point of view, the complete lack of any Allied ground force coupled with our air dominance 24 hours a day, had led the Serbian army to widely disperse. It thus did not present the type of target for which these munitions are specifically designed. Accordingly, and without extensive legal consultation, I indicated that I was not prepared to employ such weapons under the existing conditions.

This "confluence" was relatively smooth to me; the military imperative was not there, in fact their use was to some extent, counter to our stated objectives. Without taking the time to debate the legality, it was clear that the rumble strips would be sounding. Fundamentally, this was not the "right" thing to do.

Vignette: Rapids Ahead: Area Targets

One lesson that was obvious from before the outset of the campaign was that if you are going to war in the Balkans, don't do it in the spring; the weather is terrible and the impact on air operations is significant. The bad weather, coupled with SACEUR's determination that the enemy forces were assembling somewhere, despite the manifest absence of any allied ground force and the continual overhead presence of our aircraft, led to the concept of area target bombing. In essence, this is the delivery of unguided bombs, through the clouds, into relatively small areas. This is possible for most modern attack aircraft and was within the capability of my force. Accordingly, when the tactic was proposed by the Combined Force Air Component Commander (CFACC), I engaged national headquarters for approval and for the equipment and bombs to perform this mission, which were duly provided. After the first few missions against wooded areas, the area targets we were assigned occasionally included villages within portions of the assigned "area". I had significant issues with this; destroying the villages and killing the very villagers we were out to save was not the "right" thing and surely must be counter to our overall objective to save Kosovo, not destroy it. When I engaged NATO authorities, I was told that they were confident that such villages would be abandoned by the Kosovar populations as they were vested by the FRY forces. I could not accept this justification for the proposed mission. I published an order to my forces that they were not to attack any area targets that I had not specifically verified. In turn, I excised villages from any "area" target that contained one, restricting the attacks to the residual portion of the area.

In this case, I believe that arguments could be advanced against bombing villages from a command, legal, and ethical point of view. My sense of "right things" certainly made this decision easier in the fatigue and stress of the circumstances.

Vignette: Roller: Communication Centre

One day we were tasked to destroy a significant communications centre during an afternoon attack. The centre was a legitimate target with great importance and was assessed to have a low probability of collateral damage. The LOAC principles would allow attacks against such a high value target even in the face of assessments of "high" risk of collateral damage or, in other words, many civilian casualties.

Upon closer examination, my planning team relayed a concern to me. They had observed this target on a previous mission and knew that it was surrounded by immense parking lots. The size of the facility indicated the presence of hundreds of civilian workers. While civilian workers involved in providing military capabilities are legitimate targets, the attack date was during the days immediately following the inadvertent attack on the Chinese Embassy. This attack had generated significant public debates in many alliance nations over the conduct of the campaign. Clearly, during that sensitive period, an incident causing dramatic levels of civilian deaths could have provoked the level of public debate that could have had the potential to end the air campaign.

I approached the deputy of the Coalition Force Air Component Commander with my concerns, and was initially rebuffed. After being directed to the targeting cell, I was again told that the target had a low collateral damage risk, was legal, and was assigned to us. I asked why this target was tasked in the mid-afternoon, assuring a large work force and many casualties. There was no answer.

Accordingly, I refused the target, and my force was assigned a different target for that operation. The next day the chief of the targeting cell approached me; the target folder now had a unique red page that stated that this target was only to be struck in the early morning hours. A couple of days later we were again tasked, and eliminated the target without causing the elevated level of casualties and subsequent adverse public attention that would surely have resulted if we had performed the mission as originally tasked. In view of the furor that arose over the Chinese Embassy, had I not objected to this attack, we might have created such debate that the entire campaign could have been placed in jeopardy.

Vignette: Souse Hole: Lead Targeting

In another situation, the Air Component Commander was ordered by SACEUR to have every attack aircraft directed to bomb enemy ground forces in the Kosovo province. This order was manifestly ill-considered from the outset; the small size of Kosovo made it impossible for all attack aircraft missions to actually fly in this tiny space without a significant danger of mid-air collisions. Additionally, and of more consequence, not even a fraction of the airborne forward air controllers (FAC) required to identify valid targets and direct the attacking aircraft to them were available. These airborne FAC's operated slower aircraft that were better suited to loiter in the areas of possible targets and their crews were equipped with a variety of specialized equipment to aid them in identifying targets as valid military targets. To this situation I would add that the complete absence of an Allied ground force, coupled with the continuous overhead presence of attack aircraft had caused the FRY army to disperse and hide; under such conditions, no air campaign can destroy an army.

In the event, the CFACC pulled the senior national commanders together, explained the situation, and indicated that he was taking personal responsibility for authorizing the flight leaders of attacking formations to find, identify, and attack targets in Kosovo without the assistance of a FAC. I expressed my concerns with my pilot's ability to correctly identify targets as legal military targets, given their lack of FAC training and equipment. The order stood. Accordingly, I immediately wrote and published an order to my force; under no circumstances were they to find and attack targets without the assistance of a FAC. This restricted them to pre-planned attacks against validated targets and attack missions with FAC's.

Two days later, the flight lead of a formation of attack aircraft from another NATO ally spotted a column of what he believed to be military vehicles. The subsequent attacks by his formation destroyed a trailer being towed behind a tractor in a larger refugee convoy. Tragically, this resulted in the deaths of a large number of the refugees that were riding on the trailer. I pitied the poor pilot as he was paraded before the Cable News network (CNN) the next day; NATO immediately prohibited such "flight lead targeting" and I subsequently rescinded my then-redundant order.

MILITARY ETHICS: INTERNATIONAL PERSPECTIVES

Once again, from a command point of view, one could debate the effectiveness of air attacks against dispersed and hidden ground forces versus the strategic necessity of appearing to be increasing the pressure on the enemy. Legally, one could debate the ability of the crews to correctly identify a target as a legitimate military target. Fundamentally, when I was up to bat, I did not have a long debate; the right thing to do was clear to me, and I acted.

DISCUSSION AND CONCLUSION

In each of the vignettes that I have described, I believe that command accountability, the law, and ethics all played a role. In some cases, they all aligned and the way forward was pretty clear. In other cases, orders, or other factors combined to produce situations where pressure existed to act in other than a "right" way. In these, I believe that to some extent the issue was resolved on a basis of choosing to do the "right" thing.

Command in combat represents the ultimate challenge to any professional officer. The merging of life and death, command responsibility, the Law of Armed Conflict, and ethics is essential to successful command and is a nearly seamless and smooth process. A strong ethical sense, and the courage to act on it, is an invaluable attribute for a commander; one which facilitates all decision-making and which will prepare him/her to do the "right" thing on the occasion where the fog of war will exert pressure to act otherwise.

AFTERWORD

How strange life is; on the eve of combat operations in March 1999, my direct superior called from National Headquarters to express his full support and his absolute confidence in me. In that he was the very General that had put me to the test so many years earlier with respect to the recommendations in my estimate concerning the deployment of aircraft to the Balkans, I could understand his confidence.

ENDNOTES

1   In the creation of this article, I have drawn heavily on some of my earlier work, including the article "Command in Combat", published in *In Harm's Way* Canadian Defence Academy Press, as well as a book review I did on *The Nightingale's Song* and other written material I generated as a requirement for the course on military ethics entitled "Command and Conscience" for Professor Toner. I also drew from the presentation entitled "Ethics in Action" that I prepared and gave to the first CF conference on Ethics.

2   The CF-5 was a fighter-bomber that was produced by Canadair, under license from Northrup, for the Canadian Forces. It came into service in 1968 and was retired in 1995.

3   Touchstone, as defined by Professor Jim Toner, Air War College, in material he provided refers to "any test or criterion for determining genuineness or value".

4   Robert Timberg, *The Nightingale's Song* (New York: Simon and Schuster, 1995).

5   Canadian Forces Joint Publication B-GJ-005-501/FP-001 "CFJP-5.1 Use of Force for CF Operations", Aug 08, Para 213: Summary Cards. Summary cards, or soldier cards constitute direction from deployed Commanders to their subordinates which outline those elements of the Rules of Engagement that are considered to be the most essential, and the interpretation of the responses allowed. While they are drafted by the deployed commander, they must be approved by the National, Operational-Level Commander, on behalf of the Chief of Defence Staff, before being promulgated in theatre.

CONTRIBUTORS

Mie Augier, PhD, until recently, was senior research fellow and director of strategy research at the research and assessment branch (UK Defence Academy). She is a research associate professor at the Navy Postgraduate School and has also worked for government organizations, business and universities in the United States and abroad on issues of leadership, strategy, and organizational design. Her research interests include the links between economics and security; organization theory, business strategy, behavioural social science, the future of management education, and the application of interdisciplinary social science to issues of strategic assessment. She has published more than fifty articles in books and journals, including journals such as the *Journal of Economic Behavior and Organization*, *Strategic Organization*, and *Academy of Management Learning and Education*. She has also co-edited two books and several special issues of journals, and has recently co-edited a six volume set of key articles in business strategy. Her current research interests include developing an intellectual and interdisciplinary framework to study decision-making and behaviour in business and military organizations, drawing upon ideas from organizational economics, organization theory and strategic management; and researching the history and future of United States business education; and the history and future of Net Assessment and strategic thinking.

Lieutenant-Colonel Coen van den Berg started his military career at the Royal Netherlands Military Academy in 1983. Originally a military engineer, since 1994 he has served as a military psychologist after obtaining a degree in psychology at the University of Utrecht. In subsequent postings as a military psychologist, his main interests and research areas include military leadership, military ethics, psychological support across the deployment cycle, cross cultural competencies during deployment and behavioural science research within the Armed Forces. He wrote his doctoral thesis on the influence of threat on soldiers' mission related attitudes. He is currently posted as mentor for the Advanced Command and Staff Course at the Netherlands Defence College.

James L. Cook, Colonel, US Air Force, PhD, is the Permanent Professor and Head of the Department of Philosophy at the United States Air Force Academy. A foreign-area and communications-computer officer, he has served in Europe, at the Pentagon, and in Afghanistan. He earned BAs in Philosophy and Math from Brandeis and the University of Colorado at Boulder, an MA in philosophy from The Catholic University of America, and a PhD in Philosophy from the Universität-Heidelberg. His research focuses on military ethics and hermeneutics.

Dr. **Jamie Cullens** is a former Infantry officer with extensive command, staff and training experience. He saw operational service in *Kashmir* with the United Nations and in *Panama* with US forces. He also worked in the Rio Tinto resources group on Cape York from 1996 to 2001. He was appointed as the first Director of the Centre for Defence Leadership and Ethics in 2002 and was the Secretary of Defence Scholar in 2008.

Brigadier-General Dwight Davies enrolled in the Canadian Forces in 1975. He earned a degree in electrical engineering at the Royal Military College in Kingston, Ontario in 1979 and attended the Canadian Forces Command and Staff College in Toronto, Ontario, in 1990. General Davies earned his pilot's wings in 1980, completed basic fighter pilot training on the CF-5 and flew this aircraft until 1984. He also served as an exchange instructor pilot, flying the F-16 fighter aircraft at Luke Air Force Base, Arizona. Selected to pilot the CF-18 "Hornet", he commanded 425 Tactical Fighter Squadron for two years. In 1994 he was posted to the Operations division at Air Command headquarters in Winnipeg, Manitoba. In 1996, he attended the United States Air Force War College at Montgomery, Alabama and was then posted to NORAD headquarters in Colorado Springs, Colorado, where he held a variety of positions at both NORAD and USSPACECOM headquarters. He took command of Task Force Aviano in January 1999, where he commanded the Canadian air contingent during the first seven weeks of combat operations as part of the NATO air campaign against the Federal Republic of Yugoslavia. He was awarded the Meritorious Service Medal for his leadership in combat. From 1999 to 2002, he commanded 3 Wing Bagotville and then served on the Air Staff at NDHQ for one year prior to being promoted to Brigadier-General and assigned to 1 Canadian Air Division, in charge of Operations. Assigned to the Deputy Chief of the Defence Staff Group in August of 2005, he assumed a leading role in the stand-up of the Canadian Expeditionary Force Command, and was subsequently appointed its Deputy Commander. Brigadier-General Davies was assigned to his current position as Director General Air Force Development in October 2007.

Andreas Fischer received his MSc in psychology from the University of Berne, Switzerland in 2007. Since 2008, he is working as a research assistant (and towards his PhD) in the Department of Leadership and Communication Studies at the Swiss Military Academy at ETH Zurich. His primary research interest is the psychological study of morality, focusing on the examination and development of moral decision-making processes. He is currently working on the project *"Developing responsible leaders"* and is teaching leadership ethics and moral decision-making to military and civilian professionals and students.

Craig A. Foster, PhD, is a Full Professor in the Department of Behavioral Science & Leadership at the United States Air Force Academy. He completed his master's and doctoral degrees in Social Psychology at The University of North Carolina in Chapel Hill. His research focuses on issues related to social power, leadership development, and romantic relationships. He teaches a number of academic courses including Introduction to Behavioral Sciences, Statistical Principles in Behavioral Science, Social Psychology, Personality, Foundations of Leadership Development, and Advanced Leadership.

Dr. **Peter Greener** is Senior Fellow at the Command and Staff College of the New Zealand Defence Force and Adjunct Professor in the School of Public Health and Psychosocial Studies at AUT University. He was Head of the Division of Public Health and Psychosocial Studies at AUT University from 2003-2007, and Head of the Department of Psychotherapy and Applied Psychology from 1998-2003. He has a Masters degree in Public Policy and his PhD is in Political Studies with a focus on New Zealand Defence decision-making. Research interests include the aetiology, management and resolution of conflict; post conflict development and post complex emergency management; and the politics of defence decision-making. He brings to these interests the perspective of his many years experience as a psychoanalytic psychotherapist. Peter's most recent books are *Timing is Everything: The Politics and Processes of New Zealand Defence Acquisition Decision Making*, Canberra Papers on Strategy and Defence No.173, Canberra: The Australian National University E-Press (2009), and *Decision-Making: International Perspectives*, Kingston: Canadian

Defence Academy Press (2009), edited jointly with Lieutenant-Colonel Jeff Stouffer.

Miriam C. de Graaff, MSc, is employed at the Centre of Excellence for Leadership and Ethics of the Royal Netherlands Army. She is a PhD student in the field of social psychology and philosophical ethics. As a psychologist and communication-scientist, she is engaged in policy, education and research in the field of military leadership and ethics.

Lieutenant-Colonel Eri Radityawara Hidayat, is currently the Head of Planning and Budgeting at the Psychological Service of the Army. He finished his Bachelor of Science at the University of Wisconsin, Madison, USA (1986), and his Master of Business Administration at the University of Pittsburgh, USA (1987). He also received a Master of Human Resource Management and Coaching from the University of Sydney, Australia (2005). Lieutenant-Colonel Eri Radityawara Hidayat is presently a PhD candidate in psychology at the University of Indonesia. His military education includes the Indonesian Armed Forces Officer's School (1990), the Australian Military Familiarization Course (2004), the Indonesian Army's Command and Staff College (2006), and the Netherlands Defence Course (2008).

Brigadier Nick Jans is a soldier, a scholar, and a management consultant. A graduate of the Royal Military College, Duntroon, he served in the Australian Regular Army for 25 years in field artillery, training, and personnel policy development. He is currently Visiting Fellow in Leadership & Military Sociology at the Centre for Defence Leadership & Ethics at the Australian Defence College. He is a co-principle of Sigma Consultancy, a firm that specialises in HR strategy and organisational research.

Lieutenant-Colonel Psalm Lew is currently Head School Leadership Development with the responsibility to review and develop the Leadership Curriculum in all SAF schools. An Infantry Officer by vocation, he is concurrently the Commanding Officer of the 802nd Battalion Singapore Infantry Regiment. His past appointments include being the Chief Researcher of the Army Museum of Singapore, a Principal Staff Officer in the 3rd Singapore Division and Training Development Officer of the Officer Cadet School. Lieutenant-Colonel Lew holds a Bachelor of Science (1st Class Honors) in Psychology from the University of Birmingham, U.K.

Douglas R. Lindsay, Lieuteneant-Colonel, US Air Force, PhD, is an Associate Professor and the Director of Research for the Department of Behavioral Sciences & Leadership at the United States Air Force Academy. He is the co-founder and co-editor for the Journal of Character and Leader Scholarship. He received his doctorate degree in Industrial/Organizational Psychology from The Pennsylvania State University. His research interests are in the areas of leadership, leadership development, leader-follower dynamics, and followership. He has published and presented extensively in these areas.

Dr. **Jamie MacIntosh** is now the Director of Programmes at the Institute for Security and Resilience Studies (ISRS), University College London (UCL) on secondment from the UK MoD. He was most recently the Chief of Research and Assessment at the Defence Academy , serving on the Defence Academy Board for 3 years. His 25 years in public service include 10 years in the British Army, with most of his time since leaving the Army involved in leading research at the cutting edge of defence, security and resilience studies. Dr. MacIntosh has advised at Cabinet level in several countries and in operational theatres. He went on loan to the Cabinet Office in early 2001, co-authored the concept of Resilience to Crises and at the Prime Minister's direction established the Civil Contingencies Secretariat. Whilst on secondment as the Home Secretary's Personal Advisor on Transformation and National Security, his advice was instrumental in the creation of the Office of Security and Counter Terrorism (OSCT) as well as the cross-departmental Research Information Communication Unit (RICU). His major research interests include: the economic dimensions of security and resilience, risk and decision-taking in networks, developing legal frameworks for the use of force and professional education in strategy, policy, campaigning and operational art.

Craig Leslie Mantle graduated from Queen's University with his MA in Canadian history in 2002 and has been employed by the Canadian Forces Leadership Institute in Kingston, Ontario as a research officer ever since. He is also a PhD candidate at the University of Calgary where he is studying officer-man relations in Canada's army of the First World War.

Colonel Imam Edy Mulyono is currently a faculty member at the Indonesian Army's Command and Staff College. He graduated from the Military Academy in 1984. His academic qualifications include a Master of Science in Strategic Studies from the Nanyang Technological University, Singapore (2001) and a Master of Strategic Studies from the US Army War College (2008). Military courses attended included Psychological Operations and Special Forces courses in the United States (1989/1990) and the Indonesian Army's Command and Staff College (1999). Colonel Imam Edy Mulyono has also attended various seminars on current military issues both at home and abroad. He spent most of his career as a KOSTRAD officer, two of his latest positions being a Battalion

Commander and a Brigade Chief of Staff. Colonel Imam Edy Mulyono has participated in various military operations both at home and abroad, including a peacekeeping mission in Georgia as part of the United Nations Observer Mission in Georgia (UNOMIG).

Sofia Nilsson, MA, is a researcher at the Department of Management and Leadership, Swedish National Defence College, conducting research on direct/indirect leadership and stress (both civil and military contexts). She is currently working on her doctoral dissertation at Karlstad University, Sweden, focusing on the interaction of human and structural factors in management/leadership during challenging situations. She has published several journal articles, book chapters, and research reports dealing with leadership and stress. In addition, she is engaged in the higher military education of Swedish officers. She has a Master's degree in political science emphasizing the contemporary international system, diplomacy, European security, and foreign policy analysis, besides a Bachelor's degree in social science.

Chaplain **Don Parker** is the Principal Defence Chaplain to the New Zealand Defence Force. An Anglican priest of 25 years, he has trained and practiced in Psychoanalytic Psychotherapy before commencing his career in the NZDF. He has deployed on Operations in both East Timor and Tsunami humanitarian relief following the Boxing Day Tsunami of 2004. Currently he is overseeing the most significant structural change in Chaplaincy in a generation and has a strong interest in the insights afforded that change process by Psychoanalysis and management principles. He has studied in the areas of Theology, Psychology and Psychoanalysis.

Joseph E. Sanders III, Colonel, US Air Force, PhD, is the Permanent Professor of the US Air Force Academy's Center for Character and Leadership Development and he has also served as a deputy department head and professor in the Academy's Department of Behavioral Sciences and Leadership. He has been a driving force for the scholarship and practice of character and leader development at the US Air Force Academy as well as for the planning and creation of the *Journal of Character and Leader Scholarship*.

Dr. **Stefan Seiler** is currently the Head of Leadership and Communication Studies at the Swiss Military Academy at ETH Zurich. He studied at the University of Fribourg and the University of Leeds and graduated with a PhD in Educational Psychology from the University of Fribourg. His research interests include leadership, intercultural leadership, leadership ethics, moral decision making and conflict management. Prior to his appointment at the Swiss Military Academy, he worked at Credit Suisse in Zurich and in New York as a Member of Senior Management in the Human Resources Department. His responsibilities included global restructuring and implementation projects in America and Asia. Dr. Seiler serves in the Army in the rank of major (militia officer) and is a member of the military science workgroup in support of the Chief Land Forces. He was previously a company commander, followed by chief of staff and deputy commander of a pioneer battalion.

Justin C. Wright graduated from the University of New Brunswick with his MA in sociology in 2006 and was employed immediately thereafter as a Defence Scientist with the Director General Military Personnel Research and Analysis. He is currently posted to the Canadian Forces Leadership Institute in Kingston, Ontario as a research officer.

GLOSSARY

ACSC	Australian Command and Staff College
ADF	Australian Defence Force
ATI	Access to Information
BKCD	Be, Know, Care, and Do Model
BIT	Built in Test System
CCLD	Center for Character and Leader Development
CE	Continuing Education
CF	Canadian Forces
CFACC	Combined Force Air Component Commander
CFLI	Canadian Forces Leadership Institute
CNN	Cable News Network
DIT	Defining Issues Test
DND	Department of National Defence
FAC	Forward Air Controllers
FCM	The Four Component Model
FRY	Former Republic of Yugoslavia
HADR	Human Assistance and Disaster Relief
JAG	Judge Advocate General
KAQ	Knowledge-Abilities-Qualities model of Leadership
KOPKKN	*Komando Operasi Pemulihan Keamanan dan Ketertiban Nasional* (National Restoration for Stability and Order Command)
KOSTRAD	*Komando Cadangan Strategis Angkatan Darat* (Army Strategic Reserve Command)
LCM	Leadership Competency Model
LIC	Low Intensity Conflict
MAD	Mutually Assured Destruction
MJI	The Moral Judgement Interview

MRT	Mass Rapid Transit System
NATO	North Atlantic Treaty Organization
NCO	Non-Commissioned Officer
NCM	Non-Commissioned Member
NS	National Service
NSmen	National Servicemen
NZDF	New Zealand Defence Force
OPCON	Operational Control
OSI	Occupational Stress Injury
PITS	Perpetration-Induced Trauma Syndrome
POI	Protection of Installations
PROI	Professional Role Orientation Inventory
PTSD	Post-Traumatic Stress Disorder
REB	Research Ethics Board
ROE	Rules of Engagement
ROB	Rules of Behaviour
RSS	Republic of Singapore Ship
SACEUR	Supreme Allied Commander Europe
SAF	Singapore Armed Forces
SAF	Swedish Armed Forces
SARS	Severe Acute Respiratory Syndrome
SCLD	SAF Centre for Leadership Development
SME	Subject Matter Expert
SOB	*Staat van Oorlog en Beleg* (State of war and siege)
SSRRB	Social Science Research Review Board
TCPS	Tri-Council Policy Statement
TNI	*Tentara Nasional Indonesia* (Indonesian National Defense Force)
TNI AD	*Tentara Nasional Indonesia Angkatan Darat* (Indonesian National Army)
UK	United Kingdom

UN	United Nations
US	United States
USAFA	United States Air Force Academy
USPACOM	United States Pacific Command

INDEX

MILITARY ETHICS: INTERNATIONAL PERSPECTIVES

U
22
.M54
2010

0 1341 1322155 7

RECEIVED

NOV 0 4 2010

HUMBER LIBRARIES
NORTH CAMPUS